Early Childhood Creative Arts

Proceedings of the International Early Childhood Creative Arts Conference

Los Angeles, California, December 6-9, 1990

Senior Editor
Lynnette Young Overby

Assistant Editors
Ann Richardson and Lillian S. Hasko

Managing Editor
Luke Kahlich

NATIONAL DANCE ASSOCIATION
an association of the
**AMERICAN ALLIANCE FOR HEALTH, PHYSICAL EDUCATION,
RECREATION AND DANCE**

Dedication

For the children of the world
who wait with open minds and hearts.

American Alliance for Health,
Physical Education, Recreation and Dance
1900 Association Drive
Reston, Virginia 22091

ISBN 0-88314-522-7

Conference Goal Statement
International Early Childhood Creative Arts Conference

The goal of this conference was to affirm early childhood as a time for active, self-directed learning filled with the joy of playful interaction within a rich, stimulating, stress-free environment. The conference aimed to bring together early childhood and arts educators to provide a forum for dialogue among those individuals who have responsibility for designing and implementing quality educational experiences for children ages three through eight.

Unprecedented attention is being focused on the lives of children in contemporary society. This interest in and concern for the welfare of children is being expressed world-wide (for example, UNESCO's Convention on the Rights of the Child, including the right to cultural and artistic activities, and the World Summit on Children, September 1990).

A primary objective of this conference was to increase awareness of critical issues and to foster international networking to seek solutions on behalf of the children of the world. Speakers and presenters from a variety of countries were invited to be on the program, and an open invitation to attend the conference was extended internationally to all those individuals having an interest in the issues which were addressed.

The conference program was designed to:

heighten awareness of the richness provided by cultural diversity, celebrate differences and nurture uniqueness, and provide participants with strategies for infusing multicultural arts experiences into early childhood programs;

provide knowledge of the unique developmental needs and learning styles of young children ages three to four and five to eight and models for creating environments and activities appropriate for those age levels;

increase awareness of the value of the arts in the human experience and their contributions to cognitive, affective, kinesthetic, and aesthetic development; and

challenge participants to reflect on the issues surrounding assessment of young children and the arts and facilitate the exploration of child-centered, child-sensitive approaches.

Permeating the conference was a philosophical commitment to child-centered, holistic learning; the central role of play and the arts throughout the early childhood years; valuing and responding to the unique needs and contributions of all special populations of children; and the integral role which parents, community members, caregivers, and artists play in providing quality educational experiences for young children.

PURPOSES OF THE
AMERICAN ALLIANCE FOR HEALTH, PHYSICAL EDUCATION, RECREATION AND DANCE

The American Alliance is an educational organization, structured for the purposes of supporting, encouraging, and providing assistance to member groups and their personnel throughout the nation as they seek to initiate, develop, and conduct programs in health, leisure, and movement-related activities for the enrichment of human life.

Alliance objectives include:

1. Professional growth and development--to support, encourge and provide guidance in the development and conduct of programs in health, leisure, and movement-related activities which are based on the needs, interests, and inherent capacities of the individual in today's society.

2. Communication--to facilitate public and professional understanding and appreciation of health, leisure, and movement-related activities, and to disseminate the findings to the profession and other interested and concerned publics.

4. Standards and guidelines--to further the continuous development and evaluation of standards within the profession for personnel and programs in health, leisure, and movement-related activities.

5. Public affairs--to coordinate and administer a planned program of professional, public, and governmental relations that will improve education in areas of health, leisure, and movement-related activities.

6. To conduct such other activities as shall be approved by the Board of Governors and the Alliance Assembly, provided that the Alliance shall not engage in any activity which would be inconsistent with the status of an educational and charitable organization as defined in Section 501 (c)(3) of the Internal Revenue Code of 1954 or any successor provision thereto, and none of the said purposes shall at any time be deemed or construed to be purposes other than the public benefit purposes and objectives consistent with such educational and charitable status.

Table of Contents

Cover design by Kate Sternberg, Reston, Virginia

Preface

The National Dance Association takes great pride in publishing these proceedings of the International Early Childhood Creative Arts Conference held in December 1990 in Los Angeles, California. These selected articles represent a major step forward in recognizing the value of arts education for this population, sharing the information and work among the arts specialists and making it available to the classroom teacher and others interested in the early education of our children.

Within this volume are rich resources of knowledge and practice that begin to define the intrinsic connection between arts and the child while encouraging further development of quality curriculum materials and methodology. The arts are clearly a cross-cultural force for early childhood education, and it is hoped that this publication will serve as a reaffirmation for those currently working in the field as well as an inspiration and a catalyst to those searching for ways to ensure quality human developmental experiences for children of the twenty-first century.

Luke Kahlich
Former Executive Director
National Dance Association

Foreword

The National Dance Association sponsored the first International Early Childhood Creative Arts Conference for ages three to eight in Los Angeles, December 6-9, 1990. Over 350 persons attended, including people from ten foreign countries. It was a significant historical event in that it celebrated the U.S. Bureau of Head Start's 25th anniversary and brought together arts education and early childhood associations for the planning and conduct of the Conference. Cooperating groups included the Music Educators National Conference, the American Alliance for Theatre and Education, the National Art Education Association, the National Association for the Education of Young Children, the Association for Childhood Education International, the International Council on Health, Physical Education, and Recreation, and the Head Start Bureau.

The Conference focused on the unique learning styles of three- to eight-year-olds and their developmental needs. Special emphasis was placed on curriculum, assessment, the essential role of the arts in learning, multicultural awareness, needs of special populations, and the interrelatedness of the arts in the learning process.

Nationally known speakers were selected for general sessions, which were followed by small group participation and/or discussion sessions. Each cooperating association identified well-known, experienced, capable presenters for the sessions. This resulted in a rich and meaningful experience for all those present.

There were 84 presenters, 65 of whom submitted articles for proceedings. Of the 65, 34 were selected by a juried process for inclusion in these printed proceedings. The remaining titles are listed in the Appendix and may be available through the ERIC retrieval system.

The Conference presented a model for future cooperative arts and early childhood endeavors. For continued impact, it is hoped that the Conference will be replicated at many local and regional sites. The National Dance Association will be happy to assist in planning.

Grateful acknowledgment is made to the cooperating associations, the Program Planning Committee, and the Site Coordinating Committee for the success of the Conference. Special tribute is extended to Carol LeBreck, program director, and to Wanda Rainbolt, site director, for outstanding organizational abilities and devoted efforts on behalf of the Conference.

Appreciation is extended to the U.S. Head Start Bureau and the Alliance for Arts Education of the Kennedy Center for partial funding. Finally, the National Dance Association is indebted to the Editorial Committee for an outstanding effort in coordinating the proceedings.

Margie R. Hanson
Conference Director
AAHPERD Vice President
and Consultant for Children's Programs

Introduction

In March of 1991, a committee was formed and given the task of compiling a book on the conference proceedings. The work of the committee involved the review of papers either presented at the conference or representative of a session. Every paper had merit and contributed to the purpose of conference, but because of space limitations all could not be included in the final book. However, most of the papers may be accessed through ERIC.

This book of proceedings is representative of the themes and directions of the Early Childhood Creative Arts Conference. The contents stand on their own as a valuable resource for teachers, parents, and administrators.

The book is organized into four major sections. Section one, titled General Sessions, provides the reader with theoretical material in the areas of curriculum development, arts assessment, and child development. Section two, titled Specific Arts Instruction, contains many practical activities as well as theoretical discourses in music, art, dance, and drama. Section three, Model Programs, describes three well-developed arts programs. Section Four, titled Multicultural/International, includes information about creative arts programs of various countries and a multicultural perspective for program development.

The committee members wish to extend their appreciation to Margie Hanson and Luke Kahlich for their vision and determination in producing this final document. We would also like to thank Peggy Park, assistant to Margie Hanson, for successfully tackling all of the organizational tasks involved in compiling this book.

Lynnette Young Overby, Senior Editor
Michigan State University

Lillian S. Hasko, Assistant Editor
Montgomery County, Maryland,
Public Schools

Ann Richardson, Assistant Editor
Montgomery County, Maryland,
Public Schools

Acknowledgments

Program Planning Committee

Carol LeBreck, Program Chair, Department of Health, Physical Education, Recreation and Athletics, University of Wisconsin-River Falls

Carol Rogel Scott, Research Chair, School of Fine and Performing Arts, Seattle Pacific University, Seattle, Washington

Theresa Purcell, Resource Chair, Brunswick Acres Elementary School, Kendall Park, New Jersey

Margie Hanson, Conference Director, Consultant for Children's Programs, American Alliance for Health, Physical Education, Recreation and Dance, Reston, Virginia

Tom Hatfield, Executive Director, National Art Education Association, Reston, Virginia

Barbara Andress (Music Educators National Conference), School of Music, Arizona State University, Tempe

Dollie Wolverton, Chief, Educational Services, Head Start Bureau, Administration for Children, Youth, and Families, Washington, D.C.

Mary Lewis, Assistant Program Director, Head Start Program, Administration for Children, Youth, and Families, Washington, D.C.

Pat Spahr, Director of Information Services, National Association for the Education of Young Children, Washington, D.C.

Gil Brown, Executive Vice President, American Alliance for Health, Physical Education, Recreation and Dance, Reston, Virginia

Victoria Brown (American Alliance for Theatre and Education), Theatre Arts Department, Gallaudet University, Washington, D.C.

Site Coordinating Committee

Wanda Rainbolt, Committee Chair, Department of Health, Physical Eduction, Recreation and Dance, California Polytechnic University, Pomona, California

Jane Adair (Physical Education), Long Beach, California

Hooshang Bagheri (Dance), Department of Elementary Education, California State University, Northridge

Madonna Billauer (Dance), Dance Department, University of California-Los Angeles

Lynne Emery (Dance), Department of Health, Physical Education, Recreation and Dance, California Polytechnic University, Pomona

Fran Johnson (Early Childhood), SCAEYC, La Habra, California

Susie Peppers (Head Start), Educational Staff Coordinator, Kedren Head Start, Los Angeles, California

Lyn Pohlmann (Music), Seal Beach, California

Mary Louise Reilly (Music), Woodland Hills, California

Cecilia Riddell (Music), Department of Music, California State University at Dominguez Hills, Carson, California

Judy Scalin (Dance), Loyola Marymount University, Los Angeles, California

Gloria Simon-Williams (Art), Consultant, Arts for Kids, Los Angeles, California

Local Area Consultants, Advisors, and Resource Persons

LOS ANGELES COUNTY BOARD OF EDUCATION

Carol Fox, Consultant, Early Childhood Education, Los Angeles County Office of Education, Downey, California

Betty Hennessy, Los Angeles County Office of Education, Downey, California

Suzan Van Pelt, Assistant Director, Head Start State Preschool, Los Angeles County Office of Education, Norwalk, California

Diane Watanabe, Arts Consultant, Los Angeles County Office of Education, Downey, California

LOCAL ADVISORS

Phyllis Berenbeim, Orange County Department of Education, Costa Mesa, California

Anne Heidt, Arts Consultant, San Diego County Schools, San Diego, California

Vera Johnston, Consultant in Physical Education, Orange, California

Gil Leaf, Director, Los Angeles Children's Museum, Los Angeles, California

Toni Marich, Department of Dance, California State University at Dominguez Hills, Carson, California

Freddie Thomson, Clay Junior High School, Los Angeles, California

STATE CONSULTANTS

Phyllis Blatz, Executive Director, California Association for Health, Physical Education, Recreation and Dance, Sacramento, California

Diane Brooks, Art/Music Consultant, State Department of Education, Sacramento, California

Ada Hand, Child Development Unit, State Department of Education, Sacramento, California

Joan Peterson, Visual and Performing Arts Committee, State Department of Education, Sacramento, California

Cooperating Associations

NATIONAL DANCE ASSOCIATION
Marcia Lloyd, President
Luke Kahlich, Former Executive Director, NDA, 1900 Association Drive, Reston, Virginia 22091

NATIONAL ART EDUCATION ASSOCIATION
David Baker, President
Tom Hatfield, Executive Director, NAEA, 1916 Association Drive, Reston, Virginia 22091

MUSIC EDUCATORS NATIONAL CONFERENCE
Karl Glenn, President
John Mahlmann, Executive Director, MENC, 1902 Association Drive, Reston, Virginia 22091

AMERICAN ALLIANCE FOR THEATRE AND EDUCATION
Joan Lazarus, President
Roger Bedard, Executive Secretary, AATE, Theatre Arts Dept., Blacksburg, Virginia 24061

ASSOCIATION FOR CHILDHOOD EDUCATION INTERNATIONAL
Marylouise H. Burger, President
Gil Brown, Former Executive Director, ACEI, 1141 Georgia Avenue, Wheaton, Maryland 20901

NATIONAL ASSOCIATION FOR THE EDUCATION OF YOUNG CHILDREN
Ellen Galinsky, President
Marilyn Smith, Executive Director, NAEYC, 1834 Connecticut Avenue, N.W., Washington, D.C.
     20009

ADMINISTRATION FOR CHILDREN, YOUTH, AND FAMILIES
(cooperating U.S. government agency)
Dollie Wolverton and Mary Lewis

Section I

GENERAL SESSIONS

The Arts and Development

Barbara T. Bowman

My challenge is to consider the arts in relation to the development of young children. The notion of tying curriculum and instruction to developmental characteristics is certainly not new. Skilled teachers have always parlayed their understanding of how children of different ages learn into effective curriculum. It is also true, however, that educators frequently have ignored the developmental characteristics of children, thus making teaching and learning more difficult. The organizers of this conference should take credit for beginning with a discussion of development and I am honored to have been asked to start the conversation.

My interest in the arts for young children is long standing. It began at the age of four when I painted a purple elephant which was hung at the 1933 World's Fair. Although I took the lessons in piano, dramatics, ballet, and art, I remember still the intensity of my early interest in painting and the pleasure I received from having my work acknowledged by others. It is indicative of my interests that I did my first research in graduate school on children's art and wrote my thesis on the Selection of Colors in Easel Painting by Four-Year-Old Children.

My personal history, I think, helps explain my belief that the arts enrich the lives of young children and that how children acquire art concepts is worthy of study. It also explains why more of the illustrations I will use are drawn from the graphic arts than from music or dance. I hope, however, that my comments have generic relevance to all the arts, and those of you whose primary interest is in dance will find my examples sufficiently clear to be translated into your own metaphor.

I have returned to my interest in the arts in recent years because of my concern about children's educational achievement. I believe the arts are what Jackson (1987) called "cultural capital" and that they can assist children in their intellectual, social, and emotional development. It is my belief that the arts foster cognitive competence, can deepen social interaction, and contribute to the personal well-being of the individual. Unfortunately, as you know, arts education has been "the first to go" in the name of school reform. I hope a side benefit of this conference will be to further stimulate interest in the arts as a focus of educational attention.

I believe that the arts should be a part of the education of all children. Just as we expect all children to become literate, doers of mathematics, and even athletes we should also expect all children to learn about and perform in the arts. A baseline of knowledge about the arts will enrich their lives as much as a baseline of knowledge in these other domains.

This does not mean that we expect every child to become an artist or to enjoy all of the arts equally. We expect only a few children to become experts in literature, or mathematics, or athletics, and few will become artists as well. But the road to proficiency is not straight and narrow and children come to expert status in roundabout ways, some fast and some slowly. Our goal in the arts should be the same as it is in literacy and mathematics and athletics — to keep the door open as long as possible for all children to have a chance at becoming a star.

You are already advocates for the arts so I assume I do not need to convince you of their benefit. But let me briefly mention six reasons why I believe the arts are especially suited as curriculum for young children.

First, the arts encourage sensory perception. Cognitive development depends on young children using their senses to learn about the world, and the arts are a wonderful way of stimulating sensual awareness and appreciation. Visual, auditory, kinesthetic, and tactile qualities are inherent in the arts and children can learn through the arts to use their perceptions and let them form the basis for more learning.

Second, the arts provide opportunities for children to learn to represent and symbolize experience. Through representation and symbolization, humans can hold on to experience, rework it, make new sense from it, find new meanings in it. Art is very much like play. Piaget (1971) wrote that one of the qualities of play is "the deformation and subordination of reality to the desires of the self" (p. 33). Art has a similar quality. Reality can be shaped to serve the needs of the ego, thus providing the individual with the opportunity for self-healing and self-development. The arts permit the individual, through repetition, to explore and master emotional, social, cognitive, and physical experience. Like play it offers the chance to release feelings, to remember the past in order to master it, and to try out alternative solutions to problems. It integrates the affective and cognitive components of the human mind.

Third, the arts provide opportunities for children to make things happen, to do things that are valued by other people, to create, to build. All children need to feel that they can affect people and things, thus deriving a sense of efficacy, an essential attribute for a positive self-image. The arts are especially valuable for children who find it difficult to compete with other children or to learn as much or in the same way as others, who often fail in other activities, and who have few chances to be judged competent. The flexibility of the arts and their broad standards offer opportunities for achievement which can carry over into other aspects of children's lives.

Fourth, participation in group arts activities can sponsor a sense of community. Children who coordinate their activities in mutually pleasure-giving ways find satisfaction in being a member of a group. Joining in singing, playing an instrument, drawing a part of a group picture, moving like an elephant to the beat of the music, these are excellent ways for children to find pleasure in group participation. And because the arts are less constrained by right and wrong and competitiveness, they can be entered into with enthusiasm by many children who would be less likely to participate in more formal or competitive activities.

Fifth, academic skills learned in the context of the arts may form the motivation necessary for school learning. This is particularly important for children who are not primed for traditional school learning. The arts can be a powerful vehicle through which to funnel an integrated school curriculum. Children who find excitement and pleasure in the arts may become charged with the energy necessary to learn in school.

Sixth, art expands our world, evoking feelings and thoughts that both mirror and change experience. Transcending logical analysis, art touches our humanity and permits us to intuitively understand and feel the truth embedded in it. A Chinese painting, an African drum, or a Thai dance can all strike chords of feeling as they play on the various senses, thus enlarging our understanding of the human condition. Young children can begin this voyage of discovery.

In this sense, there is no better or worse art, just degrees of complexity and richness. For children, the latest popular dances and ballet, simple nursery songs and arias, books illustrated by parents and those illustrated by recognized artists, and stories and music from other cultures can heighten their sensitivity to art forms and to the world. Art can become part of their everyday lives as they connect museum and concert hall art with popular music, teen dancing, and handicrafts.

Given that the arts can be an important component of an early childhood program, how should instruction be organized? To answer that question I begin by defining more narrowly the dimensions of art that interface with development. Then, I shall consider what we know about the nature of development that bears on how children achieve the skills and knowledge about the arts. And finally, I want to focus on how developmental considerations might guide our plans for children's education in the arts.

Forms of Knowing

First, what is art? I define it as a form of knowing about the world. Using the raw data of the senses as well as the capacities to think, to imagine, and to problem solve, humans organize their knowledge about the world in different ways.

The arts are first of all deeply personal. In performing, or doing art, the individual expresses what he or she knows, what he or she can see, feel, believe, and construct from their own experience. Artists can only authentically say what they know from inside of themselves. Imitation may be a form of flattery but it is not itself art. Appreciation of the arts is also a personal experience. Art must tug at an individual's emotions, or senses, or intellect—or preferably all three—clarifying or expanding or reflecting the individual's own knowledge. Although pretending to enjoy or understand art may raise one's social status or bring higher grades in art and music appreciation classes, it will not lead to appreciation unless the individual is open to personal involvement. This means that one of the most important aspects of art education is that it must personally involve the learner.

Art is also social and reflects how groups of people organize knowledge. In the sciences, for instance, knowledge is organized to be objective, predictable, and verifiable by impersonal instruments. In the arts, on the other hand, knowledge is more personal, and creative, and verifiable only by the responses of other human beings. In expressing the attraction of art for people, Rorty wrote that we "want to keep space open for the wonder which poets can sometimes cause — wonder that there is something new under the sun which is not an accurate representation of what was already there, something which (at least for the moment) cannot be explained and can barely be described" (Stoller, 1986).

Does this mean that the disciplines of science and the arts are diametrically opposed, with no overlap between them? The answer is, of course, no. In somewhat different ways, the emotional, social, and cognitive processes that underlie doing art also underlie doing science, and I may add doing social sciences, and philosophy as well. All depend on the ability to perceive forces in the environment and in the self; all require individuals to encode their own thoughts and to decode the thoughts of others, to represent and symbolize experience in ways that others can understand; and all require people to manipulate experience to create different effects. Indeed, all disciplines augment children's abilities to think conceptually and can stimulate their interest in the various other ways of knowing.

Art, however, is not just the expression of the idiosyncratic knowledge of a single individual. Although the artist's knowledge is not empirical in the scientific sense, it is not art unless it says something to others. Art, then, is also social. While children may be born with an inherent interest in communication through art forms, as is the case with other communication skills, they require a social context to bring their inborn capabilities to fruition. From social interaction children learn to draw from and make meaning with others of their group. This means that children must learn about the arts through social interaction with others. They must learn the conventional boundaries of domains of knowledge even if we may choose to ignore them on occasion.

Culture and Development

Understanding the relationship between culture and development is an essential step in understanding the relationship of development to the arts. The arts are embedded in the meaning system —the culture—that people have developed. One of the accepted facts in development is the gradual transition from a largely personal and self-centered view of the world during infancy to a more socialized and other related one as the child grows. This developmental transition is shaped by the particular culture in which a child is reared. Children are quickly taught to make meaning within the context of their own families and communities. The activities they value, the things they pay attention to, the styles of personal behavior and social interaction they prefer are derived from their families and community intimates.

Cultural meanings are the bedrock of development not only affecting what and how children act but also determining who they are. Young children learn from their families and communities attitudes about art — who should and can do what kind of art, when, and with whom. Let me give you some examples of these differences in the response of children and communities to the arts.

Some cultures, like the United States, permit greater and longer periods of personal autonomy and independence, while others, like the Chinese, require much earlier and more complete melding of the individual with the group. In China in the early 1980s I observed a teacher teaching an art lesson to a group of preschool children. She had prepared a model of a butterfly collage and carefully, gently, led the children through the steps to create a similar one. At each stage the teacher explained what the child should do and why it would be good to do so. Community aesthetics were considered an appropriate component of the children's education. Many in the United States would be appalled that the teacher assumed so much direction over the children's art products. In this country children are more likely to be left free to decide for themselves how to represent a butterfly—or even if they want to do a butterfly at all. The value placed on political hegemony in China and independence in the United States extends to the kinds of art produced by children in each community. The arts are embedded in the political system in which people live.

Another example: I observed a second grade American classroom when a Sousa march was put on the record player. The brass band had hardly struck up the first notes before these school children were ready to march in unison and reported that the music made them feel patriotic emotions. The same notes on a bag pipe might inspire similar fervor in Scottish children. But they would not have the same meaning for a child from an island in the South Pacific or an Amazon forest. Thus, similar artistic expression may evoke quite different response in children.

Thus we find some children enjoying group dances, taking pleasure in the synchronization of movements among the dancers, while children from other communities show enormous personal creativity, taking pleasure in varying the themes of the dance or music. Similarly, children from some groups produce highly structured, adult-like graphic products, taking pleasure in only minor variation on a theme, while other children push off social interference with their products.

There is, then, no single standard for what is art, but rather art emanates from the individual and is mediated by social experiences of people with one another. These differences between communities mean that there is no single right or wrong kind of art product or supportive structure for art experience. This does not mean that there are no developmental regularities in how children learn in various cultures.

Art Instruction

Children learn from art specific education. At a simple or basic level, people can communicate across cultural differences. Because of our common humanity, sign language, facial and body movements, intonations, and styles can give us an idea of what someone means who does not speak our language or come from our part of the world. But in order to really understand the meanings of others, we need to know more; mores, traditions, and beliefs tie people together in ways that permit them to understand what is meant by what others of their group say and do. Specific knowledge is also essential for understanding the arts. Technique with different media and instruments, the conventions for using materials, and the potential of various tools are essential to doing art. In addition, since art, as other human activity, builds on the past, knowledge of the arts' history adds to understanding and appreciation of art products.

Is there any developmental order around which to organize these components of art education? I suggest four developmental characteristics that affect how we should arrange art education.

Art and Individual Development

Developmental Principle #1. Age affects performance. One has only to look at a stack of children's drawings or watch groups of children dance and sing to see that there are similarities in how children of various ages perform. For instance, children begin their graphic arts experiments with scribbling, gradually adding names to their scribbles. Children make forms in a developmental order: first lines, then circles and lines, called mandellas, suns, and radials. They gradually adapt graphic forms to labels (adults are big circles and children are smaller ones).

The younger the child the more similar is their performance; thus first pictures of all children in all cultures look quite similar. Kellogg in *The Psychology of Children's Art* has fine examples of the way in which children from different cultures show developmental similarities. They create quite different effects but use "identical shapes, designs, and symbols" (p. 107).

Children's art mirrors the changes in their thinking which move from global understanding to increased elaboration and refinement. But it is not a continuous forward progress. Children go from wholes to parts, and with knowledge of a new part, re-form their understanding of the whole. And so they go back and forth, with each piece of elaboration informing their understanding of the whole, each new understanding of a whole making the parts more meaningful.

An example from children's writing may make this process clearer. Children generally begin by learning that a set of symbols, letters, stand for their name. They learn this because teachers put their names on their papers, mothers put them in their books, older children ask about the letters in their names. At first, children will represent their names with a number of meaningless (at least to us) squiggles and announce proudly, that's my name. Gradually, they begin to grasp that there are a number of separate entities that go into their names and they begin to try to duplicate these letters. The order of the letters is often irrelevant as the child's attention is in just finding out what the letters are. Slowly, order is attended to, then size and spacing. Each new aspect of name writing must be integrated into the child's understanding of symbol systems and as this understanding increases, new parts can be added.

Children's musical skill proceeds in a similarly organized fashion. Children begin by distinguishing between music and nonmusic, and learn that how one responds to the noise of music is different from the way one responds to other noises, words for instance. Children learn to respond to words with answering words; they learn to respond to music by listening and imitating. Experimenting with their own ability to make different noises, blending sounds in varying tempos to the music they hear, children slowly make their music more elaborate and complex. Over time, children coordinate melody, rhythm and pitch, and, if the words are simple, they may even use meaningful words as opposed to just sounds. But children may be as old as six or seven before they understand that the words of music are supposed to make sense. As with graphic arts, change comes through the elaboration of basic concepts, each new part is learned and each new part learned adds to the whole and lays the stage for other new parts.

How fast children go through the sequences in acquiring skills and knowledge in music and the graphic arts depends upon the kinds of experiences they have; on what they see, hear, and use; on the amount or kind of teaching provided by adults and older children; and the perceptual acuities, muscular coordination, and cognitive competence which children bring to the art.

Developmental Principle #2. Children are active learners. Symbolizing and representing personal experience assists children to develop emotionally and cognitively. Erikson explains that children project their own meanings on their activities, using them as symbols of experience to be manipulated and reworked. By learning to symbolize their own imagining, their own fantasies, children not only learn to represent experience themselves, they also learn to appreciate and use the symbols of others—as in games, music, and stories.

Similarly, Piaget noted the importance of children constructing their own physical and logical mathematical knowledge. Concrete experience with media permits children to learn the dimensions of the physical world. How do you turn three dimensional experience into two dimensional representations. How do you exert control over the paint brush or crayon, the piano or the harmonica. How do you organize the picture within the confines of the paper? Your body within the confines of your space?

Action is the primary mode of learning for young children. Metacognition, or reflecting on action, follows direct action. Thus, children are able to tell us how to make a circle only after they have made thousands of circles. The implication of this principle is that children need time to experiment with and explore the relationship of ideas to materials and instruments and that direct experience should precede talking about concepts.

Developmental Principle #3. Children learn from others. Children are not like Topsy who supposedly just "grew." Children learn from other people and they learn best and fastest those things that the people they love and who love them are interested in and who help them acquire skills to do. It is no accident that children who come from families interested in the arts are most likely to themselves be interested in the arts. Exposure is important, but modeling from important others of how, when, and in what manner to learn about and to use the arts is equally important.

Vygotsky uses the term "scaffolding" to describe how adults and older children assist a child to build on his or her prior knowledge to make new knowledge. When mother sings a lullaby with baby and lets him complete the last line himself, she is scaffolding his musical skill. When the teacher shows a child how to wipe her brush on the side of the container to avoid dribbles of paint, she is scaffolding her painting skill. The secret of scaffolding is in helping children do something they wish to do and in a way that helps move them from one level of knowledge to the next. All of us who work with young children know that scaffolding is itself a form of art based on intuitive knowledge of individuals and general knowledge of child development.

Developmental Principle #4. Children are all different. Children have differing sensory acuities, perceptual abilities, and patterns of cognitive organization. There are differences in children's art performance and in their ability to produce and recognize quality in the performance of others. Some children from an early age are able to draw or sing or dance much better than others. A variety of explanations have been given for these differences. Individual genetic blueprints are all just a little different. Social biologists look for intersects between cultures and the inheritance of particular characteristics. Neurobiologists inform us of the role of various components of the brain in processing information from the senses and their work has helped us account for differences in thinking and acting through the dominance of one side of the brain over the other. Gardner (1980) suggests there are many different types of intelligence which optimize or minimize children's interest in and skills with particular ways of knowing. As mentioned earlier, particular cultures sponsor and inhibit particular kinds of artistic expression.

While these works have sensitized us to biological and cultural variations in people's creativity in the different ways of knowing, they do not argue for basing arts programs for young children on natural talent. As with most human achievement, a wide range of natural talent may undergird artistic performance and understanding but there is no reason to believe that all people can't reach some level of expertness and pleasure in the arts.

Developmental Implications for Teaching

Thus far I have contended that the arts are a worthy curriculum for young children, particularly for children who may be alienated from school culture. I have suggested that the arts are a unique way of knowing that is different from science and logic but not in conflict with these disciplines and that interest in the arts may stimulate interest in other forms of knowing. And finally, I have listed four developmental concepts which affect how and what young children learn.

I want to go on now to consider the implications of these points in relation to one of the current controversies regarding arts education, that is, whether the arts should be taught or simply made available to young children to perform. Should the arts curriculum for young children be characterized by a hands-off approach for the teacher and a hands-on approach for children or by an instructional program which seeks to extend and refine children's skills and knowledge?

I suggest that this is a useless dichotomy. Children learn by their own actions but they also learn from others. Personal expression is an important component of the arts and children do need to gain confidence in their ability to create symbols and represent realities according to their own feelings and thoughts. In this sense, "any tampering," as Lowenfeld said, is "likely to vitiate the quality of what was produced" (Gardner, 1980, p. 169). Young children do need acceptance for themselves and their ideas; they need to be protected from the excessive pressure of too high standards or competitiveness. In these ways early experiences in the arts need to be child-centered.

But this does not mean that children will learn all they need to know without assistance. Children need modeling and stimulation from meaningful adults to value and want to engage in the arts; they need help finding new ways of looking at and organizing information about the world, about the arts, and about themselves; they need help learning new skills to enhance their performance. A developmentally appropriate arts curriculum will have ample time for both—time for children to integrate information according to their own developmental schedule and modes of learning and time for a teacher to help them extend, elaborate on, and refine their skills and knowledge.

The classroom teacher, generally responsible for implementing the early childhood programs, is often portrayed as needing little or no knowledge of the arts since her role is non-instructional. I think this is wrong. There are many things that children can learn on their own, but much of what they need to know must come from others. Children need sensitive teachers who know and understand the concepts underlying the arts to focus their attention on the most meaningful aspects of a given art form. Teachers need to have a plan for what children should learn, even though they must implement their plans flexibly. Teachers must teach, but they need to teach informally and to individuals or small groups. Teachers need to present new ideas, but in the context of the children's interest and prior knowledge. It seems to me this speaks to teachers needing to know both development and the structure of the arts, needing to appreciate the art values of children's families and communities as well as the standards and values of the larger society.

Let me summarize then what I believe are the markers for a developmentally appropriate way to teach the arts.

1. Select a teacher who can form meaningful relationships with young children and who loves and cares about an art form or forms.

2. Provide ample time for children to explore materials without pressure to achieve a particular end product. Process, not product, is the code word here.

3. Expose the children to examples and models of art: stories and poems, records and instruments, exercises and dances beginning with the ones familiar in children's homes and communities and gradually extending these to a wide range of art works (remembering that popular music and dance are art forms due respect and enjoyment).

4. Encouragement for children to reflect about what they do and see and hear and feel. Reflection enhances the meaning of art and enlarges the viewers understanding of the world.

5. Provision of information and technical assistance within the context of the child's activities and interests. How and when will depend on the individual child and on the teaching methods used in the family and community.

No single educational strategy will meet the criteria of a developmentally appropriate curriculum. Rather, development only provides guideposts for many different strategies depending on individual and group differences.

I want to pose one more question. Is what I am suggesting as an appropriate arts curriculum for young children really art? I suspect not. Certainly not in the meaning ascribed by those advocating discipline-based art education. For them, art is a discipline—a body of knowledge—based on an array of information, skills, and values. Young children, not having these, are not in a position to create or understand the arts.

I would argue, however, for another way of looking at the question. I think we should take a leap from what we have learned about reading and writing and apply it to arts education. We have learned, for instance, that literacy does not begin with decoding but develops over a long time. Children need to hear lots of stories, to pretend to read and write, to observe the various uses for literacy in the environment, and to think of themselves as able to learn to be readers and writers themselves.

The skills and knowledge of the arts also develop. I suggest that we stop thinking about "real" art as starting only after children have all the skills to do it and think about art as having different stages. The early childhood stage is the time for children to enjoy expressing themselves, see the value of arts in their own lives, begin to think about and understand the various components of an art, and expect adults to help them learn and develop.

In my opinion, arts education should be thought of as a process that begins at birth and never ends. And the beginning is just as important as any other time. Early childhood arts education may not look like traditional instruction, but it is just as important.

BIBLIOGRAPHY

Aronoff, F.W. (1969). *Music and young children.* New York: Holt, Rinehart and Winston.

Clark, G., Day, M., & Greer, W.D. (1987). Discipline-based art education: Becoming students of art. *Journal of Aesthetic Education, 21,* No. 2, 130 -193.

Eisner, E. (1985). *The educational imagination.* New York: Macmillan Publishing Company.

Eisner, E. (1987) Discipline-based art education: A reply to Jackson." *Educational Researcher, 16*(9), 50 -52.

Eisner, E. (1988) Discipline-based art education: Its criticisms and its critics. *Art Education, 41*(2), 7-13.

Gardner, H. (1980). *Artful scribbles: The developmental significance of children's drawings.* New York: Basic Books.

Gehlbach, R. (1990). Art education: Issues in curriculum and research." *Educational Researcher, 19*(7), 10 -25.

Gombrichl, E.H. (1972). The visual image. *The Scientific American, 227*(9), 82 - 96.

Goodnow, J. (1977). *Children drawing.* Cambridge, MA: Harvard University Press.

Jackson, P. (1987). Mainstreaming art: An essay on discipline-based art education. *Educational Researcher, 16* (6), 39 -43.

Jefferson, B. (1965). *Teaching art to children.* Boston: Allyn & Bacon, Inc.

Kellogg, R. with O'Dell, S. (1967). *The psychology of children's art.* New York: CMR - Random House.

Lasky, L., & Mukerji, R. (1980). *Art: Basic for young children.* Washington, DC: National Association for the Education of Young Children.

Peery, J.C., Peery, I., & Draper, T. (1987). *Music and child development.* New York: Springer-Verlag.

Perkins, D.N., & Gardner, H. (1988). Why "zero?" A brief introduction to Project Zero. *Journal of Aesthetic Education, 22*(1), Preface.

Piaget, J., & Inhelder, B. (1971). *Mental imagery and the child.* New York: Basic Books.

Rosenblatt, E., & Winner, E. (1988). The art of children's drawing. *Journal of Aesthetic Education, 22*(1), 3 -15.

Stoller, P. (1986). *The taste of ethnographic things.* Philadelphia: University of Pennsylvania Press.

Barbara T. Bowman is the director of graduate studies at the Erikson Institute, Loyola University, Chicago, Illinois. A well-known authority on early childhood educatin, with extensive experience in teacher education, she directs the Kellogg and Borg-Warner projects which provide technical assistance to six Chicago public schools, preschool through primary.

She's Just Pulled the Blanket Over Her Face

THE ESSENTIAL ROLE OF THE CREATIVE ARTS IN EARLY CHILDHOOD

Joyce Boorman

Laura, my four-year-six-months (18 1/2 days!) old friend, sits at the table painting. She obliterates with black paint a carefully drawn face. "Why are you doing that?" asks the significant adult. With patience and a sigh of exasperation, Laura responds, "Because she's just pulled the blanket over her face!" Laura's response jolts my thoughts to Saint-Exupery and his little prince,who with equal sighs says,

> The grown-ups' response, this time, was to advise me to lay aside my drawing of boa constrictors, whether from the inside or the outside, and devote myself instead to geography, history, arithmetic and grammar. That is why, at the age of six, I gave up what might have been a magnificent career as a painter. I had been disheartened by the failure of my Drawing Number One and my Drawing Number Two. Grown-ups never understand anything by themselves, and it is tiresome for children to be always and forever explaining things to them![1]

And so it is with a sense of both privilege and awe that we, as the grown-ups, try once again to enter into and explain the role of the creative arts in early childhood. And so I begin my task.

In Edmonton, Alberta, Canada, my telephone rings. It is Carol LeBrecht with an invitation, on your behalf, to join with you at this international conference on the creative arts in early childhood. My response is to ask for time to reflect—this is not a challenge to be lightly considered. I accept!

Then comes the time of excitement, of vision, of wanting to cry "I have a dream ..." For, along with each one of you here, committed to children, I have had a dream. In that dream there is no hunger, poverty, violence, neglect, weeping of children. But, because we do not live in that dream but in reality, it is at times difficult to reconcile giving our attention, our commitment to the creative arts in childhood when surrounded by the reality of the abuse that children suffer. Yet we must respond to the need because we have been given that responsibility. We neglect that responsibility at our peril, for art celebrates life, and we need to celebrate life. The celebration of life is the central, if oft forgotten, message of humanness and at the core of the creative arts in early childhood, for it is, in part, through their creative arts that young children ratify their childhood. It is through *their* arts that they make *their* childhood explicable to us, revealing to us their outermost and their innermost perceptions and understanding of their world.

It was in 1978 at the first International Conference on Dance and the Child when I was forcefully reminded that this celebration of life is what the child is telling us, again and yet again. Alan Cunningham had been presenting his keynote address on "The Child as Creator." Being a busy conference administrator, I came in at the end of the address to a hushed yet vibrating atmosphere. My sensibility being dulled by nitty-gritty, I remember asking a Scottish delegate, "How was the address?" Her eyes were bright with tears held back and I sensed immediately her rejection of my crass questioning in that charged atmosphere. Much later I read these words of Alan's and realized how sensitively he had placed them in a context of children's living poetry from "I Never Saw Another Butterfly," the writings of the children of Terezin.[2] He wrote thus:

> We have to remember these children were starving, and usually extremely ill. Everything took a special effort. To suggest that they were *playing* may sound to you an offensive way of trivializing their achievement, but only if we have a very diminished notion of what playing really is about. Play has purposes far beyond playing. Play can be far more serious than seriousness, and it is critical—and not for children only—to the whole scheme of life.[3]

This for me is the essential message of the creative arts—they address the humanness in each one of us. Each art is a force so powerful it has a purpose far beyond the art itself; it *is* essential to the whole scheme of life.

Sometimes, as I have attempted to reconcile, with university students, these conflicting concerns—on the one side societal and cultural concerns of hunger, poverty, violence, abuse of children and on the other the positive force of the creative arts—I have thought of the "necklace of protection or the amulet of joy." Each time a child experiences the strengthening power of joy, delight, enlightenment, becomes stronger for that momentary or sustained contact with a deeper sense of self, then that child is strengthened. One moment of joy added to another and then another, a circlet of beads—a circlet of protection, protection against the ennui of life, against that which Rachel Carson described as "the boredom and disenchantment of later years, the sterile preoccupation with things that are artificial, the alienation from the source of our strength."[4]

The creative arts should be a place of strength, a place of joy. I have witnessed this deep joy, which goes far beyond mere pleasure, as young children have ventured into creative dance. There is a deep centering that occurs in delighted outbursts or quiet tranquillity of spirit as children are "put back into their skins" and find an emotional balance. Perhaps this is close to the joy of which Tolkien speaks:

> This joy is not essentially escapist nor fugitive. In its fairy tale "other world" setting, it is a sudden and miraculous grace never to be counted on to recur; it denies universal final defeat giving a glimpse of Joy, Joy beyond the walls of the world.[5]

In the exploration of that place of joy, so essential in the creative arts, there are several significant adults, one of the most important being each one of you. For let us remind ourselves of the story of The Giving Tree.[6]

You are all familiar with the story of the giving tree that, once a shelter and playhouse for a young child, gradually over years gave branches, limbs, fruit, and blossom until finally, a foreshortened trunk, it could still give a resting place for the young boy who returned as a lonely elderly man, who could sit in the sun and feel its warmth.

There was such an old tree stump in my childhood. It stood in an asphalt playground in an English infant school in the poorer area of town. Whenever the sun shone at playtime, we would clatter down the spiral iron staircase attached to the outside wall of our classroom. Then six, seven, eight, or was it more, of us, would stretch and clamber to sit on the stump. But most important of all, there came to sit with us the most significant adult in our young school lives: our classroom teacher. There, our backs pressed snugly against each other, our scraggy ankle- socked legs swinging we would sit triumphantly with our teacher. We were safe, we were secure, we were momentarily inviolate.

It occurs to me today that how often perhaps we have forgotten, negated, or simply overlooked how very, very important we are to children in those moments when we cease to instruct, but continue to teach simply by the warmth of our presence in the lives of young children. I KNEW, with my six-year-old wisdom, that I was going to grow up and become a teacher. And I DID! But now, as I reflect, it seems that listening, seeing, nurturing, sharing teacher was calling forth more than my desire to be a teacher. She was helping each of us children to uncover a special blueprint that is ours alone—unique to each one of us.

I believe in the creative arts this is a primary, central process—you are the listening, seeing, nurturing adult who responds. You are the cornerstone of that process. You are in many instances the child's first audience, you are the nodding approval. As Elizabeth O'Connor says:

> Her encouragement does not make us think we are better than we are. It simply enables us
> to do what we do as well as we can.[7]

You are vital to the creative arts process because this is a process of evocation and response—the children's articulation of their known world, their inner and outer worlds. In this process of evocation and response, as you unfold the world in stories, open doors into the wonderment of music, and help the young child's eyes become excited by color, you are laying foundations that will not easily crumble.

Today, perhaps more so than in the past, parents and other significant adults are a vital part of sharing this process. So I would like to share with you verbal snapshots of four of my dancing children's parents. I have chosen the children from the early childhood ages and beyond, reaching into the teenage years. This is because I believe we must always remain conscious and alert to the vertical links of early childhood with teenage and adult years. We cannot slice early childhood horizontally, for life is both warp and weft. We must consider early childhood in the context of the horizontal and the vertical strands. So my snapshots unfold:

Anna with the Bubble Gum. Anna's bubble gum is a bright shiny pink. In she hurtles, skips, leaps, bounds, and the large pink bubbles POP! Anna, all of seven years old, knows full well that at any moment the gum will be headed for the garbage can, but she is delightedly determined to have the last chew. But it is with Anna's mother that my thoughts are directed. Energy the same as Anna's; outgoing, warm, supportive, she has patiently watched Anna grow in her dance for several years. Through sharings and concerts she has smilingly supported us each time saying, "This is wonderful, I wish I could understand it but I'm just too left brain." For Anna's mother is an educational administrator who firmly believes her thinking to be linear, convergent, logical. and specific.

Then after several more years of growing in dance Anna is twelve and her mother nods and smiles through a Christmas concert. But this time she says, "This appeals to me so much more than when she was younger. I am beginning to understand the meaning in the dance, the music is familiar to me, I can see now where it belongs." Supportive as Anna's mother had been throughout Anna's early childhood, it had been difficult for her to understand the importance of the work. Now, as the gap closed between her adult understanding and Anna's work, she could recognize its place; the dissonance had been lessened.

Parents deal each day with dissonance, particularly perhaps in childhood's play and the creative arts. We have to bridge this gap. We have to make the creative arts in early childhood accessible to the parents' and adults' understanding. We have to communicate not in the private, mysterious language of the arts, but within the general everyday language of all of us.

Ruth with the Tears. But let us look at Ruth, who was four going on five and she stood sobbing outside the room (studio). In black leotard, bare-legged, and with the thinness and fragility of childhood, she was cold and shivering. The scenario came down to what Mother termed "A Battle of Wills" and Mother had every intention of winning as she stormed off with, "I'll be back at 9:30!" It took time to gentle the sobs, warm the child, and persuade her into the room where she huddled on the floor. Near the end of the half-hour, Ruth was up and skipping and beaming—the sun was back in her life. Not all of childhood's tears can be so easily dried. But I pondered Ruth's mother more than the child.

At class end the mother returned and seeing Ruth's happiness was convinced her earlier actions had been justified. For Ruth's mother the creative dance class had had spin-off values. It is, perhaps, the spin-off values that have misled us so often in children's creative arts. Distinct from the nurturing values, the instrumental values, the value of the art form itself, the spin-off values have woven their own web of deceit. Ruth's mother was enmeshed in that web. In September Ruth did not return to dance.

The Angry Father. "If you are going to take him in there I am going to leave!" So began, in 1968, our first registration for young children in Saturday morning dance classes at the University of Alberta. Illumined forever in my memory I both see and hear that angry father as he addressed his wife, his young son standing silently by. This father was being challenged by the situation, his role identification was being disturbed, but I suspect mostly that he simply did not understand. Each one of us here has at some point or another been challenged in exactly the same way by a parent, an adult, a peer, who does not understand.

It is April 1989, and the Alberta Children's Creative Dance Theatre has just completed its spring performance. The senior class, mostly adolescents of 14 to 16 years, have culminated the performance with a powerful work, "The Good Friday Theme." A grandfather approaches me and, paraphrased, tells me, "That was wonderful. If you had told me several years ago that I would ever give up the hockey series for this and enjoy it, I'd have said you were mad." I resisted my desire to respond appropriately and smiled, could it be said, sweetly? Not minutes later a father approached me and the conversation was quite different. "I came to the dress rehearsal and now I am glad I saw that twice. This time I saw more, I understood what was happening, and I appreciated it at a deeper level!" There were 23 years of changing societal and cultural contexts between the first angry father and the last father: the difference between the fear of not understanding and the willingness to be vulnerable to learning.

For me the main reflection on all these snapshots is that these comments were not necessarily directed specifically to the creative dance context. The fathers, grandfather, and mothers were concerned with *themselves*, not the dance. What amazed the grandfather was *his own change*, what had to be articulated for the second father was *his* growth. What Anna's mother needed was the security of the recognizable. What Ruth's mother needed to know was that she was right. It was fascinating that on reflection none had mentioned their children or the dance. It was not upon reflection Anna's growth, Ruth's growth, or Neil's growth that were their concern. It was *their* growth. And in adult growth lies one of the challenges that confront us in children's creative arts.

As we approach this challenge of the creative arts in early childhood education, we shall have to be concerned with developmental phases of adult participation, from in-touch sharings, to mutual participation, to conscious distancing. We shall have to be alert that in our zeal for sharing children's work we do not eradicate the child in favor of adult expectations and fears. We shall have to examine the physical spaces in which children's arts take place, recognizing that those spaces immediately impose an atmosphere upon the adult that enters through the doors. We shall have to persuade adults that they do not "take off their responsibilities" with their shoes and leave them outside, that children's work is not a matter of "polka-dot bikinis," visually, musically, or physically, but that this is a special situation in which they can come to know their children in a very different way, a way which can reveal yet another facet in the unique blueprint of their child. We have to ensure that adults recognize that children's art has to be more than mere entertainment; it has to go beyond the "cute" and become evocation and response between child and adult: a mutual giving and receiving.

Are these then three phases of adult development--engagement, embracement, and convincing? Engagement is sometimes a given, particularly with a parental and family group. Embracement is the reaching out to enfold in the evocation and response. To convince needs the changing of adult understandings and perceptions. In the coming decade it is with this third phase that we shall engage, to convince. We have to become significant adults who can view our small protagonists and their creative arts endeavors with respect. We have to be able to recall the way things look to the small and powerless. We have to be their advocates, interpreters, liaisons, agents, and go-betweens as we bring the world of the significant adult and the world of the young child's creative arts in touch with each other. We have to be able to articulate the significance of the creative arts to parents, to colleagues, to administrators, to politicians, to translate into words the leaping, flying, whirling, falling patterns of the moving child, the splashes of red, orange, black, shouting joyfully to us from the paper, the delicate traceries of pencil, the squealing, chanting, whispered words that fall randomly upon our ears. For explain them we must. So let me cautiously and on tiptoe approach cognition!

Phases of Symbolic Representation

I can only begin to unravel cognition for myself if I combine the writings of Elliot Eisner[8] and David Best[9] and meld them with my own daily work with children. For me, cognition is intimately interwoven with symbolic representation—child the symbol maker.

Symbolic representation appears to evolve through phases of *intrinsic satisfaction.* The phase when the young child literally splashes actions into space, color onto paper, sounds into silence. The phase when Janet and James learn that they can change their world, that their actions have consequences. The phase when we, the careful observers and responders, watch and listen, gleaning knowledge of their growth.

Then, with leaps and bounds comes the second phase—open-sense making. Meaning is not fixed. As Langeveld tells us:

> We see how things in this world have no fixed meanings. What an open-sense making is a knife, is suddenly a bridge, a roadblock, a soldier, a house.[10]

For the child, there is the ordering, reordering, the continual manipulative play of sounds, colors, movements, things. For us again, the quiet watchers, there often occurs in this unconscious and transitory reordering a breathless delight as our adult world becomes surprised and enriched because of viewing something anew through the eyes of the child.

Then comes fixed-meanings and later conscious-distancing. Throughout these phases is the foreshadowing, the end that gives the beginning meaning. I understood this as I came to dance, because, if I truncated the symbolic representation in children's dance and did not recognize its foreshadowing of the mature form of representation, then I would have problems with understanding its cognitive essence. I had to understand the skipping action symbolically, that in the context of the four-year-old the skipping, leaping, flying, falling actions were the symbolic representation that would range from raindrops, candy canes, sky horses, and giants' brooms. In the context of the eight-year-old, the action context was nightmares in closets, sheriffs and cowboys, lightning and thunder, and in the context of the twelve-year-old, anger, delight, warriors of the night. The context would mature, the action was the symbolic material to be manipulated in accordance with the contextual need of expression and communication, the images, the ideas, the feelings of the child. It has to be understood that this is in direct opposition to preparing children for the future, for they can indeed only be children and should be nurtured as such. (Perhaps it is the erosion of childhood that has eroded us as adults and the children are in rebellion for our stealing of their childhood.)

But this, for me, is cognition, the symbolic representation of childhood that foreshadow the symbolic representation of adulthood. If the creative arts are not central to the young child's curriculum, then we have lost this myriad symbolic representation. With this loss we lose also a vast pool of cognition.

It was around about this point in reflecting upon cognition I decided to leap ahead and come to the end of the first draft. With a sense of the whole could I then remedy some of the parts? Through words trying to reach out to you, to draw an image for you but with words, I have been slicing the world in one way—asking you to know the world through our communication with words.

This is the issue that is so vital to Elliot Eisner's views on symbolic representation and cognition. He states it so clearly in his article, "The Role of the Arts in the Invention of Man":

> Symbol systems within our culture are nonredundant, that is, what one comes to know through one symbol system one cannot know in the same way through another. What one can come to know through poetry has no literal equivalent in prose; what one can know through prose cannot be replicated through pictures; what one can know through pictures cannot be duplicated in dance. Humans have invented and exploited each symbol system because they perform a unique cognitive function.[11]

To me this kind of understanding is dynamite! Particularly, if you realize that my whole teaching career has been devoted to explaining creative dance for children. Creative dance—a unique cognitive function—Wow! But the moment I grasp symbolic representation as I watch Melissa, Vladimir, Samantha leap—whirl—skip, fly, fall within the context of symbolic meaning, I am in the presence of cognition. Exciting stuff. So as our children slice their world in differing ways, the better to understand it, we must hear Eisner's words: "Incompetence in any one of those symbol systems exacts a price that exceeds the borders of its own cognitive domain."

If the price is high in the cognitive domain we must ask ourselves, is it even more highly priced in the affective and social and imaginative tapestry of early childhood? And if a high price in childhood, is this our children's destiny as adults? For Saint-Exupery writes of such adults:

> I heard them talking to one another in murmurs and whispers. They talked about illness, money, shabby domestic cares. Their talk painted the walls of the dismal prison in which these men had locked themselves.... Nobody grasped you by the shoulder while there was still time. Now the clay of which you were shaped has dried and hardened, and naught in you will ever awaken the sleeping musician, the poet, the astronomer that possibly inhabited you in the beginning.[12]

If we as educators neglect the creative arts in education, we are responsible for helping to turn the key of that dismal prison in which children will grow. We will be a part of the process whereby the clay hardened about them and the poet and poetry within them dies.

Symbolic representation, however, pushes us to the frontiers of structural knowledge of the subject matter with which the children deal as they shift toward the five- to eight-year-old range, the second phase of early childhood.

Melissa is growing into a six-year-old. She has chosen to sit on the floor. The shape she has carved with her body is angular. Fingers are stretched with the smallest windows and doors of space gleaming between each finger. Elbows make sharp, jagged edges to her choice of shape. The music softly echoes through the room. Very gently, with great care, concentration, intensity, and precision Melissa starts to turn. The spirit trapped in the icicle by the wicked wizard of winter has started to escape. Now traveling and turning, Melissa freezes. She is a lone spirit. But then another comes to join her. Shapes change, melt, mold, for the myriad of shapes to be made by two is far greater than by one. So the spirits of the icicles meet, belong, know each other, are joined by more and more until an exuberant band of spirits escape the final clutches of winter. Imagination, affect, awareness of each other, all is happening to Melissa—a far deeper layering of growth than the mere cute or superficial enactment of a children's story, for Melissa had been helped over an ever maturing process to control and express the idea, the images, the feelings inherent in this fantasy. Now she owned them and in owning them they were her next stepping-stone, the foreshadowing of the next phase of growth, cognitive, emotional, imaginal, social.

Knowledge of the Structure of Arts

But, without growth in the structural knowledge and development of each art, are our creative arts, perhaps, a little like this story?

> A woman traveling in India chanced upon a maker of brass bowls. She picked up one of intricate design and asked its price. "Two annas." She thought of a friend who ran a "gifte shoppe" in America and of the profit she could make. "Ask him," she said to the interpreter, "how much they will be if I take fifty like this." The maker pondered. "Four annas each." "But," said the bewildered woman, "tell him if I take so many they must be less, not more." The craftsman answered, "Tell the lady that if I repeat myself so many times I must have much money, for I shall need to go away into solitude so that my spirit can re-create itself."[13]

Our children do not have this freedom to go away and re-create themselves if we give them in education a meaningless series of repetitive tasks. Knowledge of the structure of each art is essential as I discovered or rediscovered recently in England when on supply teaching. Let me anecdotally elaborate:

My phone rings at 8.00 a.m. "Yes," I would go to —— school. Into my car I would trundle and through streets, lanes, countryside, or town I would go, eventually and hastily to park within the school's proximity. Into the school and into the classroom! From Key-Phonics to Infant Math, through registers and dinner money, into assembly, out of assembly, into "Miss ... Miss ... MISS," "My pencil needs sharpening Miss," "He hit me Miss," "She punched me Miss," "I need paper M-I-S-S," "What shall I do NOW Miss?" The day surged onward, the voices rose, deafened, abated, strident, piercing young vocal chords declaiming life and its rights. And amid the noise the hastening ones with limbs askew whacking the air, emerged the rare, quiet spirit, withdrawn, sheltering, unnoticed unless "the listening eyes" could search out and draw out the solitudes.

Somewhere in each day I would explore the creative arts with the children. One day it was creative dance, albeit in the classroom. Everything I knew from years of experience with my children in the Alberta Children's Creative Dance Theatre is invalid! The children come to the experience eager but without background. Fortunately, I know the structural development of creative dance and can swiftly adapt and give the children the beginning experiences but in a developmentally acceptable context. Then I venture into painting, paper sculpting, glue, paste, beans and barley! I make every beginner's mistake ever recorded. The children are delighted. Hours after everyone else has gone home I am still washing paintbrushes, crawling under desks to find crayons, sticky paper, beans and barley. Not only had my classroom management skills been sorely tested, but nothing *cognitive, emotional, or social* could possibly have occurred because I DID NOT KNOW the structural development of these disciplines and the concomitant process of learning involved.

The creative arts are highly cognitive, affective, and social experiences for early childhood when taught knowledgeably. But knowledgeably they must be taught. And when taught knowledgeably, what have my young protagonists taught me of the creative core of the arts which I shall call creativity?

As I reflect upon the children who over the years have taught me so much and given me some of their wisdom, where do I take my stance? They have with patience and forebearance taught me that there is a *processional order* to the creative arts that exists in the lives of children. Through creativity children express their loyalty to this processional order. We can, in our own field, nurture or negate this processional order, but fortunately for us, children will *never totally surrender it to us*. Children have taken me by the hand and led me, step by careful step, to the real belief that all children possess the kernel of creativity. That they guard or share that creativity very carefully. Because their creativity is paradoxically both very vulnerable and very strong, they will if necessary *create a fortress to defend it*, or, as Kathryn said,

> You don't see me. You see only my skin, hair and eyes. The real me is hiding down in the cellar and I won't come out until I know you won't embarrass me.[14]

If they have to build that fortress, that citadel, to defend their creativity, our children may emerge later as the adolescent, the university student we teach, the adult mistakenly labeled as "lacking in creativity." When this occurs, we have to go on that archeological dig, using with care all the tools and techniques available to us, to help bring that creativity out of the *fortress* where the child buried it for safety.

The children have led me to champion their need for creative arts they *can own*, forms that permit them to be other than miniature adults. Forms that ratify *their* creativity and imagination and recognize that their art has *purposes far beyond the act of the art itself*. They have reaffirmed for me that in the theories of art I am an "instrumentalist." That art at its best is there *to serve* the children we teach. That as an instrumentalist I have in the creative arts forms that best serve the creative process and creativity in children.

And with great generosity, they have from time to time given me the *keys to their kingdom* and allowed me to enter. To enter their world that stands astride reality and imagination, creating from reality the imaginative and from imagination, reality. For where do we nurture their creativity but from the world of fantasy and imagination?

Where, then, have Ruth, Krista, Jenny, Ben, and the endless number of children led me over the years as I reflect upon them and creativity? To a belief that has been so beautifully stated by Gertie in *The Dollmaker:*

> He's been a-waiten there in the wood, you might say, since before I was born. I jist brung him out a little—but one of these days, jist you wait an' see, we'll find the time an' a face fer him an' bring him out-a that block.[15]

Before I conclude I would like to mention the thirteenth fairy at the christening of Sleeping Beauty. Today that thirteenth fairy brings budget cuts, curriculum disasters, teacher shortages, truncation of the creative arts. We must hope that this thirteenth fairy of education will not be allowed to put our children to sleep for the next hundred years!

But let us banish the thirteenth fairy and finish with a poet's words, a poet who might have been writing about the contemporary single parent, a poet who, if we attend, speaks to us of the beginnings of children's creative arts. This young child has been banished to bed for having disobeyed his parent—and so Coventry Patmore writes:

> Then, fearing lest his grief should hinder sleep,
> I visited his bed,
> But found him slumbering deep,
> With darkened eyelids, and their lashes yet
> From his late sobbing wet.
> And I with moan,
> Kissing away his tears, left others of my own;
> For on a table drawn beside his head,
> He had put within his reach,
> A box of counters and a red-veined stone,
> A piece of glass abraded by the beach,
> And six or seven shells, a bottle with bluebells,
> And two French copper coins, ranged there with careful art,
> To comfort his sad heart.
> So when that night I prayed
> To God, I wept, and said:
> "Ah when at last we be with tranced breath,
> Not vexing Thee in death,
> And then rememberest of what toys
> We made our joys
> How weakly understood
> Thy great commanded good,
> Then fatherly not less
> Than I whom Thou moulded from the clay,
> Thou'll leave Thy wrath, and say,
> 'I will be sorry for their childishness.'"[16]

Endnotes

1. Saint-Exupery, A. (1943). *The little prince.* New York: Harcourt, Brace and World.

2. *I never saw another butterfly. Children's drawings and poems from Terezin Concentration Camp 1942-1944.* New York: McGraw Hill.

3. Cunningham, A. (1978). The children of Terezin. Keynote addresses and philosophy papers. In *Proceedings of the International Conference on Dance and the Child.* Ottawa: Canadian Association for Health, Physical Education and Recreation.

4. Carson, R. (1956). *The sense of wonder.* New York and Evanston.

5. Tolkien, J.R. (1964). *Tree and leaf.* London: Allen and Unwin.

6. Silverstein, S. (1964). *The giving tree.* New York: Harper and Row.

7. O'Connor, E. (1971). *Eighth day of creation—Gifts and creativity.* Texas: Word Book.

8. Here I am referring in particular to three works by Elliot Eisner:
(1980). The role of the arts in the invention of man. *New York University Education Quarterly, 11*(3); (1978). What do children learn when they paint? *Art Education, 35*(8); (1978). The impoverished mind. *Educational Leadership.*

9. Here I am referring in particular to Best, D. (1974). *Expression in movement and the arts.* Lepus Books.

10. Langeveld, M. (1964). *Studien zur Anthropoligie des Kindes.* Tuebingen: Neimeyer Verlag.

11. Eisner, E. (1980). The role of the arts in the invention of man. *New York University Education Quarterly, 11(3).*

12. Saint-Exupery, A. (1939). *Wind, sand, and stars.* New York: Reynal and Hitchcock.

13. Wickes, F.G. (1963). *The inner world of choice.* New York: Harper and Row.

14. McIlveen, E. (1990). *Cotton candy chatterbox: Verbal snapshots of childhood.* Vancouver: Credo.

15. Arnow, H. (1954). *The dollmaker.* New York: Macmillan.

16. Patmore, C. *The toys.* Source unknown.

Joyce Boorman is professor emeritus, University of Alberta, Edmonton, Alberta, Canada. She was chairman of the First International Conference on Dance and the Child and instrumental in the subsequent formation of Dance and the Child: International.

A Developmental Approach to the Early Childhood Curriculum

Lilian G. Katz

What does it mean to take a developmental approach to the education of young children? This paper discusses ways of looking at the concept of development and at some principles of pedagogical and curriculum practice that would take the concept into account.

Criteria of Appropriateness

There are many criteria against which a pedagogical or curriculum practice may be evaluated and judged appropriate. For example, a curriculum might be judged in terms of its educational, cultural, physical, ethical, logistical, psychological, or financial appropriateness. However, to look at it developmentally means to address those aspects of pedagogical and curriculum practice that change as the learners get older and accrue more experience.

For example, the principle that the younger children are, the more curricular time should be allocated to informal rather than formal activities and instruction addresses development by saying that as children get older, it is appropriate to subject them to greater amounts of formal instruction. However, use of a "time out chair" for punishment is not a developmental criterion, because such a pedagogical strategy is never appropriate, no matter what age or experience the child has acquired. (That is not to say that a child should not be withdrawn from on-going action in order to calm down and regain control of impulses, but this should not be used as punishment.) Furthermore, I say that use of a "time out chair" is inappropriate by applying criteria of psychological, ethical, or humane appropriateness, rather than developmental ones.

The Concept of Development

Evaluating a practice as developmentally appropriate must take into account two equally important but different dimensions: the *normative* and the *dynamic*. The normative deals with what is typical at each age and the distribution of particular characteristics across a given age group. The dynamic dimension addresses the course of development and change within an individual as time and experience accrue. This dimension has in turn three aspects of equal importance. One is concern with sequence and what is learned first, next, and so on, sometimes referred to as stages of development. Another aspect is the concern for both positive or negative delayed effects of early experiences. In other words, some early experiences do not impact on feelings or behavior until a later date when they seem to reappear like playing an early tape recording; however, the immediate impact of the experience is not apparent at the time of its occurrence. The third aspect of the dynamic dimension is cumulative effects of frequently repeated positive and negative experiences. The benefits or risks of these experiences increase with their frequency, but may seem ineffective or benign if they occur rarely.

In light of the two different dimensions of development, a major principle of practice is that just because children can do something does not mean that they should. The question of what children *can* do is a normative one; the question of what they *should* do is the dynamic one. Some believe that the developmental appropriateness of a curriculum activity can be assessed by the children's response to it (e.g., whether they are having fun or are bored). But such normative assessment is insufficient to judge the developmental appropriateness of the curriculum. The critical developmental criterion is the best judgment we have about the potential long-term cumulative effects of the experience. Principles of practice that satisfy criteria of developmental appropriateness must take both dimensions of development into account.

Four Categories of Learning Goals

In principle, education at every level must address four types of learning goals: knowledge, skills, dispositions, and feelings.

Knowledge during the early years can be broadly defined as information, ideas, stories, facts, concepts, schemas, and other such "contents of mind" that make up much of the content to be covered in a curriculum.

Skills can be defined as small units of action or behavior that are easily observed, for example, walking along a balance beam or writing one's name or drawing a house. Mental skills included in this category can be fairly easily inferred from observed behavior that occurs in small units of time or on a given single occasion, such as counting the fingers on a hand. Mental processes difficult to infer from observed behavior might include skills and many other kinds of information processing as well.

Dispositions, usually omitted from lists of educational goals, are broadly defined as relatively enduring "habits of mind," or characteristic ways of responding to experience across types of situations, for example, curiosity, generosity, quarrelsomeness, and so on. Unlike attitudes, they involve behavior and motivation. One can have an attitude without behaving or acting upon it. But a disposition implies high or reliable motivation to act on the habit of mind.

Feelings include feelings of belonging, self-confidence, and unlovability (Katz, 1985). It is not clear which feelings are learned from experience. Surely many of them, such as anger, sadness, and frustration, are temporary reactions to situations and experiences. But feelings of competence and incompetence or of acceptance or rejection in the school or classroom situation could be learned in that they are associated with the context and are typically aroused by it and in it.

These four categories of goals are achieved in different ways. Children can be helped to acquire knowledge by being informed about and alerted to relevant phenomena. Skills may be learned partly from observation, imitation, trial and error, instruction, and optimum amounts of drill and practice. Lessons and workbooks can be used to aid the acquisition of skills.

Dispositions, on the other hand, are not likely to be learned from instruction or lectures, but rather from observation and emulation of models. The dispositions are then shaped and strengthened by being appreciated and acknowledged. In general, strengthening dispositions relies on manifestations, followed by positive responses. If, for example, we wish to strengthen children's dispositions to be curious, we must provide opportunities for children to act upon or otherwise express their curiosity, followed by our appreciation with appropriate responses. Of course, not all dispositions are desirable, and some have to be responded to in such a way that they are weakened. Among the dispositions to be strengthened in early childhood are cooperativeness, curiosity, resourcefulness, and the disposition to be absorbed and interested in worthwhile explorations and activities.

Some Risks of Academic Pressures on Young Children

Among the issues surrounding whether young children should be in the public schools is the fear that they will be introduced to the formalized instruction and academic school work associated with elementary grades. The issue is not whether young children *can* start school work early. The fact that children can do something is not sufficient justification for requiring it of them. While there is no compelling evidence to suggest that early introduction to academic work guarantees long-term success in school, there are reasons to believe that it could be counterproductive.

Damaged disposition hypothesis. Certainly young children can be successfully instructed in beginning reading skills, but the risk of such early achievements, given the amount of drill and practice required, is the undermining of children's dispositions to be *readers.* This view, referred to as the "damaged disposition hypothesis," suggests that the early introduction of academic or basic skills may undermine the development of children's dispositions to use the skills thus acquired (Katz, 1985).

The damaged disposition hypothesis seems to be a reasonable interpretation of some of the results of longitudinal studies (e.g., Karnes et al., 1983; Miller & Bizzell, 1983; Schweinhart et al., 1986; see also Walberg, 1984). Some studies suggest that early pressure on young children to perform academic tasks introduced through direct instruction (e.g., practice in phonics, work book exercises) appears quite harmless, or even beneficial, in the short term. But, as developmentalists, we are obliged to take into account potential long-term consequences of early experiences, no matter how benign they appear to be at the time they occur.

Results from longitudinal studies suggest that curricula and teaching methods should be approached so as to optimize the acquisition of knowledge, skills, and desirable dispositions and feelings and that these are mutually inclusive goals, giving each type of learning equal weight. It is clearly not very useful to have skills if, in the process of acquiring them, the disposition to use them is lost. On the other hand, having the disposition without the requisite skills is also not a desirable educational outcome. The challenge for educators—at every level—is to help the learner with both the acquisition of skills and the strengthening of desirable dispositions.

Homogeneity of treatments. Another risk in emphasizing academic or basic skills in preschool programs is the use of a single teaching method and curriculum. Use of a single instructional method (a homogeneous treatment) with a group of children of diverse backgrounds and developmental patterns produces heterogeneous outcomes. For those desired heterogeneous outcomes of education, such as all children having the disposition to be readers, the treatment is likely to have to be heterogeneous.

It is reasonable to assume that when a single teaching method is used for a diverse group of young children, a significant proportion of them is likely to fail. It also seems to be a reasonable hypothesis that the younger the children are, the greater the variety of teaching methods that should be used (Durkin, 1980; see also Nelson & Seidman, 1984). For reasons of stability and practicality, however, there are likely to be limits upon how varied the teaching methods can be. This hypothesis is derived from the assumption that the younger the group, the less likely they are to have been socialized into a particular and standard way of responding to their environment and the more likely it is that the children's background experiences related to their readiness to learn are unique and idiosyncratic rather than common and shared.

Academically focused curricula typically adopt a single pedagogical method dominated by workbooks, drill, and practice. Even though such approaches often claim to "individualize" instruction, what is typically individualized is the day on which a given child completes a task, rather than the task itself! I suspect that very often "time on task" for the children in such programs could be called "time on deadly task." After a year or two of such schooling the effect on the disposition to learn is likely to be deadening!

Learned stupidity. Another risk that may attend introducing young children to academic work prematurely is that those children who cannot relate to the content or tasks required are likely to feel incompetent. College students are apt to fault the instructor for content or tasks that are difficult to grasp or perform. For young children, however, repeated experiences of being unable to relate to school work are likely to lead to the self-attribution of stupidity, or "learned stupidity." Such children are then very likely to bring their behavior into line with this attribution.

Interaction as a Context for Early Learning

One of the most reliable principles suggested by developmental research is the enhancement of young children's learning through interactive processes (Brown & Campione, 1984; Glaser, 1984; Karmiloff-Smith, 1984; Nelson, 1985; Rogoff, 1982). In addition to learning through trial, error, and observation, young children gain a great deal, cognitively as well as socially, through interaction with each other, with adults, and with aspects of their environment.

Research also suggests that children's learning is best served by active rather than passive activities. A weakness of including conventional academic tasks in the "pushed down" elementary school curriculum is the resulting reduction of interactive processes.

Development of Communicative Competence

Early childhood is widely recognized as a critical period in the development of communicative competence, in self-expression and understanding others. Contemporary insights indicate that all three basic functions of language (communication, expression, and reasoning) are strengthened when children are engaged in conversation, rather than simply passively exposed to language. Virtually all aspects of communication are most fully developed when children engage in conversations with adults and other children (Wells, 1983).

In conversation, the content of each participant's responses is contingent upon the others', in a sequential string of interactions. It may very well be that the contingency of the responses of adults to children in and of itself has a powerful effect on the development of their intellects. Conversation is more likely to be prolonged when adults make comments to children than when they ask them questions (Blank, 1985).

The work of Bruner (1982) and others suggests that conversation is most likely to occur when children are in small groups of three or four, with or without an adult present. Most teachers of young children recognize the difficulty of encouraging conversation during a large group session; they expend much effort reminding children that another child is still speaking or that their turn has not yet come!

Children are most likely to engage in conversation when something of interest occurs in context (Bruner, 1982; Clark & Wade, 1983). I watched a kindergarten teacher attempting to engage a class of five-year-old children in a discussion by asking each in turn, "What is your news today?" Each child struggled to find something worthy to report to disinterested and squirming classmates! Perhaps some of these children were learning "to listen" as the teacher intended, but many appeared to be learning "to tune out" their stammering classmates.

Development of Interest

An important disposition of concern to educators of young children is interest, or the capacity to "lose oneself" in an activity or concern outside of oneself. Interest refers to the capability of becoming deeply enough absorbed in something to pursue it over time, with sufficient commitment to accept the routine as well as novel aspects of work. Sometimes called "intrinsic motivation" (Morgan, 1984), "continuing motivation" (Maehr, 1982), or "self-directed learning" (Benware & Deci, 1984), this disposition appears to be present in the normal human at birth and is affected by a variety of social-psychological processes throughout childhood.

Recent research has illuminated the effects of different kinds of feedback on learners' intrinsic motivation, or what I refer to as the disposition called interest. Research on the so-called "overjustification effect" suggests that when children are rewarded for tasks in which they had initially shown interest, the reward is followed by loss of interest. In such cases, rewards undermine children's interest. The overjustification effect refers to metacognitive processes assumed to be occurring in children's minds, suggesting that children respond to such rewards by saying to themselves, "It must be wrong to like doing X, if I am given a reward for doing it" (Deci & Ryan, 1982). Since this effect applies especially to those activities children originally find interesting, it suggests that teachers should exercise special care not to offer rewards for those activities young children spontaneously enjoy, find attractive, or are easily encouraged to engage in.

A parallel line of research suggests that general positive feedback may serve to increase productivity but not interest (deCharms, 1983). General positive feedback includes vague comments like "very good," "well done," and the decorative smiling face or gold star. On the other hand, specific positive feedback, particularly if it includes information about the competence of the performance, serves to strengthen interest. The latter is called a "tribute," the former, an "inducement." A tribute is associated with increasing interest in the task, whereas an inducement leads to loss of interest once the positive feedback becomes unavailable. Academically oriented programs typically emphasize general positive feedback, ostensibly to give children feelings of success and to spur productivity. While this strategy appears to induce young children to keep working at disembedded, decontextualized, and often very trivial tasks, research on the effects of rewards strongly suggests that children may suffer academic "burnout" after two or three years of experience with general positive extrinsic rewards.

Curricula and teaching methods that attempt to provide children with constant amusement, fun, and excitement also risk undermining the development of children's disposition for interest (see Katz, 1977b). Thus, the teacher's role in strengthening children's dispositions to be interested in relevant and worthwhile phenomena is complex and highly critical. Children's dispositions toward sustained interest and involvement can be strengthened when children are encouraged to engage in projects that call for effort and involvement over time and provide contexts for extension, elaboration, and continuation of work and play (Rosenfield, Folger, & Adelman, 1980).

The disposition to lose oneself in an activity may also be threatened by frequent interruptions. Thus, the daily program for young children should allow for flexibility rather than fragmentation in the allocation of time to various activities.

Social Competence

Although definitions of social competence vary in details, they generally include the capacity to initiate, develop, and maintain satisfying relationships with others, especially peers. Social competence does not require a child to be a social butterfly. It is not a source of concern if a child chooses to work or play alone, as long as he or she is capable of interacting productively and successfully with another when desired or when appropriate.

However, contemporary research indicates that if a child has not acquired minimal social competence by the age of about six (give or take a year), the youngster is more likely than others to be a school dropout (Gottman, 1983; Parker & Asher, 1986). That child will also be at significant risk in young adulthood in terms of mental health, marital adjustment, and other aspects of social life in which interpersonal competence is required (Asher, Renshaw, & Hymel, 1982).

The acquisition of social competence involves many complex processes beginning in early infancy. It should be noted that inappropriate, as well as appropriate, social responses are learned through interaction. Weaknesses in social competence may be intensified during such interactions unless adults help the child alter maladaptive patterns. In the preschool period, inadequate peer-interactive skills are unlikely to be improved through formal instruction or even coaching, but can be modified by the intervention of a knowledgeable teacher (see Katz, 1984). Fortunately, a range of techniques that teachers can use to foster the development of social competence is now available (Burton, in press; Katz, 1984).

The Recursive Cycle

It is useful to think of social competence as having the characteristics of a recursive cycle, the principle being that, once an individual has a given behavior or characteristic, reactions to him or her tend to increase the chances that he or she will display more of that behavior or characteristic. For example, children who are likable, attractive, and friendly tend to elicit positive responses in others fairly easily, and because they receive such positive responses, they become more likable, attractive, and friendly. Similarly, children who are unattractive, unfriendly, and difficult to like tend to be avoided or rejected by others, and in response, they tend to behave in ways that make them even more unattractive, increasing the likelihood that they will more often be avoided or rejected, and the cycle becomes well-established. This general principle can be applied to many kinds of behavior and learning, but especially to social behaviors (see also Patterson, 1986).

The principle of the recursive cycle confirms the point made earlier that young children should be engaged in interactive processes, especially in the company of teachers who have specialized training and competencies in helping young children maximize the educative potential of such interaction. A young child cannot break a negative cycle alone since the capacity to understand the cause of his or her social difficulties and make the necessary adjustments is virtually nil. Adults must intervene to break faulty cycles by teaching young children more productive peer interactive patterns *in situ* during ongoing social interaction in the early childhood setting.

Recent experience suggests our response to children's needs in the early development of their social competence can help put them on a positive cycle and relieve much of the anguish that inevitably accompanies social difficulties in childhood. If we wait until a child is 9 or 10 years old and is making life for him or herself or for others difficult, we may need substantial resources from a mental health agency to intervene, and still may be too late. Insights from recent research on children's social competence suggest that preschool teachers' concern with social development is well placed and should be given as much weight in planning and teaching as is concern for children's intellectual development.

Specific Implications for Preschool Programs

Many people suggest that the choice for curriculum is to have either an academic or a socialization focus. Some of the risks of introducing academic tasks to young children have already been indicated. But the alternative is not simply to provide spontaneous play, though all children up to about seven or eight years of age can probably benefit from spontaneous play.

Rather, the data on children's learning seem to suggest that what is required in preschool and kindergarten is an intellectually oriented approach in which children interact in small groups as they work together on a variety of projects that help them make sense of their own experience. These projects should also strengthen their dispositions to observe, experiment, inquire, and reconstruct aspects of their environment.

Research on the impacts of different kinds of early childhood curricula also support the view that preschool and kindergarten programs should provide opportunities for interaction, active rather than passive activities, in which children have ample opportunity to initiate activities that interest them (Koester & Farley, 1982; Fry & Addington, 1984). The benefits of informal interactive teaching methods are especially striking in the long term, and notably discouraging in the short term (Miller & Bizzell, 1983; Schweinhart, Weikart, & Larner, 1986).

According to Walberg (1984), a synthesis of 153 studies of open education, including 90 dissertations, indicates that:

...the average effect [size for open education] was near zero for achievement, locus of control, self concept, and anxiety (which suggests no difference between open and control classes on these criteria); about .2 for adjustment, attitude toward schools and teachers, curiosity, and general mental ability; and about a moderate .3 for cooperativeness, creativity, and independence. [These statistics, derived from a meta-analysis, represent a modest positive effect on the variables listed for open compared with traditional formal classes.] Thus students in open classes do no worse in standardized achievement and slightly to moderately better on several outcomes that educators, parents, and students hold to be of great value. (Walberg, 1984, p. 25)

In sum, insights derived from developmental and related curriculum research support the view that a significant proportion of the time children spend in preschool and kindergarten classes should be allocated to the kind of project or unit work characteristic of pedagogical methods that are intellectually-oriented and informal. This classroom approach was known in the 1960s as open education, the integrated day, or informal methods.

The Value of Project Work for Young Children

Contemporary research suggests the project approach is a particularly promising strategy for fostering children's interactions. A project is a group undertaking, usually around a particular theme or topic, and involves a variety of kinds of work over a period of several days or weeks.

Types of projects. During the preschool period the most common types of projects are *reconstructions* of environmental aspects within the preschool or primary school setting; *investigations* of aspects of the environment, including various ways to report the findings of the investigations to classmates; and *observations* of aspects of the environment plus preparing ways to present what was learned from the observations to others in the class. Many projects may be various mixtures of the three basic types.

A topic or theme for a project, depending in part on the ages of the children, may be introduced by the teacher or children, or evolve from discussions they have together. There may or may not be a project leader who coordinates the activities of the group, and membership of the project group may fluctuate, although it may be beneficial to require stability in group membership or to encourage the members to carry their part of a project through to completion.

Project phases. Projects usually have three phases, which are likely to blend into each other. First is a planning phase during which children and staff discuss the elements of the project, develop plans and procedures for obtaining the materials, building the elements, or carrying out the investigations and observations. This phase also includes discussions about what information to obtain during field trips or site visits and provides ample opportunities for rich discussion and for children to display and generate interest in the project.

A second phase consists of constructing or building the parts of the project, gathering information or making observations, or making pictures by which others in the class can know what has been learned. A third phase includes role playing or taking the roles appropriate to the various elements of the project. During this period, extensions and elaborations on elements of the project may be undertaken. Almost any aspect of the environment can become the focus of a project. Many opportunities for cooperative social interaction occur in all three phases of a project.

I recently heard about a group of kindergarteners who undertook a detailed study of their own school bus. There is no special virtue to studying a school bus, in the sense that some test will ever examine the knowledge the children gained from the project. What is important is that the bus is part of the children's own daily environment and that they learned a lot about it: the correct names of various parts of it, a simple understanding of how it works, and what features of it contribute to their safety.

It is especially important that projects provide a context in which children's dispositions to observe, inquire, and become interested and involved in a sustained group effort can be strengthened. In such projects the teacher alerts children to a wide range of potentially interesting aspects of a topic that will take several days or even weeks of continuous probing and exploring. The fact that children are expected to tell and explain what they have learned to their own classmates is likely to encourage persistence in attaining information and reaching for adequate understanding (see Benware & Deci, 1984).

In sum, the project approach can be valuable for young children because it addresses their intellects. It can strengthen a variety of important dispositions and provide both rich content for conversation and a context for peer interaction in which cooperative effort makes sense. Projects are also culturally relevant in that they stem from the children's own interests and environments. But it should not be overlooked that another virtue of the project approach is that it can make teaching interesting—something unlikely to be characteristic of the more formal academic approaches to early childhood education.

Conclusion

Many educators and parents fear that programs for young children provided in public schools will inevitably offer experiences that too closely resemble the formal academic approach appropriate for the elementary school years. Indeed, there is some concern also that many programs for young children outside of the public schools offer programs oriented toward academic goals. Although the research bearing directly on these issues is as yet scant, we have learned much from developmental studies bearing indirectly on curriculum issues. It seems to me that the alternative to an academic approach is not simply to provide endless play, but pleasant spontaneous play as well. The appropriate contrast to the academic approach is an *intellectual* approach.

The inclusion of project work in the curriculum is consistent with the intention to engage young children's minds in improving their understandings of relevant phenomena in their environment and to provide a context in which the development and application of their social competencies are strongly encouraged. Both intellectual and social development can be well served by the project approach, whether it is offered in a public or private group setting.

I have suggested that the project approach is not only developmentally appropriate, it is also culturally appropriate. Since it can make teaching interesting, it provides a context in which children can observe adults intellectually engaged and interested in what they are doing.

References

Benware, C.A., & Deci, E.L. (1984). Quality of learning with an active versus passive motivational set. *American Educational Research Journal, 21*(4), 755-765.

Blank, M. (1985). Classroom discourse: The neglected topic of the topic. In M.M. Clark (Ed.), *Helping communication in early education,* Education Review Occasional Publication No. 11, 13-20.

Brown, A.L., & Campione, J.C. (1984). Three faces of transfer: Implications for early competence, individual differences, and instruction. In M.E. Lamb, A.L.Brown, & B. Rogoff (Eds.), *Advances in developmental psychology,* Vol. 3. Hillsdale, NJ: Lawrence Erlbaum Associates.

Bruner, J. (1982). *Under five in Britain,* Vol 1, Oxford Preschool Research Project. Ypsilanti, MI: High/Scope Foundation.

Burton, C.B. (in press). Problems in children's peer relations: A broadening perspective. In L.G. Katz (Ed.), *Current topics of early childhood education,* Vol. 7. Norwood, NJ: Ablex.

Carnegie Corporation of New York. (1984). *Child care and the role of the public schools: Report of a conference.* ED 264 013.

Carpenter, J. (1983). Activity structure and play: Implications for socialization. In M.B. Liss (Ed.), *Social and cognitive skills: Sex roles and children's play.* New York: Academic Press.

Clark, M.M., & Wade, R. (1983). Early childhood education. *Educational Review, 35*(2), 15.

Consortium for Longitudinal Studies. (1983). *As the twig is bent...Lasting effects of preschool programs.* Hillsdale, NJ: Lawrence Erlbaum Associates.

deCharms, R. (1983). Intrinsic motivation, peer tutoring, and cooperative learning: Practical maxims. In J.M. Levine & L.G. Katz (Eds.), *Current topics in early childhood education,* Vol. 4. Norwood, NJ: Ablex.

Deci, E.L., & Ryan, R.M. (1982). Curiosity and self-directed learning. In L.G. Katz (Ed.), *Current topics in early childhood education,* Vol. 4. Norwood, NJ: Ablex.

Donaldson, J. (1983). Children's reasoning. In M. Donaldson, R. Grieve, & C. Pratt (Eds.), *Early childhood development and education*. London: Guilford Press.

Durkin, D. (1980). Is kindergarten reading instruction really desirable? In *Ferguson lectures in education*. Evanston, IL: National College of Education.

Fry, P.S., & Addington, J. (1984). Comparison of social problem solving of children from open and traditional classrooms: A two-year longitudinal study. *Journal of Educational Psychology, 76*(1), 318-329.

Glaser, R. (1984). Education and thinking: The role of knowledge. *American Psychologist, 39*(2), 93-1104.

Gottman, J.M. (1983). How children become friends. *Monographs of the Society for Research in Child Development, 48*(3), 1.

Haskins, R. (1985). Public school aggression in children with varying day-care experiences. *Child Development, 56*, 689-703.

Karmiloff-Smith, A. (1984). Children's problem solving. In M. Lamb, A. Brown, & B. Rogoff (Eds.), *Advances in developmental psychology*, Vol. 3. Hillsdale, NJ: Lawrence Erlbaum Associates.

Karnes, M.B., Schwedel, A.M., & Williams, M.B. (1983). A comparison of five approaches for educating young children from low-income homes. In Consortium for Longitudinal Studies (Ed.), *As the twig is bent...Lasting effects of preschool programs*. Hillsdale, NJ: Lawrence Erlbaum Associates.

Katz, L.G. (1977a). Early childhood programs and ideological disputes. In L.G. Katz (Ed.), *Talks with teachers*. Washington, DC: National Association for the Education of Young Children.

Katz, L.G. (1977b). Education for excitement. In L.G. Katz (Ed.), *Talks with teachers*. Washington, DC: National Association for the Education of Young Children.

Katz, L.G. (1984). The professional early childhood teacher. *Young Children*, July, 3-9.

Katz, L.G. (1984). The professional preschool teacher. In L.G. Katz (Ed.), *More talks with teachers*. Urbana, IL: ERIC Clearinghouse on Elementary and Early Childhood Education.

Katz, L.G. (1985). Dispositions in early childhood education. *ERIC/EECE Bulletin*, Vol. 18, No. 2. Urbana, IL: ERIC Clearinghouse on Elementary and Early Childhood Education.

Katz, L.G. (1986). Current perspectives on child development. *Council for Research in Music Education Bulletin, 86*, 1-9.

Katz, L.G. (in press). Current perspectives on child development. In L.G. Katz (Ed.), *Professionalism, development and dissemination: Three papers*. Urbana, IL: ERIC Clearinghouse on Elementary and Early Childhood Education.

Koester, LS., & Farley, F. (1982). Psychophysical characteristics and school performance of children in open and traditional classrooms. *Journal of Educational Psychology, 74*(2), 254-263.

Maehr, M.L. (1982). Motivational factors in school achievement. ED 227 095.

Morgan, M. (1984). Reward-induced decrements and increments in intrinsic motivation. *Review of Education Research, 54*(1), 5-30.

Nelson, K. (1985). *Making sense: The acquisition of shared meaning.* New York: Academic Press.

Nelson, K., & Seidman, S. (1984). Playing with scripts. In I. Bretherton (Ed.), *Symbolic play: The development of social understanding.* New York: Academic Press.

Parker, J., & Asher, S. (1986). Predicting later outcomes from peer rejection: Studies of school drop out, delinquency and adult psychopathology. Paper presented at the Annual Conference of the American Educational Research Association, San Francisco, March.

Patterson, G.R. (1986). Performance models for antisocial boys. *American Psychologist, 41*(4), 432-444.

Prescott, E., & Jones, E. (1972). *Day care as a child rearing environment.* Washington, DC: National Association for the Education of Young Children.

Rogoff, B. (1983). Integrating context and cognitive development. In M.E. Lamb & A.L. Brown (Eds.), *Advances in developmental psychology,* Vol. 2. Hillsdale, NJ: Lawrence Erlbaum Associates.

Rosenfield, D., Folger, R., & Adelman, H.R. (1980). When rewards reflect competence: A qualification of the overjustification effect. *Journal of Personality and Social Psychology, 39*(3), 368-376.

Schweinhart, L.J., Weikart, D.P., & Larner, M.B. (1986). Consequences of three preschool curriculum models through age 15. *Early Childhood Research Quarterly, 1*(1), 15-46.

Walberg, H. (1984). Improving the productivity of America's schools. *Educational Leadership, 4*(8), 19-30.

Wells, G. (1983). Talking with children: The complementary roles of parents and teachers. In R. Grieve & C. Pratt (Eds.), *Early childhood development and education.* London: Guilford Press.

Lilian G. Katz is professor of early childhood education and director, ERIC Clearinghouse on Elementary and Early Childhood Education, University of Illinois, Urbana-Champaign. She is editor-in-chief of the *Early Childhood Research Quarterly* and author of a monthly column in *Parents Magazine* titled "Three and Four Year Olds - As They Grow."

The Assessment Dilemma

Doris O. Smith

Summary of Presentation

Because of my work on the California School Readiness Task Force and on the California Early Primary Assessment Advisory Committee, I feel eminently qualified to discuss the assessment dilemma with you. By that I mean I have many observations and questions but not so many answers. I do believe that professionals in the the art areas have much to teach us about informal assessment.

Lynn Kagan from Yale has said that some reports indicate two out of three respondents report they are having trouble implementing developmentally appropriate practices in early childhood programs (Kagan,1989). I submit that a major explanation for this barrier lies in the overemphasis and reliance on standardized test scores in our programs. Fortunately, a strong movement toward developing authentic assessment in lieu of standardized tests is occurring.

For your consideration, here are some key questions and principles which have been presented to the California Early Primary Assessment Advisory Committee.

1. Should one assessment instrument be selected for use across the state or should guidelines be provided to local districts to aid them in selecting the best assessment instruments and procedures for their specific priorities?

2. What should be assessed?

3. Should assessment for accountability be different from assessment for instructional purposes?

4. Can authentic assessment be used to meet the evaluation requirements for Chapter I. What impact does authentic assessment have on cultural and diversity issues?

In looking at assessment one should consider a continuum going from standardized tests to performance samples and to observations. Standardized tests are located on one end of the continuum and are identified as artificial while observations over time are located on the opposite end and identified as authentic, with performance samples in the middle of the continuum. Authentic assessments are characterized by the use of samples over time rather than information gathered at one sitting. They assess real learning, involve problem solving, are embedded in the curriculum, and are process-oriented. Artificial assessments are characterized by samples in only one time frame or context. They assess segmented skills, test for a "correct answer," do not necessarily relate to the curriculum, and are product-oriented.

Authentic assessments focus on complex intellectual challenges not on fragmented bits of knowledge. Students' habits and repertoires are investigated rather than eliciting simple one-shot responses. Authentic assessments use multifaceted scoring systems and multiple samples. They exist in harmony with school aims. That is, they are in tune with the theory base, philosophy, objectives, and curriculum in use. They provide a means for assessing individual strengths instead of just right and wrong answers.

In early childhood programs, authentic assessments are being implemented through writing portfolios, problem solving tasks in math, emergent literacy read aloud tasks, reading running records, and, most importantly, by recording developmental milestones over time through use of teacher observations and anecdotal records.

One may find examples of a child's work, records of a child's progress over time, anecdotal records, and photographs of constructions in portfolios. The advantages of using portfolio assessment are that it allows for documentation in various formats, helps the teacher monitor "real learning," helps the teacher plan effectively, provides a basis for parent conferences, and emphasizes developmentally appropriate curriculum.

We must ask ourselves the following questions about making decisions regarding assessment of young children.

1. Does the assessment fit with the goals of developmentally appropriate curriculum for young children?

2. Where does the assessment fit on the authentic-artificial continuum?

3. Does the assessment provide important information regarding a child's concept development?

4. Does the assessment allow the teacher to obtain information regarding a child's performance in more than one time frame? In more than one context?

5. In reporting the results of this assessment to parents, will the growth the child is making in regard to important developmental considerations be emphasized? (Herrell, 1990)

There are some excellent resources available to support the movement toward authentic assessments. The National Association for the Education of Young Children has published a position paper titled *Guidelines for Appropriate Curriculum Content and Assessment in Programs Serving Children Ages Three to Eight* (NAEYC,1990). The National Association of Elementary School Principals has published *Early Childhood Education and the Elementary School Principal,* calling for developmentally appropriate assessment practices in early childhood programs (NAESP, 1990).

Further causes for the assessment dilemma come from an analysis of the relationship between learning and development. Most early childhood educators and I presume many art specialists see the world primarily from a constructivist perspective. We talk about constructing knowledge, teaching for thinking, problem solving, and understanding. School learning, we believe wrongly, focuses on producers and performers, getting the right answer, success without understanding. The constructivists and the school learning people get nervous when they are asked to move out of their camps. There is a mismatch of children's minds and school curriculum. The discussions about art as a discipline are examples of this dichotomy between learning and development.

What we are really talking about is the relationship between school learning and development. We are asking ourselves hard questions:

Are school learning and development unrelated?
Are school learning and development identical?
Does school learning precede development?
Does development precede school learning? (Liben, 1987)

Art specialists and early childhood educators have come together at this conference to investigate this relationship.

Vygotsky says that if two children are developmentally the same (say eight years) and then, after given some assistance, one child measures twelve developmentally and the other child, with the same assistance, measures nine, we now have some important information about those children. The ZPD (zone of proximal development) is the distance between the actual developmental level as determined by independent problem solving and the level of potential development as determined through problem solving under adult guidance or in collaboration with capable peers. Developmental measures reflect past accomplishments while the ZPD focuses on future potential. Vygotsky tells us what the child can do today with assistance will become his/her own in the future.

Vygotsky agrees that school learning should be matched in some manner with the child's developmental level but one cannot understand the child's developmental level unless one considers the actual and the potential developmental level. In order to be responsive to the child's region of sensitivity to instruction, the expert (instructor) must continually define and refine a theory of the child's existing state of learning. But we should not overlook the fact that children also create and extend their own zones of competence without aid from others. In these cases one could say that the child is interacting with an imagined internalized audience.

Vygotsky's theory focuses on the sociocultural context of development. Development is inseparable from human and social activities. Central to Vygotsky's theory is a stress on both the institutional and cultural activities. ZPD is where culture and cognition create each other. Contexts create learning and development. Pedagogical (school) learning is controlled not by the instructor or the learner but by both. The child does not have a ZPD but rather shares one with an instructor. Activities are not the heart of teaching—children are!

Good school learning exists in the ZPD. It is the scaffolding which the learner uses in constructing knowledge. It is extraordinarily sensitive because it can be misused so easily. It must be fluid, bidirectional, interactional, dialectical, and ever-changing from both directions.

By understanding the importance of constructivism as compared to instruction (invention versus convention) and by becoming aware of the ZPD teachers are made aware of the importance of becoming excellent observers. We will never be aware of the child's potential or actual development if we don't start looking.

Thus, in summary, we are saying that in aligning school learning with developmental principles we must use authentic assessment practices in our early childhood programs.

References

Brown, A.L., & Reeve, R.A. (1987). Bandwidths of competence: The role of supportive contexts in learning and development. In Liben (Ed.), *Development and learning: Conflict or congruence?* Hillsdale, NJ: Lawrence Erlbaum Associates.

Herrell, A. (1990). *Assessment in early childhood programs*. Draft Report. Sacramento, CA: California State Department of Education Child Development Division.

Kagan, S.L. (1989, November). Presentation at the National Association of Early Childhood Teacher Educators Annual Meeting, Atlanta, GA.

National Association for the Education of Young Children. (1990). *Guidelines for appropriate curriculum content and assessment in programs serving children ages three to eight*. Washington, DC: Author.

National Association of Elementary School Principals. (1990). Early childhood education and the elementary school principal. Alexandria, VA: Author.

Rieber, R., & Carlton, A. (Eds.). (1987). *The collected works of L.S. Vygotsky,* vol.1. New York: Plenum Press.

Rogoff, B., & Wertsch, J. (Eds.). (1984). *Children's learning in the "Zone of Proximal Development."* San Francisco: Jossey-Bass.

Strauss, S. (1987). Educational-developmental psychology and learning. In Liben (Ed.), *Development and learning: Conflict or congruence?* Hillsdale, NJ: Lawrence Erlbaum Associates.

Vygotsky, L. S.. (1978). *Mind in society: The development of higher psychological processes,* M.Cole, V. John-Steiner, S. Scribner, & E. Souberman, Eds. Cambridge, MA: Harvard University Press.

Doris Smith has taught preschool, indergarten, and primary grades and is now coordinator of early childhood education programs in the School of Education and Human Development at California State University-Fresno. She has served on the California School Readiness Task Force and the Child Development Division Early Childhood Assessment Advisory Committee.

Roundtable Discussion Summary

There was group consensus that assessment is essential and desired but controversy centers around the kind of assessment to be used—how, when, by whom, for what goals and purposes. Assessment must be a flexible, responsive process involving many parties and flowing in many directions—from student, teacher, parent, administrator, and other outside sources. Teachers must have ownership in the formulation of assessment to buy into the concepts and expectations and to make sure that appropriate assessment is developed related to curriculum being taught and to the goals for the students. Teachers need to be part of continual revisions relating assessment to goals and curriculum. They need to know what assessment can do for them as instructors and for their programs.

Teacher preparation and education regarding various assessment tools is essential. Teachers need to learn the language that enables them to record observations in a nonjudgmental, descriptive method.

Teacher training for all teachers needs to be revamped to make sure education psychology is cogent. The arts educators said they need extensive knowledge in development. We all need to plan for developmentally appropriate curriculum. Specialists, early childhood teachers, and parents should all be involved.

The child's motivation and growth must be a basic part of objectives for arts education in early childhood. In observing children's behavior teachers might note the length of time a child perseveres at a certain activity, the frequency with which a child returns to an activity, and the enthusiasm level related to an activity to determine how meaningful that activity is to the child, that is, how much "joy, satisfaction and meaning" (Stinson) the child does derive. Several participants emphatically reminded us that the arts are nonverbal and concluded we should not ask children about their work.

Nonverbal very young children can be observed for input regarding their response to arts to determine the growth they are experiencing. Portfolios may also be a valuable tool. Some said children who can verbalize can share their feelings regarding their work but this must not be done in such a way as to disrupt the creative process. Observations by others (than the teachers) may be sought. Parents and others can observe and compare results. A combination of several sources and methods (triangulation) is preferred.

The time factor regarding teachers' ability to assess student progress is a problem that might require restructuring of the daily schedule and even the desired outcomes of curriculum. Students may need to be given more free time to allow them the opportunity to make free choices of various activities and to allow teachers an opportunity to observe the choices students make.

In response to the question of what is the cost of assessment in the arts and where does the time come from, participants emphasized the importance of collaborative efforts between classroom teachers and art specialists. Many said that the specialists should be used to train the classroom teachers in the disciplines and teachers would then integrate the arts activities into the regular curriculum. Authentic assessment would then follow as part of the regular day. It was stated that specialists should come into the classrooms and the teachers should stay, thereby expanding the parameters of experience.

Other comments:

In China children are not formally assessed under age seven. Then assessment generally is shared through descriptive comments rather than grades.

What is measurable is generally what will be taught in public schools so it is important that arts education have assessable outcomes. Teachers and administrators are held accountable. To be effective, arts education advocates need to be able to speak the language of those who look for assessable outcomes in arts education.

Assessment through Observation:
A Profile of Developmental Outcomes
(Ages 5-8)

Elizabeth Jones and Jane Meade-Roberts

Teacher observations of children's work and play, together with portfolios of children's work, provide the richest information about a child's growth to be used both for record-keeping and curriculum planning and for reporting to parents. Organization of observations within a framework of developmental outcomes provides comprehensive data and, in the process, educates teachers in developmental theory.

With teacher involvement in the process, a developmental profile/report card can be designed to incorporate curriculum objectives within a context of developmentally appropriate practice. Each point on the profile is described in positive rather than deficit terms, as a legitimate stage of growth. Each child's growth is charted over the course of a year. Profiles overlap from one grade to the next.

Data collection for a profile not only directs teachers to observe children's learning, it challenges them to find the time to do it. In this process, more autonomy for children in the classroom is created.

The Process of Profile Development

The typical report card asks teachers to rate children as more or less satisfactory in a number of categories. Such evaluation is inconsistent with developmentally appropriate practice, in which teachers observe and respond to children's growth through sequential stages, each of them "satisfactory." At San Vicente School in Soledad, California, kindergarten teachers developed a new report card at the request of the principal, Joan Hillard. These were the steps in the process.

1. Brainstorming

Guided by teacher Jane Meade-Roberts and consultant Elizabeth Jones, teachers began by brainstorming in response to the questions: What do you look for in assessing a child's growth? How do you know if a child is ready for first grade? Their long list of items reflected the screening tests and instructional frameworks with which they were most familiar.

2. Organizing

Combining the teachers' items with our knowledge of development, the two of us created a set of categories under which to describe positively stated points in a developmental sequence. We identified subcategories under literary and numeracy skills, physical development, and social skills. We added curiosity and creativity. We lumped a good many of the screening test items under the category of "ability to meet school/teacher expectations." We wrote descriptions of five behaviors in each subcategory and placed them along a line. We were preparing a draft for teachers to react to and change.

3. Trying it out

We took our draft back to the teachers with the request that they try rating half a dozen children (their highest and lowest achievers) on the profile, to see what worked for them and what didn't.

4. Critiquing it

At a half-day meeting we invited teachers to tell us everything they didn't like about the profile. Their major concern was, "I don't know some of those things about my children," and we talked at length about observing to find out. They also questioned the logical ordering of some items; we agreed, and made changes.

5. The report card

Items were reworded to be more understandable to parents and then translated into Spanish; the report card is bilingual. Teachers worried about parent reaction: "They won't like it. It doesn't tell them how their child compares with other children, and whether he's satisfactory or not." After a year of use, however, teachers' feelings were positive: "It is self-explanatory, unlike the ordinary report card. I don't have to explain why I gave a C. In the parent conference I can really talk about the child—a story she has written, a typical day with choices she has made."

The teachers created the profile and they review it each year for possible changes. As a cooperative task requiring active teacher involvement in both design and implementation, profile development has proved remarkably effective in raising issues, generating critical thinking, and identifying points for growth.

Sample Profiles for Two Children

Of the two children whose profiles are shown here (pages 46-49), Sean has developed furthest in literacy, fine motor skills, and ability to meet school and teacher expectations. He is relatively immature in large motor development and in social skills with peers. Erminda, in contrast, is relatively immature in her understanding of literacy and numeracy but highly developed in social and large motor skills and in creativity. Both these children, rated here

Student Name __Sean__   Teacher _____

Date _____   Child is using Spanish _____ English __✓__

Soledad
Profile of Developmental Outcomes
for Kindergarten

LITERACY SKILLS

Oral Language

1	2	3	4	5
Is non-verbal in school	Uses language to satisfy basic wants and needs	Often uses language in play and conversation with peers	Clearly describes real or imaginary situations using complex descriptive language	Speaks in whole sentences using a well-developed vocabulary

Drawing

1	2	3	4	5
Scribbles	Draws a face	Adds arms/legs to face	Adds body with arms/legs	Adds details (e.g. hair, ears, hands, feet)

Writing

1	2	3	4	5
Scribbles and pretends to write	Uses letters or letter-like signs to represent writing	Spontaneously writes own name including all letters	Spontaeously copies words	Can invent spelling of words using phonetic clues

Reading

1	2	3	4	5
Reads own name	Recognizes beginning letter of first name when written in other places	Recognizes and names other letters and numerals	Recognizes and reads sight words including signs, labels, key words, teacher-created word lists, and/or words in books	Uses knowledge of letter sounds to sound out words

Attitudes toward literacy

1	2	3	4	5
Not yet interested in books or writing	Demonstrates focused interest in picture books	Demonstrates interest in written language (e.g., asks about or reads signs, names, words in class, labels, words in books	Spontaneously practices writing letters and numerals	Demonstrates interest in writing correctly.

NUMERACY SKILLS

Problem-solving using classification

1	2	3	4	5
Randomly manipulates objects	Spontaneously orders by likenesses and differences	Recognizes or creates simple (AB) patterns using a variety of materials and/or symbols	Recognizes or creates complex (e.g., AABAAB) patterns using a variety of materials and/or symbols	Can classify by more than one attribute at a time (e.g., size, and color).

Problem-solving using number

1	2	3	4	5
Calls numerals at random	Counts by rote	Demonstrates understanding of one-to-one correspondence (e.g., counts objects accurately)	Is able to use knowledge of counting to solve real problems	Demonstrates conservation of number (e.g., understands that # of objects remains constant)

CURIOSITY AND CREATIVITY

Curiosity

1	2	3	4	5
Watches silently	Asks cautious questions	Asks questions constantly	Asks questions appropriately	Uses resources to find answers to questions (e.g., experimenting, taking risks, solving problems on own)

Sean

Creativity

1	2	3	4	5
Waits to be told what to do	Explores available materials	Invents simple dramatizations or projects with provided materials (e.g., blocks, art, housekeeping area)	Asks or looks for not already available materials to accomplishe project or play ideas	Works competently on notably complex, creative, imaginative, self-intiated tasks

PHYSICAL DEVELOPMENT
Large motor

1	2	3	4	5
Runs	Jumps	Hops on one foot	Catches a ball with arms and chest	Can catch a ball with hands only

Fine motor

1	2	3	4	5
Scribbles with crayon or pencil	Is able to use scissors	Colors inside lines Cuts on lines	Draws/writes accurate lines (e.g., reproduces shapes, letters & numerals. Hold writing tool correctly	Good coordination result in consistently neat work

SOCIAL SKILLS
With peers

1	2	3	4	5
Usually observes play of others	Usually plays alone or is involved in parallel play	Is developing cooperative play skills	Socially self-confident plays effectively with other children	Has well-developed skills of leadership and cooperation in play

With adults/in group

1	2	3	4	5
Accepts situations rather than ask for adult help	Communicates with adults primarlily to get help	Speaks spontaneously and freely with adults	Participates in group activities and conversation	Is sensitive to and articulate about the needs of others

ABILITY TO MEET SCHOOL/TEACHER EXPECTATIONS
Attention Span

1	2	3	4	5
Has rapidly changing focus of attention	Can focus attention on self-selected tasks	Can Focus attention on teacher-selected tasks	Works independently on self-welucted and teacher-selected tasks	Can follow complex directions and maintain focused attention for long periods.

New Learning

1	2	3	4	5
Chooses to observe rather than participate	Has strong preference for familiar tasks	Willing to try new task	Masters new tasks quickly	Masters new tasks independently, demonstrating ability to build on previous knowledge

Social Knowledge

1	2	3	4	5
Knows colors	Knows shapes	Knows personal information (address, birthdate, etc.)	Knows names of letters and numerals	Knows days of week, months of year

Student Name **Erminda**   Teacher_____

Date _____   Child is using Spanish ✓   English _____

LITERACY SKILLS

Oral Language

1	②2	3	4	5
Is non-verbal in school	Uses language to satisfy basic wants and needs	Often uses language in play and conversation with peers	Clearly describes real or imaginary situations using complex descriptive language	Speaks in whole sentences using a well-developed vocabulary

Drawing

1	2	③3	4	5
Scribbles	Draws a face	Adds arms/legs to face	Adds body with arms/legs	Adds details (e.g. hair, ears, hands, feet)

Writing

1	②2	3	4	5
Scirbbles and pretends to write	Uses letters or letter-like signs to represent writing	Spontaneously writes own name including all letters	Spontaeously copies words	Can invent spelling of words using phonetic clues

Reading

①1	2	3	4	5
Reads own name	Recognizes beginning letter of first name when written in other places	Recognizes and names other letters and numerals	Recognizes and reads sight words including signs, labels, key words, teacher-created word lists, and/or words in books	Uses knowledge of letter sounds to sound out words

Attitudes toward literacy

1	②2	3	4	5
Not yet interested in books or writing	Demonstrates focused interest in picture books	Demonstrates interest in written language (e.g., asks about or reads signs, names, words in class, labels, words in books	Spontaneously practices writing letters and numerals	Demonstrates interest in writing correctly.

NUMERACY SKILLS

Problem-solving using classification

1	2	③3	4	5
Randomly manipulates objects	Spontaeously orders by likenesses and differences	Recognizes or creates simple (AB) patterns using a variety of materials and/or symbols	Recognizes or creates complex (e.g., AABAAB) patterns using a variety of materials and/or symbols	Can classify by more than one attribute at a time (e.g., size, and color).

Problem-solving using number

1	②2	3	4	5
Calls numerals at random	Counts by rote	Demonstrates understanding of one-to-one correspondence (e.g.,counts objects accurately)	Is able to use knowledge of counting to solve real problems	Demonstrates conservation of number (e.g., understands that # of objects remains constant)

CURIOSITY AND CREATIVITY

Curiosity

1	2	3	④4	5
Watches silently	Asks cautious questions	Asks questions constantly	Asks questions appropriately	Uses resources to find answers to questions (e.g., experimenting, taking risks, solving problems on own)

Erminda

Creativity

1	2	3	4	5
Waits to be told what to do	Explores available materials	Invents simple dramatizations or projects with provided materials (e.g., blocks, art, housekeeping area)	Asks or looks for not already available materials to accomplish project or play ideas	Works competently on notably complex, creative, imaginative, self-intiated tasks

PHYSICAL DEVELOPMENT
Large motor

1	2	3	4	5
Runs	Jumps	Hops on one foot	Catches a ball with arms and chest	Can catch a ball with hands only

Fine motor

1	2	3	4	5
Scribbles with crayon or pencil	Is able to use scissors	Colors inside lines Cuts on lines	Draws/writes accurate lines (e.g., reproduces shapes, letters & numerals. Hold writing tool correctly	Good coordination result in consistently neat work

SOCIAL SKILLS
With peers

1	2	3	4	5
Usually observes play of others	Usually plays alone or is involved in parallel play	Is developing cooperative play skills	Socially self-confident plays effectively with other children	Has well-developed skills of leadership and cooperation in play

With adults/in group

1	2	3	4	5
Accepts situations rather than ask for adult help	Communicates with adults primarlily to get help	Speaks spontaneously and freely with adults	Participates in group activities and conversation	Is sensitive to and articulate about the needs of others

ABILITY TO MEET SCHOOL/TEACHER EXPECTATIONS
Attention Span

1	2	3	4	5
Has rapidly changing focus of attention	Can focus attention on self-selected tasks	Can Focus attention on teacher-selected tasks	Works independently on self-selected and teacher-selected tasks	Can follow complex directions and maintain focused attention for long periods.

New Learning

1	2	3	4	5
Chooses to observe rather than participate	Has strong preference for familiar tasks	Willing to try new task	Masters new tasks quickly	Masters new tasks independently, demonstrating ability to build on previous knowledge

Social Knowledge

1	2	3	4	5
Knows colors	Knows shapes	Knows personal information (address, birthdate, etc.)	Knows names of letters and numerals	Knows days of week, months of year

in the fall semester of their kindergarten year, are developing normally within their different styles of being in the world. Their teacher values their strengths and their choices, while also encouraging them to practice the activities in which each is less developed.

Authors' Note: For a more detailed account of the profiles see the Pacific Oaks Occasional Paper titled *Assessment through Observation* or Meade-Roberts, "It's All Academic," in E. Jones (Ed.), *Reading, Writing and Talking with Four, Five, and Six Year Olds* (1988). Both are available from Pacific Oaks College Bookstore, 5 Westmoreland Place, Pasadena, CA 91103, phone 818-397-1330.

Elizabeth Jones is a member of the Human Development faculty of Pacific Oaks College, Pasadena, California.

Jane Meade-Roberts is a teacher in the San Vicente School (K-2), Soledad, California.

Promising Practices in Arts Education Assessment

Susan W. Stinson

Assessment is one of the most troubling issues for all educators, one we cannot ignore in current times. It is particularly troubling for arts educators, who used to be able to ignore the issue, at least when dealing with young children. There are few experts in arts education assessment for early childhood, and I am not one of them; thus I do not have any ideal solutions to share in this presentation. Instead I will be reviewing what I find to be some of the most exciting developments in arts education assessment and discussing their application to young children.

I must admit at the outset that I often find myself agreeing with Maxine Greene, who commented recently to me, "Why do we have to assess everything? Can't we just accept some things as important?" I think back to when my own children were young and we took trips to the zoo and other interesting places. My children and I were engaged together in something we each found interesting. I trusted that they learned during these experiences, but I felt no need to assess *what* or *how much* they learned. I *knew* it was a good way for us to spend the afternoon. I think the luxury of experiencing without assessing is still open to parents, but it is increasingly not open to teachers.

While I acknowledge the need for assessment in education, I am concerned about how we do it and what we use it for. Assessment is all too often used to categorize and rank children like appliances in the Sears catalogue, according to who is good, better, and best—and even who is not good at all. I mistrust quantitative and summative evaluation for this reason. It changes the way I choose to be with children, in which I value them as unique persons with their own qualities and abilities—and, yes, their own limitations—which make each of them wonderfully different from anyone else in the world. So when I speak of what I see as the most promising proposals for assessment, they are largely qualitative and formative in nature.

The Theory of Multiple Intelligences

The work of Howard Gardner with Project Zero at Harvard University has provided the theoretical basis for the other projects I will discuss. Gardner's work at Project Zero has emphasized what he calls the Theory of Multiple Intelligences—the theory that, as a species, human beings carry out at least seven different forms of knowing. These include intelligences dealing with language, logic and mathematics, music, spatial information, bodily-kinesthetic information, knowledge about other persons (interpersonal), and knowledge about oneself (intrapersonal) (Gardner, 1983). All normal persons possess all of these forms of intelligence, but we each have different profiles. Schools emphasize certain forms of intelligence over others, and clearly not all are tested on the Scholastic Aptitude Test. Because of this, we currently classify children as more or less intellectually capable, instead of recognizing that all are capable in different ways. One of Gardner's important ideas about assessment, then, is that it should reveal multiple forms of intelligence.

A second important principle about assessment that Gardner puts forward is that assessment should, for the most part, take place in context. To use his illustration, if we want to know students' aptitude or ability in chess, the best way is not to devise tests of isolated skills and knowledge, but to watch them play chess in a familiar, nonthreatening environment. If they do not know how to play chess, we teach them. With enough time spent observing the children play chess, it will be fairly clear which students demonstrate ability in chess—at that moment in time. It will also be clear who is demonstrating interest in chess, which is essential to develop whatever ability is there. Furthermore, the children will not have lost any time from the chess curriculum in order to be tested on their ability to play. With this vision of assessment in context, creating procedures for assessment becomes intimately involved with curriculum development.

Three Kinds of Artistic Thinking

In addition to the theory of multiple intelligences and the principle that assessment should reveal these intelligences in the context of interesting curricular activities, Gardner has contributed to a theoretical understanding of artistic thinking. He finds three kinds of artistic thinking, which he names production, perception, and reflection. (These three activities are described in more complex ways in the literature that has arisen from Gardner's work; my description here is a simplified one.) Production involves doing art—such as dancing and making dances. Perception involves looking at one's own work and that of others, discriminating elements or qualities of, in the case of dance, performance and composition. Reflection involves looking at oneself as well as one's work, particularly over time— recognizing one's goals, one's own process, what choices one has made and why. Unlike advocates of some current approaches to arts education, Gardner is clear that production— art-making—ought to be central. This is particularly true under age ten or so (Gardner, 1989). Production involves thinking *in* the art, as distinguished from thinking *about* it. For example, how can I change from this shape to that one, with a sense of smoothness? How can I create a particular mood through my movement?

I have reviewed literature on two projects which are developing the theoretical base contributed by Gardner into practice. Project Propel is a collaborative effort among the Arts and Humanities Division of the Rockefeller Foundation, Harvard's Project Zero, the Educational Testing Service, and the Pittsburgh Public Schools. Propel has developed two educational vehicles, referred to as Domain Projects and Process Portfolios. Domain Projects are sets of exercises focusing on a particular aesthetic concept; they allow students to manipulate artistic materials over several curricular sessions, making different choices which reveal their learning. Process Portfolios are collections of a child's artistic work such as that produced by Domain Projects—not just the final products or the "best" work, but all the attempts along the way. We can see evidence of the child's artistic growth in observing his or her work over time. Even more important, the Portfolios serve as a basis for the child's artistic perception and reflection. Teachers ask questions of the children, for example, "Which of these two paintings do you consider the better work? Why? How would you describe your artistic style? How would you compare your style to that of Georgia O'Keefe (or any other artist)? What changes have you observed in your style?" Eventually children begin to ask their own questions. Process Portfolios use the medium that is relevant for each particular art form; in the case of dance, videotape is used.

As someone involved with dance education thoughout the lifespan, I am excited about the potential for these procedures. We are incorporating them increasingly into our undergraduate and graduate programs in dance at my university. However, I find them of limited applicability to early childhood education. Young children enjoy repeating favorite activities, but I find them much more excited about making a new dance than about reworking one that they did yesterday. They may have some interest in watching themselves on video, but not in analysis of the video image. Even if they were, their vocabulary for analysis would be very limited.

Gardner (1989) offers an observation that is particularly relevant at this point. He notes that, in most areas of learning, an individual's ability to comprehend or understand develops in advance of his or her productive ability. However, this is not always true in the arts, in which comprehension appears to lag behind performance or production. The art work of young children often impresses us with its richness, but they may not have very much to say about it. Of course, this does not mean that we do not talk with young children about their art and listen to their comments. Just as we label objects in the preschool classroom long before we expect children to read them, we similarly introduce vocabulary that describes their dance, such as "Micah's doing a smooth glide; Maria's using quick changes." Eventually, when children are ready, they will be able to "read" their own dances and those of others, just as they will be able to read the symbols we call words.

Assessment at the Preschool Level

While Project Propel has limited applicability to early childhood, Gardner and his colleagues have another project focused directly on assessment at the preschool level, including but not limited to assessment in the arts. Project Spectrum is a collaborative endeavor of Project Zero, Tufts University, and the Eliot-Pearson Children's School in Massachusetts. Like Project Propel, Spectrum has evolved into a curriculum; assessment activities seem incorporated into the classroom as naturally as the housekeeping corner. Most of these activities fit a workshop or open classroom structure, in which children select activities they find interesting. Gardner (1989) notes that, in such a structure, preschool children are capable of a great deal of self-generated learning and development in the arts. Further, he comments,

> As is the case with natural language, this acquisition can occur without explicit tutelage on the part of parents or teachers....In this respect artistic learning stands in sharp contrast to most traditional school subjects. (p. 73)

In Project Spectrum, Process Portfolios are kept of the children's drawings. Videotapes are made of the twice weekly creative movement sessions to create a similar portfolio. However, instead of the children analyzing and reflecting upon the work in the portfolios, it is the adults—the researchers and teachers—who study the children's art work as it develops over time. As Gardner and two fellow researchers write, "Carefully observing videotapes of these sessions, we can follow each child's ability to adapt, invent, and replicate movements as he or she dances and plays the numerous movement games" (Wexler-Sherman, Gardner, & Feldman, 1988, p. 81).

The goals of Project Spectrum, as cited by these researchers, seem important:

> By providing enriching materials across a broader, more diversified range of content areas, we seek to provide conditions under which children can discover and reveal their own distinct proclivities and interests. At the same time, by eliciting and recording an array of abilities generally overlooked by traditional IQ tests, we hope to provide a greater number of children with the sense of self-worth and competence that arises from exposure to and connectedness with materials suited to their specific abilities. (p. 80)

In other words, a child who demonstrates considerable bodily-kinesthetic intelligence would be able to learn mathematical concepts through whole body activities, and likely be more successful at it.

Certainly there are limitations and potential for abuse of the procedures developed in Project Spectrum, just as in any other form of assessment. One danger mentioned by Gardner (in press) is that of too early labeling, potentially tracking a child into a particular path as a result of interest and ability demonstrated at age four. This risk, he notes, may be reduced in two ways. One is to stress to parents and teachers that the descriptions only refer to a particular moment in time; in young children, profiles of abilities may change a great deal from one year to the next. The second procedure for reducing risk is to maintain the assessment procedures each year. Gardner states:

> So long as students continue to be exposed to a variety of inviting materials and exercises, and so long as assessment is not a one-shot affair, there is every reason to believe that the cognitive profile will evolve...and that subsequent reports will capture the new profile accurately. (p.22)

I am aware of another limitation not mentioned in the articles I surveyed, one growing out of the time that I spend in watching and analyzing videotapes of university students' choreography and teaching. I find this task quite tiresome and am fortunate that I rarely have to do it for more than two hours at a stretch. I try to imagine screening a semester's worth of videotapes of creative movement with four-year-olds, one hour for each week, in order to observe and analyze John's development in dance. I would have to watch each video fully and intently for the times that John would be in the sight of the camera. Then I would have to watch the videos again for Tomika, and for Osceola, and for every other child. I can imagine graduate research assistants spending this much time watching videos, and perhaps even researchers with large grants.

However, most early childhood teachers that I know have chosen their profession because they like being with young children. Being with a video is not as satisfying, despite the importance of assessment. Further, the time spent in front of a VCR would have to be taken from time spent on other tasks with and for children, or additional personnel must be hired. I wonder if parents and school administrators could justify such priorities for assessing an area of learning that, despite its potential for personal meaning, is still not highly valued by society. All of the assessment procedures suggested by Gardner are labor intensive, but viewing videotapes takes much more time than looking through a portfolio of writing or drawing

It was this kind of practical limitation that led a committee I recently chaired, appointed by the National Dance Association to develop curricular guidelines for dance for young children, to reject a video portfolio as the basis for assessing the development of young children in dance. Instead we proposed the development of an instrument which we named a "Descriptive Dance Profile." We defined a descriptive dance profile as consisting of periodic descriptions of a child's work in dance, what the child is doing and not doing. This kind of description

> requires a teacher who knows the children by name, has good observational skills and a language for recording observations, and has the time in his/her schedule to keep records immediately after observations. (National Dance Association, p. 16)

We noted that

> (T)he time factor could be eased if the teacher specifically observed one to three children during each dance session, recording these comments immediately afterwards. The process could further be facilitated by a coding instrument that did not require lengthy verbiage. (p. 16)

The committee has recommended that the National Dance Association develop such an instrument and field test it for classroom use.

In one sense, recording the descriptions is the easiest task. More difficult is analysis of the data, to determine whether the child is learning. There are, to my knowledge, no research-based indicators of development in children's dance, although our committee suggested some. Gardner and his colleagues are still in the process of developing such indicators for assessing the Process Portfolios. It is clear that a great deal of research will be necessary to accomplish this task.

However difficult it might be to assess whether children are showing evidence of learning in dance, perhaps an even greater issue is how to tell if and when a child's learning is unsatisfactory. As a committee, we asked ourselves what all children needed to know in dance by the end of early childhood. We concluded that, since

> ...the primary reason for dance to be in the early childhood curriculum is for children to find joy, satisfaction, and meaning....(T)here is no level that every person of any age <u>must</u> attain. If young children experience good creative dance teaching (as previously described), the vast majority will desire to engage in the experience and will learn. Even without indicators of continued learning, however, one must assume the child's level is satisfactory as long as it is a source of joy, satisfaction, and meaning [to that child]. The teacher's responsibility is to provide the environment and structure through which the child may continue to develop—when the child is ready to do so.If the child is indicating frustration or dissatisfaction with what he or she knows/can do in dance, the teacher needs to explore both why the child is not progressing to his/her own satisfaction and the source of the dissatisfaction...and then take the appropriate action. (p. 16)

Some arts educators might argue with our conclusions and believe that young children should be able to fail dance just as they can fail other subjects. The document we created clearly does not contain the final answers to assessment, even in dance education. Despite his extensive work and that of his colleagues, Gardner would be the first to note that their work, too, is still in progress. Probably there will never be final answers to the many issues involved in assessing arts education, but I am grateful to all of those who help us ask the important questions.

References

Gardner, H. (1983). *Frames of mind: The theory of multiple intelligences.* New York: Basic Books.

Gardner, H. (1989). Zero-based arts education: An introduction to ARTS PROPEL. *STUDIES in Art Education: A Journal of Issues and Research, 30,* 71-83.

Gardner, H. (in press). Assessment in context. In B. Gifford (Ed.), *Report of the commission on testing and public policy.*

National Dance Association. (1990). *Guide to creative dance for the young child.* Reston, VA: National Dance Association.

Wexler-Sherman, C., Gardner, H., & Feldman, D.H. (1988). A pluralistic view of early assessment: The Project Spectrum approach. *Theory Into Practice, 22,* 77-83.

> More detailed information about the projects mentioned in this article may be obtained from Harvard Project Zero, 323 Longfellow Hall, 13 Appian Way, Cambridge, MA 02138 .

Susan W. Stinson teaches in the Department of Dance, University of North Carolina at Greensboro. She has written extensively in the area of movement and dance education in early childhood.

Assessment as Dialogue: Involving Students in the Assessment Process

Nancy Alison Place

We are just beginning in our school district to study alternative forms of evaluation for language arts and mathematics. I'd like to discuss some tentative thoughts about this work in progress, present a strategy that we are finding useful, and ask a question. I'll focus on a type of assessment that should be of particular interest to people concerned with the arts and early childhood.

One of the assessment strategies we are studying is the use of portfolios, something with which many of you are familiar. In the world of visual arts, portfolios are a way for artists to collect and show their work. Portfolios, as they're being talked about for assessment purposes, are composed of student work selected for a specific purpose and collected over time.

As an elementary teacher I have always kept a folder of children's work throughout the year. The wonderful thing about this type of collection is the growth it shows over time, particularly with younger children. I didn't really understand the possibilities of portfolios, however, until I heard Dennie Wolf speak. She works with Arts Propel, a joint project of the Pittsburgh Public Schools, Educational Testing Service, and Project Zero at the Harvard Graduate School of Education. The purpose of the project is to "demonstrate that it is possible to assess the thinking processes characteristic of the arts and humanities in rigorous, but undistorted, ways" (Wolf, 1989, p. 36). The tool they've been working with is a "process portfolio," which is a collection of student work that includes:

1. Work selected by the student including all early drafts leading up to a final work.

2. A range of work that shows a diversity of technique and style. This could include pieces that are successful and those that are not.

3. Reflections by students on their work. This might include a journal of their progress and critiques of other artists.

As I listened to Dennie Wolf I realized that portfolios were a lot more than collections of student work over time. The important part was the involvement of the student in both selecting the work and analyzing the process of creating it. Portfolios seen in this light seemed a wonderful way to foster conversation between student and teacher and between students themselves, as well as a wonderful way for students to become more conscious of the process of learning.

My question is: This process was developed for high school students. How does it translate for elementary school children? And for our purposes today: Is any of this appropriate for young children of kindergarten and primary age? What can children say about their own work? How metacognitive can they be? Would young children simply pick a piece because they like the subject (I like my picture because I like my dog)?

I'd like to show you some work from Jill Boyd's kindergarten classroom in our district. The students made collections of their art throughout the beginning months of school. Prior to parent conferences, Jill asked them to select one or two pieces that they liked best and then tell why they liked them. In turn, Jill picked one piece and said why she picked it. Her concern was not only to validate the children's work but also to expand their language and their thinking about what it might be possible to see in the art work.

Some of the children did focus on the subject of their work. Sam (all of the children's names have been changed), who is a very kinesthetic painter (he enjoys the large brush movement of easel tempera painting), said about his painting of brown and white swirls, "I like the ghost." About another painting (also swirls of brown and white) he said, "I like the story it makes." (Jill had written his words about a ghost on the painting.) Jill's comment about the watercolor wash she picked was, "I like how soft the colors are. They blend."

Some of the children have very strong emotional ties to their work. Carie said of her painting with the three large red hearts surrounded by blue and green, "The heart—it's like loving me." Jill picked a water color which featured pastel straight and curving lines and talked about the interesting things that Carie had done with the lines.

Carl, who spends most of his painting time mixing and experimenting with colors, chose a painting in which colors were combined in swirls on the page and said, "It looks neat because the colors are mixed up." Jill also commented on his use of color when she picked a painting in which mixed colors in light shades were surrounded by darker mixed colors and said, "I like how you used dark colors in the back with a bright color swishing though it." It's interesting to compare Sam and Carl's work because although they look very similar (abstract swirls of paint moving through the pictures), the purposes behind each of the paintings are very different. Sam enjoys the kinesthetic experience; Carl is engrossed in experimenting with the mixtures of colors. Without teacher observations, or the children's commentary of their work, this would not be evident.

Bob is a serious painter, conscious of his work. He usually does a series of paintings of the same topic (houses, faces, flowers), varying each one slightly. He picked a purple house painting, complete with windows and a door, and said, "I like the door handle because I made a good circle." About one of his face paintings he said, "The yellow hair—it's long." Jill's comment about the picture she chose, a large green and yellow flower, was "You moved from lines to blocks of color to a mixture of both."

Allison is an artist who gets a lot of attention for her work. About the painting she picked, a girl with a multi-colored skirt, she said, "It's a girl, I like her skirt." Jill commented on the painting she picked, multi-colored flowers and other plants, saying, "You have lines and big areas of color. That makes it more interesting."

I'd also like to show you a picture that Allison did just two days ago. This picture is abstract with lots of lines and swishes of color. If you hadn't seen Allison's earlier work you might think she was a beginning painter. Her earlier pictures show a great deal of control of the medium. For Allison, this recent work represents a new playfulness with the medium and in her use of color. Because we can see her paintings over a period of time, this becomes evident.

I was quite surprised by the ability of the children to be reflective about their work. They focused on what was important to them—and what was important varied with each child. For some children, like Sam, the question of selecting a work and commenting on it was seemingly irrelevant; but for most of the others the question had importance. While Carie's response was tied to a strong emotional response to the subject of the painting, other children (Bob, Allison, Carl) were intrigued by the craft of painting and talked about the aspect of their work they were currently investigating.

So here's the question. On the one hand it seems to me that the more consciousness people have about their own learning processes, the more empowered they are. Selma Wasserman in her book *Serious Players in the Primary Classroom: Empowering Children Through Active Learning Experiences* says: "To hold power for deciding for oneself about the quality of one's work, including what its strengths and weaknesses are—is the greatest level of personal power." I am also reminded of Mary Budd Rowe, who in her book *Teaching Science as Continuous Inquiry: A Basic* writes about crapshooters and bowlers. Crapshooters are people who feel that the events of life are totally random, that there is nothing they can do personally to affect the outcome; it's all a throw of the dice. Bowlers are those people who think they can develop some skills that will affect the outcome of their lives. Rowe argues strongly for education which supports people in becoming bowlers, and certainly self-evaluation of one's own learning process is part of this.

On the other side, does asking young children to do this type of self assessment impede the natural learning that they're doing? They act in the moment; does asking them to step outside themselves inject an element of self-consciousness which creates a barrier to doing this? Jill asks, "Do they have to come up with something because I'm asking them? Am I putting them on the spot? Do they really need to be 'master players' (Betty Jones's term) first?" How much metacognition is appropriate for five-year-olds?

References

Camp, R. (1990). Thinking together about assessment. *The Quarterly,* Spring, 8-14, 27.

Levi, R. (1990). Assessment and educational vision: Engaging children and parents. *Language Arts,* 6 7(3), 269-273.

Rowe, M.B. (1978). *Teaching science as continuous inquiry: A basic*. New York: McGraw Hill.

Wasserman, S. (1990). *Serious players in the primary classroom: Empowering children through active learning experiences*. New York: Teachers College Press.

Wolf, D.P. (1989). Portfolio assessment: Sampling student work. *Educational Leadership, 46*(7), 36.

Nancy Alison Place is a language arts curriculum specialist in the Program and Personnel Services Division of the Belleview, Washington, Public Schools.

Three A's: Arts, Art Education, and Advocacy

Lauren Tewes

You may be wondering why I was chosen to speak to you this morning. I haven't the education most of you have. I'm not a teacher or a principal. I didn't write a book. I don't head any committee and I'm not even a parent. So, what am I doing here at your conference?

Well, I think we all share one important feature. We care about children and we recognize that the future of our society, and indeed, of mankind, lies with today's and tomorrow's children. The information they receive and eventually pass on is the future of the world.

The world today is definitely in turmoil. With most major countries ready at any moment to go to war, the world economy being unpredictable, and the family structure changing drastically and rapidly, how can we justify our concern for the arts education of preschool children? Because kids grow up, and these self-confident, expressive adults can improve our world and secure civilization.

I firmly believe that the appropriate release of emotions is the most important stepping stone to building a strong sense of self and character. Children who can express how anger feels, how love sounds, how embarrassment or confidence looks, has a good chance of learning to express themselves appropriately in all aspects of adult life. One of my major gripes about my own childhood is that I was taught how to be a good child—and I was a good child— but very little attention was paid to how to live a rewarding and responsible adult life. What a shock it was to me to find that I was good at being something that only lasted about 16 years.

Expressing emotions is what day-to-day life is really about. How do you feel about a traffic jam? A news report? A flower in your garden? The smell of coffee? The comfort of your own bed? And how do you express those feelings? Healthy people talk, or sing, or paint, or dance to express joy and anger. We all know that being unable to express emotions appropriately causes people to gain weight, develop ulcers, do drugs, and hurt others.

One of the most important gifts you have in your profession is a chance to give society a future population of well-adjusted, expressive, artistic citizens.

I have attended a few of the sessions offered at this conference, and one of the phrases often heard was "it builds self-confidence." Aren't healthy children born with confidence? Don't they enter the world screaming and kicking and demanding that their own needs be met? Why should we bother building their confidence? Because society chips away at that natural self-confidence almost immediately, and we know that to be productive and happy in our demanding world, the one comfort and strength to rely on when we are challenged is our inner self-knowledge and confidence that we can solve problems, that we can answer the questions: How do I feel about this? How can I express my feeling in order to release the tensions and improve my situation?

I want to congratulate you and thank you for accepting the challenge of using creative arts to unlock emotion, thereby enriching society's children. The tools you give your students now benefit all of us. A child may know, when verbal skills fail him or her, that writing will fill in the gaps of communication, or maybe drawing or dancing will unlock the door to expression. That child knows there are alternatives in life, and he or she will look for them. Inability in one area does not equal failure in all areas.

I am very aware of the change in home life situations for children in the past 20 years or so. You, as educators, cannot be sure that the person you met in a school-opening conference is really going to be that child's care-giver throughout the school year. Divorce, death, jail, desertion, abuse, financial disaster—or war—all of these elements can remove a parent from a child's life. How many children do you teach who are cared for by single parents? Foster parents? Grandparents? Relatives or even friends? Lots!

I'm not here to judge the quality of care from these diverse groups of adults. I only want to acknowledge the reality of the world today. There are a lot of kids who need the comfort and stability of dealing with their emotions in a safe, creative way. So, here's my challenge to you. I believe that every adult who has a relationship with a child, be it as relative, teacher, neighbor, or friend, can contribute to and help develop that child's artistic expansion. If we, as responsible adults, see a child often enough to have gained the child's trust and respect, we have a wonderful opportunity to be creative with that child. This is not a painful task I am suggesting. We also get to share the joys of artistic expression.

As teachers, you may feel you have your hands full of children. You do! As parents and grandparents, your plate is even fuller. But, by sharing what you know with your friends and family, by spreading around the inspiration you have received at this conference, and by artistically challenging yourself and your neighbors, you will improve our world. By freely expressing your own artistic feelings, you will enrich society. By sharing your own opinions with others, you will help to develop discriminating audiences. As an artist, I thank you for that. An educated, opinionated audience is the most fun to perform for and the easiest to please.

This has been a wonderfully enlightening conference! Such a rich selection of information was offered here. I feel very special to have been allowed to attend your sessions, and feel more secure knowing that there are interested, innovative professionals such as yourselves teaching today's children, with the joy and love you have shown here.

Lauren Tewes is best known for her eight-year role in the television series Love Boat, although she has a long list of performances in film, television, and theatre to her credit. Since 1986 she has directed ten stage productions at theatres in Los Angeles and Studio City and maintains an active public service schedule.

Section II

SPECIFIC ARTS
INSTRUCTION

MUSIC

Developmentally Appropriate Music Experiences for Young Children

Barbara Andress

Music is a part of most young children's early experiences in the home and in various child care programs. It is often not the lack of abundant music, but rather the quality of the experience that must be questioned. Those parents for whom music is important find many ways to help their children hear and perform music. However, many families depend almost solely on the music of television, radio, and recordings to determine their children's musical repertoire and values. Prekindergarten music is predominantly guided by care providers and teachers who have limited or no musical skills. These are often responsible individuals who recognize the importance of music and do plan music into their weekly schedule. The musical content for these sessions is often based on commercial entertainment recordings, rather than on more appropriate "performable" materials that are available for the age group. The result is that in both the home and care environment, the majority of music models for children are recording artists rather than educators. Far too often, little or no regard is given to the developmental appropriateness of the musical experience.

Music educators for the past several years have been extending their range of educational commitment to include concerns for the prekindergarten child. We have studied child growth and development and coupled this information with musical ideas to be experienced and understood at a given level. This research is reflected in the MENC publication, *The School Music Program: Descriptions and Standards* (1986), where appropriate music education goals are defined for children ages birth-four. We have been involved in action research to determine viable methods and materials that can be effectively used to communicate age appropriate ideas in a concrete, real, and relevant manner to these young learners. We are aware that pushing the current public school music program downward seldom meets the developmental needs of younger children; rather, the experiences must be tailored to the unique learning styles of the age group. Such experiences are based on understanding the child's cognitive, physical, social-emotional, language acquisition, and multicultural backgrounds. This developmental information coupled with musical information provides the necessary foundation required to formulate an effective prekindergarten child-centered music curriculum.

Understanding the Child's Developmental Needs

Many researchers and educators have contributed information that provides insights to understanding the young child's developmental needs. It may be helpful to briefly allude to a few significant ideas/people as a means of justifying a proposed structure for a comprehensive early childhood music learning environment.

Cognitive Growth. What is our best guess as to how the child thinks or processes information? For an understanding of cognitive growth we can look in part to Piaget and his colleagues (1969). Useful information may be found in the descriptions of the child in the sensory-motor (birth-two) and preoperational stages (two-seven). Within these stages the child explores and forms various schemata about things and ideas in his/her world, moving from concrete to more abstract thought processes. The child develops cognitive understanding in an environment that enables him/her to assimilate, accommodate, classify, order, improvise, and perform. One implication that may be drawn is that early activities should involve sensing and doing experiences, e.g., allowing the child to simply assimilate a musical sound, evolving at a later time to playing accommodation games by categorizing the sound into a musical grouping.

Social-Emotional Growth. Many disciplines explore the child's social/play behaviors: psychology, anthropology, sociology, child development, physical education, and education. There is a consensus that play is the young child's primary method of learning. Understanding how play/social interaction develops provides key information for setting the learning environment. We need to look for this information in the writings of J. Piaget (1962), M. Parten (1932), J. Frost (1984), B. Sutton-Smith (1977), and G. Fein (1981).

Parten's ideas afford us a sequence of play behaviors that move the individual by steps from self-involvement to group interaction:

Onlooker - just watches
Solitary - independently plays without reference to what other children are doing
Parallel - independent, but plays with toys like those of others
Associative Play - with other children, but no organization
Cooperative Play - with others in small/large groups organized for a particular purpose.

Young children go through a mastery process when at play that involves sensing-doing, exploratory manipulation, improvisation, imitation, and conscious effort to control for a planned effect. To facilitate this process the early childhood music program must provide for hands-on, real, and life relevant experiences.

Musical Development. Researchers have also been looking into the musical behaviors of young children. Such questions as how children acquire songs of their culture provide us with keys to selection/creation of developmentally appropriate literature and a sense of the expected musical response. Sources that deal with vocal development and song acquisition include Davidson et al. (1980), Papousek (1981), and Scott (1970). In these readings one encounters notions about children and their spontaneous singing, the influence of imitative vocal play between adult and child, how and when the child deals with the global properties of a song, and the prekindergarten child's perception of pitch leading to mastery of a song.

Educational Practice. Several thinkers in the field of early childhood and psychology are providing excellent guidance for the profession. Two people worthy of our attention are:

David Elkind addresses concerns for the emotional stability of the child in works such as "The Hurried Child" (1981) and questions educational practices in "Miseducation, Preschoolers at Risk" (1987). His developmentally appropriate program would include *permeable learning* areas where subject matter is not fragmented but interwoven into the child's daily activities and *special interest* areas where children may choose to become involved.

Lilian Katz (1987) suggests goals and ways of organizing the curriculum. Katz proposes that a major outcome of all early childhood programs should be that children acquire *dispositions* for learning. Dispositions means that the child forms positive attitudes and enduring habits of mind as a result of the interaction in the preschool environment.

A Prekindergarten Tripartite Music Learning Environment

Synthesizing the many facets of early childhood development coupled with our knowledge of music education leads us to formulate a curriculum plan that is delivered in a *tripartite* music learning environment. The plan involves the following steps:

STEP 1: Determine the child's developmental stage (level of social play, level of cognitive understanding).

STEP 2: Plan developmentally appropriate activities that involve the child in acquisition of knowledge, skills, dispositions, and feelings.

STEP 3: Implement a tripartite system for delivering musical understandings in the learning environment, wherein each side of the triangle is supportive of the total framework for dispensing learning. Emphasis within the system shifts depending on the age group being serviced; however, all three environments are utilized at all age levels. The special interest areas with free choice opportunities for one on one interaction will be more conducive to musical play of the very young two- and three-year-olds, whereas cooperative play activities are more usable by older three- and four-year-olds.

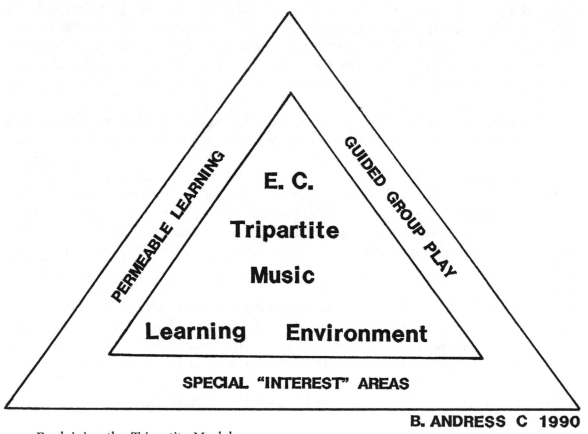

Explaining the Tripartite Model:

Side 1 - Permeable Learning. Learning experiences based on construction, projects, and frames within the context of the total early childhood curriculum experience.

Side 2 - Special "Interest" Areas. Preset topical area plays used by children, such as table plays, music corner, or a dancing place.

Side 3 - Guided Group Experiences. The teacher directs large group interactive play such as when participating in Circle Time activities.

The teacher's level of involvement in this system moves between that of a facilitator, interactor, and direct teaching. The function of a *facilitator* includes planning and presetting all environments: free choice, permeable, and large group. As an *interactor* in the play, the teacher becomes playmate, clarifier, and labeler and strives to stimulate the child's curiosity. Much of life's music is performed and shared in a group setting and thus the *direct teaching* in the guided group setting is a very real and relevant activity for young children. This is a good time for social interaction, acquisition of musical repertoire and understandings, increasing performance skills, and experiencing the joy of making music with others.

The Tripartite System in Practice

A tripartite system for providing music experiences allows us to effectively meet the individual developmental needs of young children as well as serve the group process. The following are examples of activities that might be used in a tripartite learning environment.

A Setting for Permeable Learning

> *Topic:*   Transportation
> *Play Setting:*   Construction
> *Music Play:*   Wheels on the Bus - traditional song
>   Take Me Riding in a Car - Woody Guthrie

Materials: two cardboard boxes; five 14" cake/pizza cardboard circles; several wooden dowel "pegs" or masking tape, poster paint (optional), several small chairs for car/bus seats; strips of cloth for seat belts.

Creative Construction Challenges:
Invite children to construct the front and back of a bus: Front - one box, two wheels and one circle for a steering wheel (steering wheel may be attached or placed unattached on top of the box to be picked up and used in a driving position during the play). Back - one box, two wheels. Children attach wheels to boxes using wooden pegs (teacher predrill holes) or masking tape. One flap of the front box may be left up for a windshield. Children may paint or paste additional details on the bus (lights, license plates), add horns/other sounds, or use the materials imaginatively as is. The various parts are then arranged to create a front of the bus, chairs in a line for seats, then the back of the bus box. Strips of cloth may be tied to chairs to create seat belts.

The Play:
1. Children will have many dramatic, musical, and nonmusical ways of playing in the bus. When appropriate, intervene and sing "The Wheels on the Bus." Provide a few instrumental sounds such as a horn and sand blocks for windshield wipers.

2. Suggest that the bus may become a car. Some chairs may need to be removed. Introduce songs such as "Take Me Riding in the Car, Car." Add important new verses such as "Buckle up my seat belt...."

3. Encourage children to create their own riding in bus or car dialogue song play. Sing questions: "Where is this bus going?" "Who is on the bus?" Song play that includes numbers and names usually elicits a ready response from young children.

4. Introduce children to the book "The Wheels on the Bus" by Maryann Kovalski (Joy Street Books, Little Brown and Company, 1987). Repeat the story inviting children to help sing the verses of the song as they appear.

Special "Interest" Area Play

Topic: Traditional songs to sing and play: Three Blue Pigeons
Materials: A three step stair, bells (E-D-C), mallet; pigeon patterns; popsicle sticks.

Preparing the Environment:
1. Create three steps from blocks of Styrofoam
2. Use individual resonator bell blocks (E-D-C)
3. Prepare three blue pigeons from the pattern or have children create their own pigeons. Popsicle sticks may be attached to each bird so that they may be pressed into the soft styrofoam in an upright position.

The Play:
1. Place the three blue pigeons in the play area. Encourage children to make up dialogue songs about the blue birdies: how they fly; sit in a tree; chirp to each other. Interject traditional songs such as "Blue bird, blue bird through my window...."

2. Another time, place the three blue pigeons on the steps and sing the song "Three Blue Pigeons." At the end of each verse one pigeon flies away until there are no pigeons remaining on the "wall." Children remove pigeons accordingly. The teacher needs to be aware that the children may become more centered on flying the pigeons than on singing the song.

3. More mature children may play by adding bells to the game: E on the highest step; D, middle step; C, lowest step. Demonstrate for children that they can play the bells from highest to lowest as they sing the first words of the song "Three Blue Pigeons." After children play the pattern several times, encourage them to sing and play the entire song game.

4. Inherent in the play is the musical concept that sounds move downward by steps. At this stage, the concept is dealt with at a sensing-doing level rather than direct labeling for the child.

SING AND PLAY

THREE BLUE PIGEONS

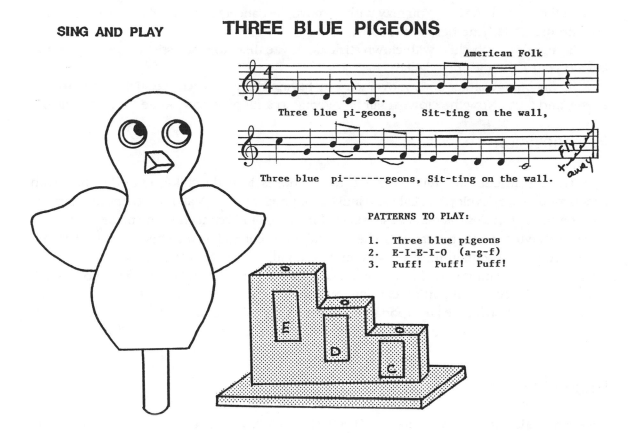

American Folk

Three blue pi-geons,   Sit-ting on the wall,

Three blue pi-------geons, Sit-ting on the wall.

PATTERNS TO PLAY:

1. Three blue pigeons
2. E-I-E-I-O (a-g-f)
3. Puff! Puff! Puff!

Guided Group Play: Circle Time

Topic: Music Play

Musical Understanding: Music moves with an underlying beat

Material: March from the "Dance of the Comedians" by Kabalevsky, two round stickers for each child. (Record Source: Holt Music - Book 2., Holt Rinehart and Winston, Inc., 1988.)

Preparation: Draw smiling clown faces on each of the stickers before the group session.

The Play:

1. As a part of the Circle Time activities, introduce children to Kabalevsky's march by involving them in imitative play. Invite children to watch your funny clowns as the music is heard. Place one sticker on each of your index fingers and improvise an easy to follow rhythmic dance for the finger clowns. Begin by hiding the clowns behind your back. Bring the right hand finger clown out, moving side to side with the beat. Continue this dancing gesture for a time, then hide the finger behind the back. Perform the same ideas using the

Section II - Specific Arts Instruction: Music   71

left hand finger clown. Later both fingers may come out to dance completing the music. The form of the music is AABA. You may wish to move the dancers accordingly or focus attention only on the underlying beat of the music.

2. Provide each child with clown stickers. Invite them to place stickers on fingers and imitate your clown as they dance.

3. Encourage larger body movements by having children place the stickers on elbows, knees, and feet. Now the clowns will be moving to a funny elbow, knee, or foot dance.

In Conclusion

The music educator must respond to the needs in early childhood education with programs that are developmentally and individually appropriate. Materials for these programs must be concrete, relevant, reflect a sensitivity for multicultural concerns, and present the finest of musical styles and performances. The curriculum is centered on the child's needs. To meet those needs the program must provide more than just Circle Time opportunities for music interaction. Music must permeate the daily activities of the child and allow for free choice small group experiences. A tripartite learning environment provides a comprehensive approach allowing music to become an important part of the child's life. Children are the carriers of our musical tradition. Let us be sure they will carry a tradition worthy of our culture.

Resources

Davidson, L., McKernon, P., & Gardner, H. (1982). The acquisition of song: A developmental approach. In *Documentary report of the Ann Arbor symposium: Applications of psychology to the teaching and learning of music*. Reston, VA: Music Educators National Conference. 1982.

Elkind, D. (1987). *Miseducation, preschoolers at risk*. New York: Alfred A. Knopf.

Fein, G. (1979). Play in the acquisition of symbols. In L. Katz (Ed.), *Current topics in early childhood education*. Norwood, NJ: Ablex.

Frost, D. , & Klein, B. (1979). *Children's play and playgrounds*. Austin, TX: Playgrounds International. (Originally published by Allyn & Bacon).

Katz, L. (1987). Early education: What should young children be doing? In L. Kagan & E. Zigler (Eds.), *Early schooling: The national debate*. New Haven, CT: Yale University Press.

MENC Committee on Standards. (1986). *The school music program: Descriptions and standards* (2d. ed.) (pp. 17-20). Reston, VA; Music Educators National Conference.

Papousek , M. & H. (1981). *Musical elements in the infant's vocalization: Their significance for communication, cognition, and creativity* . Munich: Max-Planc Institute of Psychiatry.

Piaget, J. (1951). *Play, dreams, and imitation in childhood* . New York: Norton.

Parten. M. (1932). Social participation among preschool children. *Journal of Research in Music Education,* 37, 48-60.

Sutton-Smith, B. (1977). Play as adaptive potentiation. In P. Stevens (Ed.), *Studies in the anthropology of play*. Cornwall, NY: Leisure Press.

Barbara Andress is professor emeritus of music at Arizona State University, Tempe. She has taught and supervised music at the elementary school level and co-authored the basic textbook series *Holt Music (K-8)*. She is a member of MENC's National Task Force on Music in Early Childhood.

Music in Early Childhood

John M. Feierabend

It should not come as a surprise that early training in the arts can make a marked difference in the later development of an individual. Although this is being confirmed by an increasing number of research studies, most parents and teachers remain uninformed on the importance of readiness training in the arts.

Music, perhaps more than the other arts, has traditionally been integrated into early childhood curricula. Early childhood specialists have embraced the integration of music into their curricula and rationalized its use because of the extramusical benefits in the areas of social, cognitive, motor, affective, and creative development. In addition, standard developmental stages are often measured by testing a child's ability to perform tasks easily learned through musical activities.

For example, in the *Developmental Profile II,* physical development is measured on the basis of hopping forward on one foot, jumping rope, or whistling a recognizable tune—all activities naturally explored in children's singing games.[1] The profile's social development subtest measures a child's ability to clap hands (pat-a-cake) or to take turns playing games. Its academic development subtest measures cognitive development through such tasks as rhyming words, and communication development is assessed through such things as the ability to repeat all or parts of nursery rhymes, sing songs, rhyme words, and create original songs. What better way do we have to assist these developmental abilities than to provide guided musical experiences during the formative years?

A recent educational trend is the "whole language" approach to language skills in the early elementary years.[2] The idea is that speaking, reading, and writing are most naturally nurtured by using words and concepts from the child's experience without overemphasizing correct spelling or grammar. The emphasis is on supporting self-expression, gradually working toward refinement in much the same way that early speaking skills naturally evolve from enthusiastic attempts to refined precision.

To follow this philosophy in music, we would use songs that have traditionally emerged from the child's world. The use of traditional children's folk songs and rhymes ensures a natural flow of musical language and textual content relevant to the young child's interests. A further support for the use of traditional children's folk songs and rhymes can be found in the recent interest in cultural literacy—the theory that all educated people who share the same culture should have a common body of knowledge.[3] Is an individual tuned into the American

Reprinted with permission from July/August 1990 issue of *Design for Arts in Education*.

culture if he or she has not shared a standard repertory of traditional American children's songs and rhymes—songs like "Twinkle, Twinkle" and "The Eensy Weensy Spider"? Folk songs from other cultures might also be included to begin fostering multicultural insights.

Music for Music's Sake

Whether the music is used to reinforce the whole-language approach, to nurture cultural literacy, or to assist in the natural development of social, cognitive, motor, affective, or creative skills, one basic prerequisite remains: Can the child be successful with music? If music activities are to be the vehicles to facilitate "extramusical" learnings, care must be given to develop primary music skills, comfortable singing, and rhythmic moving. Furthermore, music must not be justified solely for its ability to facilitate skill development in other areas. Nurturing music skills should be considered essential in early childhood simply because of the richness it brings to one's life.

Our society assumes certain musical behavior from all of us throughout our adult lives. We are expected to dance at weddings, cheer at sporting events while clapping hands in time with the crowd, sing "Happy Birthday" to friends and relatives, or share a lullaby with an infant. Although all people should have such minimum musical competencies, some will be more deeply involved with music as consumers of recorded and live music, while others will become performing musicians. Regardless of our ultimate level of involvement with music, the success of our musical experiences may depend on the musical nurturing we received during our preschool years.

Success in singing and moving to music involves a type of intelligence independent of other intellectual skills. Early childhood specialists most commonly consider music activities in light of the ways they benefit extramusical skills rather than for the development of musical skills for their own sake. In his thought-provoking *Frames of Mind,* however, Howard Gardner has helped us understand the importance of recognizing the variety of separate intelligences each of us possesses: linguistic, logical-mathematical, musical, spatial, bodily-kinesthetic, interpersonal, and intrapersonal.[4]

Gardner challenges us to nurture all our capabilities, including musical intelligence. Instead of judging overall intelligence by considering only one or two areas, Gardner suggests that we each have our own profile of strengths and weaknesses among all seven intelligences. If one person is exceptionally intelligent in one or two of the seven (say, music and bodily-kinesthetic) and only average in the others, is such a person any less intelligent than another who might have two other exceptional intelligences (for example, linguistic and logical-mathematical)?

Until recently, society has not placed equal emphasis on each of the seven intelligences. Many educational psychologists are awaiting with great interest the results of Project Zero, a model school in Boston based on Gardner's theories. Students are involved in a schedule that places equal emphasis on each of the seven intellectual realms. Because this curriculum was only recently put in place, no results have yet been reported. The concept, however, is already being replicated in several other locations. Directors of early childhood programs might wish to consider adopting the Project Zero concept for their preschool children.

Music as a Separate Intelligence

The theory of multiple intelligences suggests that music is an independent intelligence that may be helped or hindered by the influence of parents and early childhood specialists. According to Gardner, all children deserve to have all seven intelligences nourished so that they may function at their full potential. If any are overlooked, essential learning stages may be missed in early childhood and the potential intelligence may diminish.

This concept of diminishing intelligence has been supported by the research of Edwin Gordon at Temple University. In 1965, Gordon began to explore music intelligence through the development of a music aptitude test, *Musical Aptitude Profile* (MAP).[5] Designed for students aged 9 to 18, the test measures the ability to retain a short melody "in your mind" and then compare it with a second melody. Gordon defines the ability to hear music that is not physically present as "audiation" and determines the level of musical aptitude by the ability "to audiate." He found that each individual tested rarely scored similarly on the tonal and rhythmic subtests. In general, those who score superbly on one part of the test will have average scores on the other part. According to Gordon, we are each stronger in one kind of music intelligence than in the other.

As Gordon retested students as they progressed through junior high and high school, he discovered that they retained the same levels of audiation ability. A 12-year-old student who performed at the fiftieth percentile would be likely to perform at the fiftieth percentile at 18. Our audiation as adults resembles our audiation as nine-year-olds. Furthermore, it appears that participation in a music ensemble such as band, orchestra, or choir has little effect on audiation ability after age nine. While students may learn to perform better and develop musical coordination skills through the school years, they cannot actually enhance their basic aptitude for mentally retaining tonal or rhythmic patterns. More recent research on children younger than nine years old produced more startling findings.

Music Aptitude Testing

In 1978, Gordon developed a simplified version of MAP for children between the ages of five and nine. The *Primary Measures of Music Audiation* (PMMA) contains two parts: one measures tonal audiation and one measures rhythmic audiation.[6] When Gordon administered the tests in subsequent years to the same students between the ages of five and nine, he discovered that music audiation scores would decline if the children did not receive musical stimulation. In school districts where there was no general music in the elementary curriculum, or where the program did not stress singing and rhythmic moving, Gordon consistently found similar results.

Of great importance was the finding that the greatest loss in audiation occurred between the ages of five and six. There was a significant, though less severe, decline in audiation scores between the ages of six and seven. Audiation scores continued to decline each year the student aged, but less significantly. From eight to nine there was only a slight loss in audiation scores, and at nine music audiation stabilized.

In one study, Gordon tested students who began public school music in the second grade (approximately at age seven). As before, students' scores declined between the ages of five and seven. Scores increased slightly from ages seven to eight, and even less from eight to nine. The audiation scores that then stabilized at age nine were slightly higher than those at age eight but noticeably lower than at age five. It appears that the longer the delay in music stimulation in the form of singing and rhythmic moving, the more the ability to audiate can be lost and the less will be regained.

Although there is currently no test to measure music aptitude in children younger than five years, there is a clear trend in Gordon's research. If the greatest loss in music audiation occurs between the ages of five and six, what happens between the ages of four and five or from birth to five? Children are probably born with their own level of music intelligences that begin to atrophy unless supported by a musical environment. If children have not experienced singing and rhythmic moving at home, by the time they reach kindergarten their music aptitudes have probably declined significantly. If they are given a nurturing environment starting in kindergarten, their music aptitude scores can increase until age nine. Aptitude scores can also show the greatest increase between the ages of five and six. Each year closer to nine, the increase is less noticeable.

If a school district needs to curtail a music teacher's schedule, the kindergarten is usually the first to be cut. This is obviously the worst possible year to withhold music. It would be better to scale down a junior or senior high school music program. In the upper grades, a teacher can teach more music literature or present more information about music, but in kindergarten the teacher can change the children's music intelligence for life.[7]

An additional comparative study involving audiation testing and general intelligence showed a zero correlation between Stanford-Binet IQ scores and music aptitude scores.[8] One should not assume that musical potential is based on general intelligence. The commonly believed notion that mathematical abilities and music abilities are related depends on how one defines music abilities. Logical-mathematical intelligence may be related to a theoretical understanding of music, but audiation appears to be a separate intelligence from mathematics or verbal thinking.

In another study, a low correlation was found between the music aptitude of parents and children.[9] It seems that the musical intelligence of children born to a family where parents provide musical experiences will be nurtured, but there is no guarantee that musical parents will pass on musical intelligence to their offspring. There were as many high-scoring children with low-scoring parents as low-scoring children with high-scoring parents. There were musical parents with musical children and nonmusical parents with nonmusical children. These results suggest that it is not possible to base a prediction of a child's musical talent on the parents' musical aptitude.

Aptitude Versus Achievement

Children who possess high musical aptitude may not be able to reach their full musical potential. According to Gordon, music achievement will depend on a number of factors.[10] Students need a balanced diet of music experience. This includes experiences with major, minor, and other tonalities and rhythm in duple and triple as well as other meters. A broader range of experiences will enable children to assimilate a more complete understanding of musical organization.

We learn better about what something is by learning about what it is not. Formal study of meters and tonalities is not needed at this early stage. It is, however, important that young children sing and move to music informally, much the way they work with language during the first five years of life. As with language, children should not be deprived of the whole musical picture because they are too young to understand it. Children learn and understand a great deal more than they can speak about during their first years, but we would never think of not speaking to infants and toddlers just because they cannot speak. The child will naturally assimilate the sophistication of the language, the grammar, and the dialect in a specific environment. When children begin to speak, they will attempt to reproduce those sounds or words that their lips and tongue can reproduce. Their comprehension of language far exceeds their ability to coordinate speech.

Music deserves the same natural assimilation. The broader the repertory and the more sophisticated the musical vocabulary, the richer will be the child's intuitive understanding of how music is organized. Children's early attempts at singing or moving to music may show a lack of coordination, but they should not be deprived of experiences that nurture comprehension before they are able to coordinate their activities.

Partners in Artistry

Attention to singing development and rhythmic moving is fundamental to the development of music aptitude. Still, music is more than tones and rhythms. It is spirit. No musical performance could be considered successful if only the tone and rhythms were present—those tones and rhythms must be performed with a deeply felt message. The ability to perform tones and rhythms with spirit is the direct outcome of music making at any age.

Children would never have developed a repertory of traditional songs and rhythm solely for their tonal and rhythmic pleasure. The spirit, the joy, and the magic embodied in these songs make them appealing. When nuturing a child's development, adults should ensure that the songs and text are inspired, that they embody a marriage of melody and spirit.

Adults should select songs and rhymes that suggest childhood fantasies and are based on make-believe concepts. Imagining toes as piggies, or a knee bounce as a horse ride, will do more to inspire the musical spirit of a child than a "teaching song" that derives its inspiration from a need to educate about numbers, letters, or colors. This is not to say that "teaching songs" should be excluded from an early childhood curriculum, but parents and teachers should not consider their child's musical spirit nurtured through those songs. Use "teaching songs" to teach concepts, but use inspired repertory to enhance a child's artistry. When striving to integrate music into the preschool child's life, remember that spirit and ability are partners in artistry.

Making a Difference

If we teach to enhance all of a child's intelligences, we must include the child's music intelligence. Ideally, that teaching should be provided by musically competent individuals. Regardless of musical ability, however, the best and most natural music enrichment should come from the parents. Parents should acquire collections of children's songs (or recordings if they do not read music) and memorize songs and rhymes so that children feel they are sharing a pleasurable experience with their parents rather than being made to learn a song or rhyme. Many collections of children's folk songs and rhymes are housed in the children's section of the library. Libraries also frequently present children's music programs with sing-alongs and movement activities. These are good sources from which to acquire a new song to share, but they should not be considered a substitute for the integration of music and movement into the daily routine.

Day-care and preschool teachers should plan regular music sessions. In these situations, it will be more difficult to provide the one-on-one adult-to-child interaction suited to many of the songs and rhymes, although there is the advantage of a group situation in which music games can be played that would not be practical in the home. Still, day-care and preschool teachers should try to find opportunities for each child to share songs and rhymes in a one-on-one situation. Group singing does not give children opportunities to really hear themselves and know if they can produce musical sounds without assistance.[11]

Parents and caregivers who feel insecure about their own singing abilities should use recorded music during music time, not as a substitute but as a partner. The children will be provided with a model of tonal and rhythmic accuracy from the recording and the spirit or joy of the activity from the eyes, face, and gestures of the adult.

One ideal solution for both parents and day-care and preschool teachers is attendance at organized music classes for preschool children. These classes are becoming increasingly common, and many well-trained musicians and educators are becoming interested in teaching this age group. Unfortunately, the quality of preschool music programs is uneven. Stay away from those that profess to give a child a head start learning "about" music. Learning facts about music will do little to enhance a child's audiation ability. Find programs where the instructor has a pleasant singing voice and moves rhythmically in a comfortable manner. The instructor should express a real love for songs and rhymes in a playful manner and be able to evoke spiritful singing and movement responses from children of this age.

What to Expect in the Future

Everyone is talking about early childhood education. The arts community is no exception. Several state departments of education are advocating public preschool. The Connecticut Department of Education is making an effort to address the need for improved early childhood education. During the past year, the department has extended the certification of music teachers down through nursery school. This action reflects the department's desire for colleges and universities to prepare teachers to teach this young group. Publishing companies are offering more collections of songs and rhymes for preschoolers. There is a new wave of recording artists in the hot new market of children's recording. Performances of musical artists focusing on the preschool artists such as Raffi and Sharon, Lois, and Bram are consistently sold out. Even textbook publishers are investigating music curricula for the preschool years.

Future efforts may include high school classes on parenting that incorporate the arts, or videotapes to be viewed in the hospital after delivery that show mothers how to share a lullaby or other music play with their newborn. Certainly music and the other arts should be required in any early childhood college curriculum. Some colleges are already beginning to anticipate the rising need for preschool arts specialists; others seem to be waiting for state departments of education to mandate changes. Continued advocacy and research are beginning to make a difference. Administrators are beginning to see that music and the other arts can make a difference for young children.

Caring about the whole child means caring about arts education. With the shift toward more day care, now, more than ever, parents need time and experiences to nourish their children's spirits. Music activities in the first five years are a natural means of fostering a wide variety of developmental skills. Now is the time for administrators and policymakers to recognize the many benefits the arts can offer and to understand that the arts are not as important in preschool as at other times in life. They are *more* important.

Endnotes

1. Alpern, G., Boll, T., & Shearer, M. (1984). *Developmental profile II.* Los Angeles: Western Psychological Services.

2. Goodman, K. (1989). *What's whole in whole language.* Fort Smith: Heinemann Educational Books.

3. Hirsch, E.D. (1987). *Cultural literacy: What every American needs to know.* Boston: Houghton Mifflin. See also Hirsch, E.D., *The first dictionary of cultural literacy.* Boston: Houghton Mifflin.

4. Gardner, H. (1983). *Frames of mind*. New York: Basic Books.

5. Gordon, E. (1965). *Musical aptitude profile*. Boston: Houghton Mifflin.

6. Gordon, E. (1979). *Primary measures of music audiation*. Chicago: G.I.A.

7. Teachers and administrators who would like to investigate Gordon's research on music aptitude further should refer to his book, *The nature, description, measurement and evaluation of music aptitude* (Chicago: G.I.A.).

8. Ibid.

9. Ibid.

10. Gordon, E. (1989). *Learning sequences in music*. Chicago: G.I.A.

11. Goetz, M. (1985). *Factors affecting accuracy in children's singing*. Ann Arbor: University Microfilms.

John M. Feierabend is associate professor of music education at the Hartt School of Music of the University of Hartford, Connecticut, and is coordinator of the Connecticut Center for Musical Growth and Development which oversees programs in early childhood education in music and movement, Solfege musicianship training, and the Children's Chorus of Connecticut. He is the author of several books focusing on the importance of music and movement in early childhood.

The Magical Question of "Why?"
Nurturing Thinking While Enjoying Music (5- to 8-Year Olds)

Mary P. Pautz

To teach young children is to be allowed to remain a child oneself in the most positive sense of the word. It is a joy that is not found in the world of medicine, law, or business. To be a child is to be excited about snowflakes and butterflies, to be thrilled with the opportunity to play a stumf fiddle, a triangle, or a drum, to be consumed with delight as the excitement of "In the Hall of the Mountain King" becomes too much to simply sit quietly and listen, to be excited when one discovers while singing "Bingo" that when "B-i-n" are removed "GO" is left! To be a child is to live in a constant world of wonder.

To teach is to retain the soul of a child, to possess the wonder of "why?" and nurture it in others. To teach is to understand the difference between "fun" and "joy." (Fun is external and frivolous and has its occasional place in the classroom just as it has its place elsewhere in life. Joy is profound and is the essence of what teaching and learning can be. There must be enduring joy if the wonder of learning is to be nurtured.) Children come to school with great expectations! They are coming to learn to read! They are coming to explore the world! They are coming to enjoy the wonder of music!

Is there a magic age at which the statement "play is the child's most viable method of learning" ceases to be true? At age 5? Age 6? Age 7? Age 8? How does one help children make the transition from early childhood to childhood and eventually into pre-adolescence and adolescence?

While play is beginning to be accepted as the ideal for preschoolers, it is still considered suspect once "formal schooling" begins. At a time when child-initiated centers and age-appropriate materials are receiving positive attention from many sectors involved with early childhood, the opposite is happening in kindergartens and primary schools where clay, water, and sand tables have been replaced with desks and chairs, worksheets and tests, and even remedial activities. It would seem that someone has determined that "fun and games" are okay for preschoolers but, once in school, the serious business of education begins. Somehow educators have been convinced that children "learn from the seat up."

It is time to speak up against the sharp distinction that occurs when formal schooling begins. It is true that, just as there are differences among two-, three-, and four-year-olds, there are also differences between preschoolers and primary school children. What one does and how one teaches kindergarteners IS different from how one thinks and teaches preschoolers. However, primary children are closer in need and development to preschoolers than to intermediate grade children. Perhaps then, the school model for primary grades should more closely resemble the early childhood model than it does the intermediate grade model. This intermediate model as described in *Developing Minds* (Costa, 1985) is one of recitation. "The interaction is teacher centered. The teacher controls by asking questions and reinforcing answers." This model is in use in the majority of primary classrooms as well.

As stated in this conference's goal statement it is our intent to "affirm early childhood as a time for active, self-directed learning filled with the joy of playful interaction within a rich, stimulating, stress-free environment." How can this environment be maintained while moving children forward in their cognitive, social, physical, affective, and emotional development? What aspects should be retained? (Specifically, the question posed to me for presentation at this conference was "How can thinking skills and processes be developed in music classes for children aged five through eight?") In other words, how does one reconcile the desire to maintain the environment described above and achieve the intellectual progress that is desired as children grow in age and ability to process information?

The current literature on the teaching of thinking calls for ALL teachers to make room for the teaching, modelling, practicing, and evaluating of thinking within each area of study in the school curriculum. What are the thinking skills that need to be incorporated into the music class as well as every other class? Twenty-one core thinking skills grouped into eight categories were identified by the authors of *Dimensions of Thinking* (Marzano, 1988). These have been further categorized by Barrett in *Dimensions of Musical Thinking* (Boardman, 1989) into three large categories as follows:

I.   Skills of Knowledge Acquisition:
Focusing Skills (defining problems, setting goals)
Information Gathering Skills (observing, formulating questions)
Remembering Skills (encoding, recalling)

II. Skills of Processing:
Organizing Skills (comparing, classifying, ordering, representing)
Analyzing Skills (identifying attributes and components, identifying main ideas, identifying relationships and patterns, identifying errors)

III. Skills of Transfer and Application:
Generating Skills (inferring, predicting, elaborating)
Integrating Skills (summarizing, restructuring)
Evaluating Skills (establishing criteria, verifying)

The "rich, stimulating stress-free environment" called for in the early childhood model is the perfect environment for developing these core thinking skills. However, a rich environment does not automatically produce critical and creative thinkers. DeTurk (in Boardman, 1989) lists three requirements of musical critical thinking: The critical thinker must have high quality resources available for comparison, must understand the elements of music (conceptual knowledge), and must wish to, and know how to, make an informed decision (metacognitive strategies).

Rich Musical Resources in a Stress-Free Environment

The goal of music education—helping children become musically independent learners (who also possess the disposition to interact with music because of joyous experiences)—must be clearly understood by those preparing the environment, choosing the music and activities, and participating as a musical model. Following a commitment to child-centered holistic learning will cause the music educator to reexamine some traditional practices. It is time to reconsider such basic ideas as the organization and use of time and space and the choice of materials.

Traditionally, music classes for kindergarten, first, and second grade consist of group activities that are teacher-directed. Songs are learned; group games and dances such as "The Hokey Pokey" are taught; time is spent matching pitch in an effort to achieve in-tune singing; rhythms are clapped; names of orchestral instruments are learned; children march, skip, gallop, and tiptoe; and rhythm instruments are played while a variety of recordings are heard. Ultimately it is the teacher who makes all the decisions as to the use of time, the choice of music, and the involvement of the children. How could these decisions be modified using the early childhood model? If one is serious about capitalizing on the natural curiosity of children it will mean exploring alternatives regarding use of time, space, and choice of music.

1. Use of time and space: Music activities will include free exploration; some will be child-initiated, some will be teacher-directed, and some will be teacher-guided with small groups or individuals. Instead of the traditional 30-minute teacher-led class, the time could be divided into a 5-minute gathering time in which a "hello" or favorite song is sung, a 10-minute child-initiated exploration/music center time, followed by a 15-minute teacher-led group activity. It would be during this group activity where the conceptual development would be directed by the teacher. Another option would be to have one class a week devoted to traditional group activities and another devoted to music center small-group or individual play. A third possibility would be to use the two music periods with the music teacher for group time and introduction of centers. These centers would then be housed in the regular classroom and used by the children at the discretion of the classroom teacher. Perhaps the best option of all for kindergarten classes would be for the music specialist to visit the kindergarten room daily for 15 minutes, sometimes moving around the room, interacting with children as they go about their play, and at other times, calling them together for circle or group time. In this scenario, the music specialist serves as resource person for the classroom teacher rather than as released time. Music thus could become integrated into every aspect of the curriculum.

2. Choice of musical materials: It is often disconcerting to enter a primary classroom and observe the choice of music being used in music classes. It would appear that decisions on what to use are sometimes influenced by glitzy packaging, extra-musical objectives such as teaching colors or mathematics, and worries that only up-tempo, rock-like music with synthesized accompaniment will appeal to children. Nothing could be farther from the truth. Children love to sing simple folk songs with appropriate ranges and texts; they are more entranced by the sound of the autoharp than a contrived sound track; they would rather interact actively with music than be passive spectators. It is the responsibility of the teacher to make musical decisions based on the integrity of the art rather than relying on marketing people. The teacher must be aware of language development of children and readability when looking at texts of songs for kindergarten and first and second graders. Other considerations include degree of rhythmic and melodic sophistication, length and complexity of compositions that will be used for listening, range and tessitura of songs, clear examples of concepts, and a wide variety of multicultural materials.

Conceptual Knowledge of Music

Children do not want to be entertained or spoon fed. Anyone who has been around young children has heard the statements "Let ME do it," "I can do it MYSELF," and "WHY?" more times than they wished. Children want to make music and, just as they want to learn to read books, children also want to learn to read music in their attempt to become independent. The task of the music teacher (whether that be a trained specialist or the classroom teacher) is to organize material in a meaningful, age-appropriate manner, taking into account the experiences the children bring with them to school, the quality of the music that is shared, and the cognitive skills that children possess. One example of organization is a concept bank to be introduced and continued from kindergarten through secondary school. All concepts can be introduced in a nonsymbolic manner in kindergarten. For example, while it would be inappropriate for five year olds to be singing in harmony, it would be appropriate and desirable for them to be introduced to the concept of harmony by having them physically respond to chord changes on an autoharp (changing direction when a different chord is played, etc.) or being aware whether or not there is accompaniment on a recording. (See Figure 1 on next page for concept bank chart.)

Children need to learn how to learn. There is never enough time to teach them everything they will need to know in life regarding music; therefore they must learn the strategies that will make it possible for them to generate their own knowledge—to go beyond the information given. The following are some ways a teacher can begin this process:

1. Establish an environment for learning: Music centers should be inviting, age-appropriate, and engaging. The environment should say: "This is a special place! Music is

CONCEPT BANK

Concepts Related to the Musical Whole

EXPRESSION
> Musical elements are combined into a whole to express a musical or extramusical idea.
> The expressiveness of music is affected by the way individual elements (timbre, dynamics, articulation, rhythm, melody, harmony, form, texture) interact to create a musical whole.

TIME AND PLACE (Style)
> Musical elements are combined into a whole in a way that reflects the origin of the whole.
> The origin of the musical whole (its style) is reflected in the way the individual elements (timbre, dynamics, articulation, rhythm, melody, harmony, texture, form) interact within the musical whole.

FORM
> A musical whole begins, continues and ends.
> A musical whole is a combination of smaller segments
> A musical whole may be made up of same, varied or contrasting segments.
> A series of sounds may form a distinct musical idea within the musical whole.
> A musical whole may include an introduction, interludes and an ending segment in addition to segments that may be the same, varied or contrasting.

Concepts of Individual Musical Elements

TIMBRE
> The quality of a sound is determined by its sound source.
> The quality of a sound is affected by the material, shape and size of the source.
> The quality of a sound is determined by the way the sound is produced.

DYNAMICS
> Music may be comparatively loud or soft.
> Music may become louder or softer.

ARTICULATION
> A series of sounds may move from one to the next in either a smoothly connected or a detached manner.
> The quality of a sound is affected by the way the sound begins, continues and ends.

RHYTHM
> Music may be comparatively fast or slow, depending on the speed of the underlying pulse.
> Music may become faster or slower by changing the speed of the underlying pulse.
> Music may move in relation to an underlying pulse (beat or shortest sound)
> A series of pulses may be organized into regular or irregular groupings by stressing certain pulses.
> Individual sounds and silences within a rhythmic line may be longer than, shorter than or the same as other sounds within that line.
> Individual sounds and silences within a rhythmic line may be longer than, shorter than or the same as the underlying pulse.
> Accented sounds within a rhythmic line may sound with, before, or after the accented underlying pulse.

MELODY
> A series of pitches may move up, down or remain the same.
> A series of pitches may move up or down by steps or skips.
> Each pitch within a melody moves in relation to a home tone.
> A series of pitches, bounded by the octave, "belong together," forming a tonal set.
> A melody may be comparatively higher or lower.
> Individual pitches may be higher, lower or the same as other single pitches.

HARMONY
> Chords and melody may move simultaneously in relation to each other.
> A series of simultaneous sounds may alternate between activity and rest.
> Two or more musical lines may occur simultaneously.
> Two or more pitches may sound simultaneously.

TEXTURE
> Musical quality is affected by the distance between simultaneously sounded musical lines.
> Musical quality is influenced by the number of and degree of contrast between musical lines sounding simultaneously.

Figure 1. Chart from *The Generative Approach to Music Learning: Music in the Elementary Classroom,* by E. Boardman and M. Pautz, 1989, University of Wisconsin-Madison Division of University Outreach. Used with permission.

86 Early Childhood Creative Arts

special! You are special! This a safe place! This is a place to experiment!" Centers should be set up for active engagement and exploration. They could include <u>singing areas</u> with

- props such as play microphones, "singing stumps or chairs" to encourage both the individual singing of familiar songs and vocal improvisation;

- props which serve as reminders of songs (such as a puppet which can be drawn downward into a cone for "Jack in the Box," a furry mitt with "b-i-n-g-o" on each of its fingers for the "Bingo" song, a clown with multiple pockets for the song "Pockets");

- props which serve as motivation for improvisational conversations such as toy tables and chairs for singing about playing house;

- props such as charts which remind children of favorite songs.

Visuals, when used, should be of a graphic or iconic nature. To introduce musical symbols that are meaningless is a foolish and futile endeavor. However, after multiple experiences with associating icons to sound as well as multiple opportunities to manipulate them, children will be ready for standard musical notation. (See Figure 2.)

Figure 2.

Other centers could offer <u>instrumental exploration</u>—percussion instruments, autoharps, and bells are favorites and readily available. In addition to simple exploration to determine what kind of sound is made and how it is made, simple graphics will allow six-year-olds to play their favorite songs by "reading" them.

Language arts books that have been shared in music or reading time (such as *I See a Song, City Sounds, Jungle Sounds, Color Dance, Spike, The Sparrow Who Couldn't Sing, Chicka Chicka Boom Boom, Barn Dance, The Boy of the Bells,* and *Orchestranimals*) will be enjoyed by children in language centers and will often lead to vocal and/or instrumental improvisation and composition. A dance or <u>movement corner</u> will include a tape recorder and brightly colored scarves and pieces of materials, streamers, and other props which can be used to stimulate the imagination and increase sensitivity to music. <u>Discovery centers</u> with items such as canisters containing salt, rice, and popcorn kernels encourage children to be inquisitive as they manipulate the items to determine loudest and softest as well as to match like sounds. <u>Listening corners</u> equipped with tape recorder and pillows and icons will allow children the joy of multiple repetition of favorite pieces introduced in class.

2. Organize new material meaningfully and relate it to what is known already: A teacher concerned about helping children learn to think while enjoying music will not operate with a "what shall we sing today" attitude regarding lesson planning. Instead, she/he will be aware of and use principles from educational psychology such as "Move from the concrete to the abstract, from the whole to the part, and from the simple to the complex." A teacher must think about what a five- or six-year-old knows and is interested in, what is being studied in the rest of the curriculum, and how this information can be used in structuring understanding of musical concepts. Songs are not taught in isolation but are compared and related to each other in terms of tempo, mood, melodic direction, etc.

3. Expect all children to be learners: Teachers must believe that "I can" is as important as "IQ"; that "success comes in cans—`I can sing...' and 'I can figure this out'... 'I can....'" Following William Purkey's advice, one must "invite children to celebrate their potential." A teacher can "empower" children to be independent learners rather than "enabling" them to be dependent, fearful, or apathetic. To be aware of the need to nurture thinking does not mean to negate playfulness! Rather it means being inventive as a teacher. Sometimes it is simply a matter of fine tuning what we already do as music teachers. We sing songs with children.

It is important that the children take increasing responsibility of performance. Using simple graphics, children can begin to make decisions how each verse of "This Old Man" will be sung. A simple activity is to have one child make decisions regarding dynamics and signal these decisions to the class by displaying appropriate cards (see Figure 3). Another day, articulation decisions will be made by a child. Still another day, tempo decisions are made. Eventually all decisions will be made by children and shown simultaneously. Children can be challenged to watch three children and respond to choices made. Again, the key is in the careful structuring of the lesson. The directive may be that in the beginning only one child may change cards per verse; as the children gain proficiency, all three children are allowed to change cards for each verse if they choose. This involves much more thought than simply singing the song. The joy of achievement is evident in the squeals and laughter and requests to "do it again."

Figure 3.

4. Teach children cognitive strategies: Children need to learn how to learn; they need to be taught that achievers do indeed plan, implement and evaluate strategies. As a teacher this means setting up opportunities for children to plan, rewarding and praising thinking as much as the correct answer, and using vocabulary that encourages them to become strategic thinkers and mental explorers. Children need to learn that musicians use strategies—simple strategies such as knowing that one needs to listen when learning a new song. (Anyone who has ever taught young children will testify that this is a strategy young children do not know. If you say that you have a new song for them, they will begin to sing with you even though they do not know the words nor have ever heard the melody!) Other strategies to teach children include knowing that one must choose a starting pitch, that one must set a tempo, etc. If these are never modeled consciously (that is, the teacher picks the pitch "out of the air" and never models finding a pitch on the bells or piano, never comments on the need to warm-up or tune up), then children assume that one simply opens one's mouth and sings. One need only to hear the singing of "Happy Birthday" in a restaurant or to ask someone to start the "Star Spangled Banner" to realize the problems when no attention is paid to starting pitch. Unless children learn strategies and the responsibility is turned over to them, they will remain forever dependent on someone else for initiating musical activities.

Returning to the 21 core thinking skills listed earlier, children need to learn how to predict, to classify, to identify relationships, to infer, to order, to establish criteria, to compare, etc. It is easier for a child to decide which song is faster than to describe the tempo of a single song.

What is fast to one person is not fast to another. Those concerned with how children learn suggest that one must also supply both examples and non-examples. One cannot truly learn "major" without hearing "minor," or meters of "2" without hearing meters of "3." Very young children can be taught to scan a piece of music to find same and different parts. Questions such as "What would happen if the flute had played the tune instead of the trumpet?" "How are these two compositions alike?" "Why do you think the composer...?" "Why don't we like the singing on the tape?" must be deliberately planned and asked by teachers who hope to nurture thinking in a musical context. Children need practice in thinking skills as much as they need practice in musical skills.

5. Teach children metacognitive strategies: Metacognition is a dimension of one's thinking process which refers to one's knowledge concerning one's own cognitive processes and products or anything related to them. One of the greatest things a teacher can do is to be a model thinker, a model life long learner; a model of one excited about learning; a model of one who is puzzled about an unknown, a model who thinks aloud and shares the secrets of the thinking process, comments such as "I'd better get the starting pitch from the bells." "That was hard to follow; I think I'll track with my finger," "I need to listen to that again." "This will be easy to learn because the first and second parts are the same." "This is a lullaby; I bet that it will be soft and smooth and probably played by the flute or violin." "That sounded great because our voices went up and down just like the picture of the song did!" "Wasn't that FUN! Let's do it again!" "WE could do that; let's be composers today!"

Indeed, to teach IS to retain the soul of a child, to possess the wonder of "why" and nurture it in others. To teach IS to understand the difference between "fun" and "joy." Children come to school with great expectations! Becoming an independent musician is an important part of that expectation.

Resources That May Be Helpful

BOOKS
(includes those referred to in text)

Andress, B. (1989). *Promising practices: Prekindergarten music education.* Reston, VA: Music Educators National Conference.

Boardman, E. (Ed.). (1989). *Dimensions of musical thinking.* Reston, VA: Music Educators National Conference.

Costa, A. (1985). *Developing minds: A resource book for teaching thinking.* Alexandria, VA: Association for Supervision and Curriculum Development.

Elkind, D. (1987). *Miseducation: Preschoolers at risk.* New York: Alfred A. Knopf.

Jones, B.F., et al. (1987). *Strategic teaching and learning: Cognitive instruction in the content areas.* Alexandria, VA: Association for Supervision and Curriculum Development.

Marzano, R., et al. (1988). *Dimensions of thinking: A framework for curriculum and instruction.* Alexandria, VA: Association for Supervision and Curriculum Development.

Raths, L.E., et al. (1967). *Teaching for thinking.* Columbus, OH: Charles E. Merrill Publishing Company.

VIDEOTAPES AND MANUALS

Boardman, E., & Pautz, M. (1989). *The generative approach to music learning: Music in the elementary classroom.* Madison, WI: University of Wisconsin-Madison Division of University Outreach.

MAGAZINES

Educational Leadership (magazine of the Association for Supervision and Curriculum Development)—
Issues devoted to thinking:

1990	February	1988	April	1986	April and May
1985	May	1984	September and November		

Design for Arts in Education (a bi-monthly magazine)
July/August 1990 Symposium on Early Childhood Arts Education

Kappan (magazine of Phi Delta Kappa)

SUGGESTED LIST OF CHILDREN'S BOOKS

Carle E. (1973). *I see a song.* New York: Thomas Y. Crowell.

Emberley, R. (1989). *City sounds.* Boston: Little, Brown and Company.

Emberley, R. (1989). *Jungle sounds.* Boston: Little, Brown and Company.

Jonas, A. *Color dance* . (1989). New York: Greenwillow Books.

Maddox, T. (1989). *Spike, the sparrow who couldn't sing.* New York: Barron's.

Martin, B., & Archambault, J. (1986). *Barn dance.* New York: Henry Holt and Company.

Martin, B., & Archambault, J. (1989). *Chicka chicka boom boom.* New York: Simon & Schuster, Inc.

Simon, C. (1990). *The boy of the bells.* New York: Doubleday.

van Kampen, V., & Eugen, I. (1989). *Orchestranimals.* New York: Scholastic Inc.

MUSIC EXAMPLES USED IN CONFERENCE SESSION: SOURCES

Also sprach Zarathustra (R. Strauss)   Bernstein, Encore collection, vol. 1 (CBS
                                          XMT 44723)

Children's march (Goldmark)   Holt music (grade 1)*
                                          Fennell, March time, Classette412300-4

Jack in the box   Holt music (grade 1)*

Pockets (Joe Wise)   Holt music (kindergarten)*
                                          Wise, Show me your smile

Waltz of the flowers (Tchaikovsky)   Bernstein, Nutcracker suite (CBS
                                          XMT31806)

Traditional songs:
Row row row your boat   Holt music (grade 2)*
Bingo   Holt music (grade 1)*
This old man   Holt music (grade 1)*

*Meske, E., Andress, B., Pautz, M., & Willman, F. (1988). *Holt music*. Orlando, FL: Harcourt, Brace, Jovanovich.

For further information contact: Mary P. Pautz, Music Department, University of Wisconsin-Milwaukee, Box 413, Milwaukee, WI 53201.

Mary P. Pautz is assistant professor of music education at the University of Wisconsin-Milwaukee.

Music Is Child's Play:
A Developmental Approach for
Kindergarten Music

Diane Cummings Persellin

Most kindergarten music programs center on teacher-directed large group experiences. Songs and group activities are presented by either a music specialist or a kindergarten classroom teacher. This teacher-directed approach is only part of a developmentally appropriate music curriculum for kindergarten children. Young children also need opportunities to play and explore within a musical environment at their own speed.

> Our traditional approach, involving children in large settings where they listen, play, sing, and move to heritage music materials, can no longer represent the sole part of a larger program in which children interact and make decisions about sounds, their quality, intensity, pitch, and duration. The children should manipulate and play with sounds, musical and environmental, as a means to ordering and organizing their musical world. (Andress, 1980)

Children's play is their work. During the prekindergarten years, children have been evolving through several different stages of interactive play. Parten (1930) writes that these stages form a hierarchy that includes solitary play (alone, without others), parallel play (same toy as others but no interaction), associative play (in which children are enjoying the company of others but not cooperating together), and cooperative play (highly organized group play).

A music curriculum based totally upon large group cooperative play does not take into account the developmental needs of many of the young kindergartners. These young children still need music opportunities in which they can play by themselves or in small groups in child-initiated activities. Often the music program is all teacher-directed and requires a high level of continuous cooperation from all kindergartners. How can a music program foster both the teacher-directed and the child-initiated play?

A music curriculum can involve both types of music experiences by regularly introducing music manipulatives in the large teacher-directed group situation. These manipulatives will then be placed in the kindergarten classroom in a music center for children to play and explore during their free-choice time. If a music specialist teaches music to the kindergarten class, she/he can work with the classroom teacher on the logistics such as the frequency of rotation. Examples of how these music centers work will be discussed later in this paper.

Whenever possible, the music specialist should also be in the environment with the children during their free choice time when they select centers. The music specialist can then interact musically with the children in the music center. Much of the inspiration for these centers will come from the teacher-directed music class.

The Teacher-Directed Music Class

During the teacher-directed activity time the music specialist needs to plan carefully for age-appropriate activities. "Hello" and "Goodbye" songs help establish a structure that young children need. Songs that incorporate children's names are appealing as well. At the beginning of the year, care should be taken to change activities or songs every few minutes. Some activity will help children to focus on the task at hand and should be included about every five minutes in order to get the wiggles out. Songs can be created to make transitions smoother. Children respond well to new words such as "Make a circle, Yes-sir-ee" when added to a familiar folksong such as "Skip to My Lou." This also helps reinforce the melody of this simple folk song, as well. A reward for good listening and working hard comes at the end of class in the form of a small surprise such as a puppet in the Big Music Bag. The guitar often provides a soothing accompaniment to a quiet song at the end of the music class before the children line up at the door.

Acknowledging Learning Styles When Planning for Music

As with adults, all children do not learn in the same way. Some children prefer to learn visually and delight in pictures and puppets. Other children are intrigued by sounds and prefer to learn by listening and imitating verbally. Many kindergarten children prefer to learn by moving their fingers and hands or their whole bodies. These tactile/kinesthetic learners enjoy getting physically involved in the learning. These learning styles are often combined for children who have more than one preferred way of learning. It should also be noted that young children's preferred learning styles are not constant and may vary as they develop (Persellin, 1990).

When teachers allow for differences in learning styles as they plan instruction they are enabling children to learn through a variety of means. For example, a music class with movement may be more meaningful to a young tactile/kinesthetic learner than a class that is all auditory and visual in its presentation.

As teachers, we should also be aware that our preferred teaching style may not match our children's preferred learning style. If we prefer to teach in an auditory style, that is singing, speaking, and listening, we may lose our young visual and tactile/kinesthetic learners. Learning style experts tell us that we should initially present something using our preferred teaching style and then reinforce that lesson using the other two learning styles.

Children should have many experiences working with music auditorially, kinesthetically, and visually. Visual experiences can include pictures of song lyrics or the instruments being played on a recording, or eventually an iconic or graphic representation of high and low or long and short sounds. Visual symbols of notation can later be used in the elementary grades with greater understanding after the experiential foundation has been laid in kindergarten.

Moving to Music

At the beginning of the year, children are introduced to songs and games that stress starting and stopping the movement of hands. Gradually this starting and stopping includes the whole body. Once this structure has been established, children are then ready for expressively moving with scarves, streamers, or dancing scarf dolls.

Circle games where one child travels around the circle while the children sing, such as "Circle Round the Zero," work well for kindergartners. Gradually circle games or movement activities that require more structure can be presented. Activities requiring a specific left or right response, or switching partners, are best postponed until later on in the elementary years.

Choosing Songs to Be Sung in Kindergarten

Children need to sing the very best literature. Folksongs that have been handed down from generation to generation are usually the finest sources of song material. Some composed songs are also good but should not comprise the bulk of the songs chosen. Songs should be selected because they are good and expressive and not just because they teach a lesson or because the children like them. Children will grow to love many different types of music. We sometimes underestimate children and give them only what is cute or superficial. Children need to experience beauty in their music.

Care should be taken to choose songs that the children will be able to sing successfully. If the song is pitched too low, children will not be able to sing those lower pitches and may begin to speak or chant rather than sing. If the song has large leaps that the children cannot easily sing, they may sing only the contour of the song and not be able to sing all the notes accurately. Some children cannot sing in their "high singing voices" if the song has many notes that lie below the staff in the treble clef. Children should be encouraged to listen carefully to the teacher or to the recording and then sing softly.

Many children's recordings are pitched too low for children to sing well. These songs are often good listening songs or songs to which children enjoy moving with the music. The teacher needs to choose these records and activities carefully.

Voice Exploration

Exploring different uses of their voices is fun for kindergartners. A variety of activities, songs, spoken rhymes, and games can be used to help children become more aware of the capabilities of their voices.

When some young children attempt to sing, they are in fact, speaking or chanting. This has become a habit for many of them who are unaware that there is a difference between their singing and their speaking voices. Some children are able to correct this when they become aware that there is a difference between singing and speaking. Asking the children to comment on whether they are using their singing or speaking voices is helpful. Children enjoy switching imaginary channels to their singing channels. They may need many experiences singing and making pitched sounds in their upper singing range.

One game to help children use their upper range or their high singing voices is the Copycat Game. In this game the children copy different vocal inflections first presented by the teacher. Later children can take turns being the leader. Care should be taken to model voice qualities that are high and low as well as loud and soft. Children enjoy imitating puppets as well as bird and animal calls in this game. Call and response songs, such as "Charlie Over the Ocean," are also excellent in helping children learn to listen and echo the melody.

Games that involve children taking imaginary rides on elevators or roller coasters are often effective ways to help children feel the sense of pitch rising and falling along with their bodies. Because it is usually easier for children to bring the lighter head voice down rather than force the heavier chest voice up, children may have better success with starting with the elevator on the top floor and bringing it back down to the ground. Children will enjoy moving a puppet up and down a giant roller coaster drawn upon large pieces of craft paper, as their voices match the up and down of the roller coaster ride.

Children also enjoy hearing themselves talk and sing into plastic tubing or a section of a PVC pipe that connects the ear to the mouth. Young children often do not realize what their voices sound like and this gives them immediate feedback. It is also possible for the teacher to speak and/or sing into the tube and then have the child try to imitate the vocal quality. The PVC pipe can then be placed in the music center for further exploration.

Child-Initiated Music Activities

Setting Up Music Centers

Music activities can be introduced by the music teacher and then placed in the music center for children to explore for the next couple of weeks. There are several ways of organizing the music center. One possibility is to ask children to cross their names off a class roster placed in each center. When all names have been crossed off they may then have a second turn. This assures children that they will eventually have a turn at that center. The teacher should decide how many children each center will accommodate and then post that number by the center.

Wooden instrument players created by Barbara Andress and marketed by Peripole are all enjoyed by children in music centers. These wooden manipulatives of a brass player, string player, pianist, and drummer come with several paper settings where each instrument is often found performing. For example, the string player is found in a restaurant and the drummer is found in a parade. These instrument players can be introduced one by one in music class with recorded excerpts of the instruments. The children enjoy manipulating the wooden instrument players and instruments while they listen to the musical excerpts.

Many music instruments can also be rotated through the music center. After the children have been introduced to an instrument in the music class, it can be placed in the music center. The instrument should be sturdy and should not require that the child blow into it. Hand drums, tambourines, jingle bells, and other small percussion instruments work well. An autoharp can also be fun for young children to explore.

When children have learned a song or a nursery rhyme, play mats can be created to give them a tactile/kinesthetic experience. Simple pictures of the words of the song or rhyme can be drawn on paper and then laminated. This play mat can first be demonstrated in class and then placed in the music center. A "Wee Willie Winkie" play mat works well with a clothespin doll or other small wooden dowel doll to be marched around on the play mat by the children.

The music specialist or kindergarten teacher can sing questions through dolls that have been designated as "singing people." These dolls can be created from round clothespins, PVC pipe, or pieces of wooden dowels. Houses for the dolls can be created from shoe boxes or on paper play mats. Children enjoy playing make-believe with their toys and especially enjoy singing their responses during their playtime. The modelling of the teacher making up simple sung conversation is important. Later the children will enjoy playing and improvising conversation between the singing people dolls.

Children enjoy manipulating a variety of music puppets in the music center. These puppets can range from simple stick puppets to glove puppets with different characters on each finger of the glove. "Old MacDonald Had a Farm" makes an effective glove puppet for children to manipulate while singing the song and imitating the animal sounds.

Cassette tapes can be recorded by the music teacher. Children can sing along with these tapes of two-note chants of books such as Bill Martin's "Brown Bear, Brown Bear." Tapes can be made to accompany books such as "This Old Man" or "Mary Wore Her Red Dress." Later the children can sing without the tapes. Children also enjoy making up their own songs when they are reading a book.

Once some songs or stories have been introduced in the music class, they can then be reinforced and shared with parents by creating a class book. Each child can draw and color a page to be collated to form a book placed in the music center. Children can then sing the song or tell the story as they read the book. One example of a song that makes a delightful book is "Mary Wore Her Red Dress." Each child draws a picture of themselves in their favorite article of clothing. The teacher then labels this picture for the book.

Kindergarten is a very important year for making music. Music is too important to be included only when there is extra time or when a holiday is approaching. Kindergartners need teacher-directed songs and activities as well as child-initiated play experiences. If music is a priority in the kindergarten and if care is taken in planning meaningful age-appropriate experiences, a young child begins to love music as an important part of life.

RECORDED MUSIC

Bach, J.S. Piano minuets, musettes and marches (many are from the Anna Magdalena Notebook).
Britten, B. Young person's guide to the orchestra. 4AE 34460
Chopin, F. Piano waltzes and preludes
Classical Jukebox, Vol. I. MLT 45736.
Feierabend, J. Music for very little people.
Go for Baroque: Greatest hits of the 1700s. RCA-VICS-1687.
The King's Singers: Kids' stuff. 4DS 47870.
Mozart, W.A. Piano minuets.
Peter, Paul, and Mary. Peter, Paul, and Mommy. Warner 1785.
Pinto, O. Run, Run, Scenes from childhood.
Sharon, Lois & Bram. Elephant show record. EC 0308.
Raffi. Singable songs for the very young. CL 0202.
Raffi. In concert: Shake my sillies out. CL0235.
Tchaikovsky, P. Nutcracker Suite Ballet.
Vaughan Williams, R. March past of the kitchen utensils. The Wasps.

CHILDREN'S BOOKS

Dudley, D., designer. (1989). *This old man*. Compass Productions.
Hellen, N. (1990). *Old MacDonald had a farm*. Orchard Books.
Martin, B., & Archambault, J. (1989). *Chicka, chicka boom, boom*. Simon & Schuster.
Martin, B. (1983). *Brown bear, brown bear*. New York: Holt, Rinehart, Winston.
Wood, A. (1982). *Quick as a cricket*. Child's Play International.

RESOURCE BOOKS

Andress, B. (1980). *Music experiences in early childhood*. New York: Holt, Rinehart, and Winston.

Andress, B. (Ed.). (1988). *Promising practices: Prekindergarten music education*. Reston, VA: Music Educators National Conference.

Boardman, E., Andress, B., Pautz, M., & Willman, F. (1988). *Music* (kindergarten teachers edition). New York: Holt, Rinehart, Winston.

Boswell, J. (Ed.). (1985). *The young child and music: Contemporary principles in child development*. Reston, VA: Music Educators National Conference.

Choksy, L., & Brummit, D. (1987). *120 singing games and dances for elementary schools*. Englewood Cliffs, NJ: Prentice-Hall, Inc.

Feierabend, J. (1986). *Music for very little people*. Boosey & Hawkes.

Feierabend, J. (Ed.). (1990). *Tips: music activities in early childhood*. Reston, VA: Music Educators National Conference.

Fox, D. (1987). *Go in and out the window*. New York: Metropolitan Museum of Art.

Kealoha, A. (1989). *Songs of the earth: Music of the world*. CelestialArts.

Parton, M. (1930). Social participation of preschool children. *Journal of Abnormal and Social Psychology, 23*.

Peery, J., Peery, I., & Draper, T. (1987). *Music and child development*. New York: Springer-Verlag.

Persellin, D.C. (1990). *Effective teaching by visual, auditory, and kinesthetic presentation*. Texas Music Education Research.

Regner, H. (1982). *Music for children,* Vol. 1, Preprimary. Schott Music Corp.

Sharon, L., & Bram. (1989). *The all new elephant jam*. New York: Crown Publishers.

Wirth, M., Stassevitch, V., Shotwell, S., & Parker, P. (1983). *Musical games, fingerplays and rhythmic activities for early childhood*. Parker Publishing Company.

Yamamoto, J. (1980). *Raffi singable songbook*. New York: Crown Publishers, Inc.

MUSIC MANIPULATIVES

Andress, B. Music play unlimited. The World of Peripole. Browns Mills, NJ 08015-0146. 1-800-443-3592.

Hugg-a-planet. XTC Products, Inc. Larchmont, NY 10538. 914-833-0200.

Diane Cummings Persellin is associate professor and coordinator of music education at Trinity University, San Antonio, Texas.

Environments for Exploring Music and Dance

Susan Kenney

Creating a stimulating, interactive environment may be a teacher's greatest contribution to the development of preschool children. Interactive environments foster new skills and promote curiosity, positive attitudes, cooperation and independence (see Katz, 1989; Greenman, 1988). Music and dance are important components of the young child's environment. The following environments provide a variety of materials for children to freely explore accompanied by teacher guidance, as children expand their knowledge and skills in sound and movement. The first part of this presentation will demonstrate musical environments, then dance environments will be explored (beginning on page 108).

Creating a "Sound Environment"

The young child's world is bombarded with sounds. Learning to make sense of the sounds, to describe and organize them is part of the child's work Environments filled with sound-making objects, where children can freely make sounds, hear sounds, and respond to sounds will aid them in their musical development. The following ideas can transform traditional learning centers into sound-oriented spaces and make the outdoors into a natural setting for sound exploration.

Adapting Early Childhood Play Centers

The Book Center—A picture book of "The Farmer in the Dell" may encourage children to "sing" the book rather than "read" it. (Other titles are suggested in Resource 1 at the end of this article.) A woodblock and mallet placed next to a "Hickory Dickory Dock" book encourages a child to make a tick-tock sound while looking at the book and chanting the rhyme. A cassette tape of a folk song might be placed in the environment so the child may listen to the song while looking at the book. Children may enjoy the delightful sounds of the King's Singers singing "This Old Man" as they look at a picture book of the same title, but caution should be used in selecting recorded songs. Folk songs or songs that are folk-like in length and musical simplicity allow for children to learn to sing the song rather than just listen. Singing that is precise and in a range that encourages children to use their head voice will provide a good model for children to imitate. Simple, uncluttered, imaginative accompaniments provide interesting sound colors that children can identify and sometimes imitate. Avoid renditions where the singing is inaccurate or the accompaniments too complex. (See Resource 2 for suggested recordings.)

The Block Center—Blocks may become musical instruments when a mallet is placed nearby. Children will begin "playing" the blocks to hear the different sounds that come from each block.

The Playhouse Center—Place a taped lullaby in a tape recorder near the doll's bed. (See Resource 2 for suggested lullaby tapes.) Let the child turn on the tape, sing, and rock the baby to sleep.

The Dress Up Center—Music will naturally lead to dancing when the child is "dressed up." Great masterworks can become part of the child's environment in this setting. (See Resource 3 for a list of suggested music.)

The Doll House Center—Small dolls can walk up the tone bell stairs when the tone bells are placed near the doll house. The steps can be "magic musical steps." Each time the doll walks up the steps it sings a song about going up (sing "I am going up up upstairs."). Each time the doll comes down, the song is about going down. After the teacher demonstrates, children may imitate during their free play.

The Clay Center—Children will often move rhythmically as they work with clay. As a child pats or rolls the clay, chant:

Pat, pat, pat the clay
Make a round flat shape.
Tap, tap, tap the clay
Hear the sound it makes.
Roll, roll, roll the clay
Make a nice long snake.
Mold, mold, mold the clay
Let's see what you make.

The Hammer Bench—Some early childhood play settings include a large block of wood or a bench with pegs where children can hammer steadily. Accompany a child's hammering with a recording of the "Anvil Chorus." (See Resource 3.) The strong steady beat of the music provides a delightful accompaniment .

Outside Sound Exploration—The Tree Branch Orchestra

The out of doors is a wonderful environment for sound exploration. All that is needed is a tree (evergreens work well because of their many low branches), twine or strong string, and a variety of percussion instruments. Include membrane instruments such as hand drums and tambourines; metal instruments such as triangles, varied lengths of conduit pipe, and cymbals; and wood instruments such as wood blocks, sticks, and xylophone bars. Hang the instruments securely from the tree, with a string long enough to allow children to reach the instruments. Mallets may be hung in the same way, close to each instrument, and with a string long enough to allow the mallet to freely move when a child uses it to strike an instrument.

1. Allow children to examine the instruments on the "Tree Branch Orchestra." Observe the children who are especially attentive to the sounds. Listen for comments about the qualities of sounds. Free exploration may continue for several days, while other activities are also available. Some children may wish to take an instrument from the tree and march, freely making sounds. Some may begin to sing as they march, some may twirl and dance. And of course, some will watch.

2. After children have explored the "Orchestra," begin describing sounds they make and guide their exploration. As children make sounds, describe them as ringing, clicking, high, low, etc.

3. Encourage children to make sounds that are loud and slow, loud and fast, soft and slow, soft and fast, get louder or softer or faster or slower.

4. Help children notice that some instruments are made of wood, some metal, some membrane. Begin categorizing instruments by their material. Older children may enjoy making a list of which instruments fit which categories. Help children notice the difference in sound between the wood and metal and membrane instruments.

5. Invite children to be an orchestra of woods, metal, and membranes. Choose one child as conductor. Discuss with the conductor how he/she will let each section know when to play and to stop playing. Will each group play separately? Will all three ever play at the same time?

6. Hide one wood, one metal, and one membrane instrument. Tell children that their section may march and play when they hear the correct instrument. When their instrument stops, they must stop marching. Play each instrument one at a time to let children practice listening.

7. Invite children to imagine a soldier marching (or show a picture of a soldier). Discuss how the soldier moves. Ask a child to find a sound that might represent a soldier marching. When the child plays the sound, describe it. If the sound seems to match the description of a soldier marching, ask the children to march like soldiers when the child plays the instrument. Continue with other pictures or ideas such as:

> an elephant walking or running
> a worm crawling on the ground
> a sound that will wake up a sleeping child
> a sound that will help the baby go to sleep
> a scary sound
> an angry sound
> the sound of a giant walking
> the sound of a child running
> the sound of someone tip-toeing
> the sound of money falling on the table
> the sound of a dancer spinning.

Using the above ideas, create a story, letting the children supplement with sound. Invite some children to "act out" the story while others make the sounds.

8. Discover how Mussorgsky used sounds to tell a story. Explore the idea of a chicken trying to hatch from an egg. What would it sound like? How would it move? If the farmer were watching and waiting, how would he pace around the egg? Ask a child to find a sound that represents the chick trying to peck at the egg shell, while another child pretends to be the chick inside an egg. Find a sound for the farmer walking around the egg while a child pretends to be the farmer. Put the instruments away and listen to Mussorgsky's "Ballet of the Unhatched Chicks." Act out the story by following the music.

Extending the Experience

1. Look at books such as *Crash! Band! Boom!* by Peter Spier, or *We're Going on a Bear Hunt* by Michael Rosen. Explore ways to produce sounds suggested by either book.

2. Listen to a recording of "Fossils" by Saint-Saens. Lead children to discover the wood sounds (xylophone) and the string sounds. They might enjoy playing along on their own wood sounds (blocks, sticks, woodblock) when the xylophone plays.

3. Listen to the first section of "Allegro Vivace" by Zamfir. Horns and panpipe take turns playing in this composition. Half of the class might make toy horns and the other half blow

across the top of pieces of plastic pipe or pop bottles. The children could take turns marching with each section of the music.

4. Take a field trip to a symphony orchestra rehearsal. Notice the conductor's role, the sections of instruments, the difference in sounds of each section. If possible, arrange to let the children mingle with the orchestra players so they can see the instruments up close.

References

Andress, B. (1973). *Music in early childhood.* Reston, VA: Music Educators National Conference.

Greenman, J. (1988). *Caring spaces learning places.* Redmond, WA: Exchange Press.

Katz, L., & Sylvia C. C. (1989). *Engaging children's minds: The project approach.* Norwood, NJ: Ablex Publishing Corporation.

Kenney, S. (1989). Music centers freedom to explore. *Music Educators Journal,* October, 32-36.

Susan Kenny is a member of the faculty of the Music Department at Brigham Young University, Provo, Utah.

Resource 1. Folk Song Recordings for Children

Children love listening and singing along with recordings. The following recordings were selected because they contain songs American children should know, and because of the interesting and imaginative arrangements. Listing includes examples of songs from each tape.

All Through the Night. Paul Edwards. Revere Records. P.O. Box 41347, Los Angeles, CA 90014.
        Synthesizer lullabies for rocking baby to sleep. no singing
            All Through the Night   Brahms Lullaby* Rock-a-bye Baby
            All the Pretty Little Horses

Early Early Childhood Songs. Ella Jenkins and three- and four-year olds. Folkways FC 7630. 632 Broadway, New York, NY 10012.
        Friendly singing and talking with children. One side instrumental only.
            Skip to My Lou*   Mary's Little Lamb*   Farmer in the Dell*
            Twinkle Little Star   This Old Man*   London Bridge*

Good Morning Sunshine. Patti Dallas & Laura Baron. Golden Glow Recordings. 800 Livermore St., Yellow Springs, OH 45387.
        Many instrumental sounds in the accompaniments, including clarinet, Sax. piano, flute, piccolo, tambourine, bells, tuba, marimba, calliope, recorder, harp, drums, bass, banjo, accordion.
            Eensy Weensy Spider   London Bridge*   Sing a Song of Sixpence*
            This Old Man*   A Dance by Michael Praetorius
            Ash Grove harp solo   Irish Jig—dulcimer solo

Grandma's Patchwork Quilt. Jonathan Edwards, Cathy Fink, John McCutcheon, Larry Penn, Phil and Naomi Rosenthal. American Melody. AM-C 103. P. O. Box 270, Guilford, CT 06437.
        Variety of male and female voices, instrumental accompaniments include banjo, guitar, mandolin, bass, fiddle, harmonica
            Three Blind Mice*   Oh Susanna   A Duck Named Earl

Kid's Stuff. King's Singers. EMI Records CDC 7-47870-2.
        Men's group singing, imaginative accompaniments and sound effects
            Humpty Dumpty   This Old Man*
            I Know an Old Woman* Teddy Bear's Picnic*

Mainly Mother Goose. Sharon, Lois, & Bram. Elephant Records. P.O. Box 101, Station Z, Toronto, Canada M5N 2Z3.
        Male and female singers, some children singing, creative sounds and interpretations
            Eensy Weensy Spider   Humpty Dumpty   Hickory Dickory Dock*
            The Grand Old Duke of York*   Three Little Kittens*

Nursery Songs & Lullabies. Francine Lancaster. Lancaster Productions. P.O. Box 7820, Berkeley, CA 94707.
        Female singing, interesting accompaniment arrangements
            This Old Man*   London Bridge*   Old King Cole
            Round the Village   Mulberry Bush*

Pete Seeger Stories and Songs for Little Children. HW 1207T. High Windy Audio. Fairview, NC 28730.
        Male singer and story teller
            Skip to My Lou*   Mister Rabbit   She'll Be Coming Round the
            I Know an Old Lady*   Mountain

*Picture books with the same title listed on Resource 2.

Resource 2. Music Picture Books

This list contains some of the numerous books available for encouraging young children to sing or to learn about music. Many of the picture books can be used with recordings of children's folk songs. (See Resource 1.)

Aloysius Sebastain Mozart Mouse. Oretta Leigh. Ill. by Lulu Delacre. New York: Simon & Schuster, 1984.

Crash! Bang! Boom! Peter Spier. New York: Doubleday & Company, 1972.

Hush Little Baby. Ill. by Aliki. Englewood Cliffs, New Jersey: Prentice Hall, no date.

I'm a Little Tea Pot. Ill by Moira Kemp. Los Angeles: Price/Stern/Sloan Publishers, Inc., 1987.

Lentil. Robert McClosky. Cedar Grove, NJ: Rae Publishing Co., 1978.

Little Miss Muffet. Ian Beck. New York: Oxford University Press, 1988.

London Bridge Is Falling Down! Ill. by Peter Spier. The Mother Goose Library, no date.

Lullaby and Goodnight. Ill. by Jannat Messenger. New York: Aladdin Books by Macmillan Publishing Company, 1987.

Lullaby. Jane Chelsea Aragon. San Francisco: Chronicle Books, 1989.

Mary Had a Little Lamb. Ill. by Tomi dePaola. New York: Holiday House, 1984.

Mary Wore Her Red Dress. Ill. by Merle Peek. New York: Clarion Books/Tichnor & Fields, 1985.

Mulberry Bush. Ill. by Dorothy Crider. Chicago: Rand McNalley & Co., 1969.

Music, Music for Everyone. Vera B.Williams. New York: Mulberry Books, 1984.

Once a Lullaby. Nichol. Ill. by Anita Lobel. New York: Greenwillow Books, 1983.

Orchestranimals. Vlasta van Kampen & Irene C. Eugen. New York: Scholastic Inc., 1989.

Sing a Song of Sixpence. Ill. by Randolph Caldecott. New York: Hart Publishing Co., 1977.

Skip to My Lou. Ill. by Nadine Bernard Westcott. Boston: Little, Brown and Co., 1989.

The Backyard Band from Clancy Street. Los Angeles: Price/Stern/Sloan, 1985.

The Farmer in the Dell. Ill. by Mary Maki Rae. New York: Viking Penguin, Inc., 1988.

The Grand Old Duke of York. Maureen Roffey. Toronto: The Bodley Head, 1975.

The Gum on the Drum. Barbata Gergorich. Ill. by John Sandford. Grand Haven, Michigan, School Zone Publishing Co., 1984.

The Teddy Bears' Picnic. Jimmy Kennedy. Nashville: Ideals Publishing Corporation, no date.

The Wheels on the Bus. Ill. by Paul Zelinsky. New York: Dutton Children's Books, no date.

There Was an Old Lady Who Swallowed a Fly. Ill. by Pam Adams. England: Child's Play International Ltd., 1973.

This Old Man. Ill. by Pam Adams. England: Child's Play International Ltd., 1974.

Three Blind Mice. John W. Ivimey. Ill by Walton Corbould. London: Frederick Warne & Co. Ltd., 1979.

Three Little Kittens. Ill. by Lilian Obligado. New York: Random Horse, 1974.

Tickle, Tickle. Helen Oxenbury. New York: Macmillan Publishing Company, 1987.

We're Going on a Bear Hunt. Michael Tosen. Ill. by Helen Oxenbury. New York: Margaret K. McElderry Books, 1989.

When Bluebell Sang. Lisa Campbell Ernst. New York: Bradbury Press, 1989.

Resource 3. Recorded Masterworks

The following selections have musical forms and rhythms that can support children's movement. Most are short enough that children can attend to the whole selection, allowing them to experience the overall shape of the composition while listening to the music of great masters.

Bach. "Allegro" from *Brandenburg Concerto No. 3*. BWV 1048. Archiv Produktion. 410 500-2.
> Fast, short sounds to encourage twirling, dancing.

Debussy. *En Bateau*. BOL* #53.
> Slow, smooth, flowing music to encourage slow, reaching, round movements.

Glass. "Lightening" from *Songs from Liquid Days*. CBS Records. MK 39564.
> Sharp percussive sounds to encourage quick, direct, jagged movements.

Gounod. *Funeral March of the Marionettes*. BOL #64.
> Several sections that encourage movements such as tip-toe, march, swing, jump. Can dramatize marionette story.

Grainger. *Over the Hills*. BOL #68.
> Light, long-short rhythm to encourage skipping.

Grieg. "Morning" from *Peer Gynt Suite No. 1*. BOL #59.
> Slow, smooth sounds that grow in sound and intensity to loud, slow, swinging sounds.
> Music to encourage slow, round movements that increase in size and space.

Liadov. *Dance of the Mosquito*. BOL #52.
> Introduction is a fast, buzzing sound that might encourage spinning. Body of the music has a fast, skipping feeling.

Moussorgsky. "Ballet of the Unhatched Chicks" from *Pictures at an Exhibition*. BOL #82.
> Two kinds of music: fast, quick sounds and slower sounds. Music to help children move with quick running steps or proud walking steps. Dramatize the story.

Partch. "Daphne of the Dunes" from the record *The World of Harry Partch*. Columbia MS 7202.
> Contemporary sounds with homemade instruments.

Rimsky-Korsakov. *Flight of the Bumble Bee*. BOL # 52.
> Very fast, quick sounds to encourage spinning or other fast movements.

Saint-Saens. Selections from *Carnival of the Animals*. BOL #51.
> "Aquarium"--Slow, undulating rhythm to encourage slow motion
> "Aviary"--Fast, short, sharp sounds for fluttering, quick, short movements
> "Elephant"--Swinging, low, heavy sounds for large, heavy swinging or walking.
> "Fossils"--Xylophone, sharp, crisp, fast sounds for jerky, short, small movements.
> "Kangaroo"--Short, ascending and descending sounds that get faster and slower. Music to encourage hopping, jumping, changing speed, and ending very quietly.

Schubert. *The Bee*. BOL #64.
> Very fast, quick sounds for spinning and other fast, busy movements.

Verdi. "Anvil Chorus" from *Il Trovature*. BOL #63.
> Strong, steady beat to accompany children hammering logs, marching, etc.

Zamfir. "Allegro Vivace" from *Concerto No. 1 in G for Panpipes and Orchestra*. Philips 412 221-2.
> Fast march, alternating horns and panpipe. Music to help children listen for instrument changes. One group might march when horns play, the other when panpipe plays.

*BOL: *Bowmar Orchestral Library*. A series of recordings for use with children. Each record contains several classical pieces, many ideal for using in the early childhood setting. Available from Columbia Pictures. 15800 NE 48th Ave. Miami, FL 33014

Environments for Exploring Dance

Theresa M. Purcell

This article presents descriptions of four environments that can be used to develop dance experiences.

I. The Natural Environment

This dance lesson is based on the season of fall and can be taught either indoors or outdoors. The objective of the lesson is to reflect with one's body the different shapes and ways leaves move during the fall season.

A. Introduction

To gain background information for the specific lesson content, students are asked what they notice happening to the leaves in fall. Their responses may include the following ideas: turn different colors, fall off the trees, fly in the air, fall to the ground, spin, and dry and curl up. These ideas can be explored through movement and then used in the dance composition.

B. Exploration

1. Shapes of the leaves. Students select leaves that are different shapes and colors from the outside environment or from a previous collection. After a discussion of the different shapes and colors, students make their bodies into shapes that reflect the shapes of the leaves: round, oval, pointed, long, or curled. Students are encouraged to try a variety of different shapes.

2. Wind moving the leaves on the trees. To observe the effect of the wind on the leaves, the students can go outside and make observations in the environment, or the teacher can hold a leaf and blow on it or use a fan to depict the wind. Students then create movements that will demonstrate the effect of the wind moving the leaves. The movements chosen can occur in a forward and backward direction and a side to side direction. A light wind can be reflected using small movements of the hands, head, or whole body and a stronger wind reflected with large movements.

3. Wind spinning the leaves in the air and on the ground. Students spin their leaves at different levels, in the air tossed above their head, held in their hand as they spin the leaf in

front of their body, and on the floor. Students then create different ways to spin their body: low to the floor using the back, front, and side of their body; spinning on two feet or one foot; or jumping and turning in the air.

4. Wind blowing the leaves into the air. Students can observe leaves being blown around on a windy day or, using strong energy, toss and kick leaves into the air and then discuss how they saw the leaves moving. The strong force of the wind can be reflected in their body as a run and leap up in the air or turn during their leap.

5. The wind stops and the leaves fall to the ground. Students hold a leaf high with their hand and let it fall to the ground. They observe the path and speed of the fall. The students then create movements that demonstrate the path and speed of the leaf fall.

6. The leaves dry up from a flat to a curled shape. Students use the leaf shapes they explored earlier and begin to find ways to make their body shape change from flat to curled. Curled leaves can be used as models. Some leaves are curled tightly; on other leaves only a part is curled.

7. The wind lightly pushes the curled leaves and they roll into a giant pile. Students observe a leaf rocking as the wind gently pushes under the curled part of the leaf. The wind becomes stronger and the leaf begins to roll. A phrase is developed: rock, rock, r-o-l-l; rock, rock, r-o-l-l. The rolling together of students into a group needs to be discussed, emphasizing how the students can roll and end in a pile gently leaning on each other.

C. The Dance Sequence

The teacher describes the sequence and the students use movements from the exploration section of the lesson to express the events of the leaves. I usually use percussion instruments for the exploration section to depict the tempo or rhythm I want the students to use with their movement. For the dance sequence, I used Vivaldi's "Summer."

The dance sequence is as follows:

1. Turning colors—students perform movements that demonstrate putting on new clothes or being painted with different colors.
2. Light wind, strong wind.
3. Spinning of the leaves.
4. Flying up in the air.
5. Falling to the ground.
6. Curling up.
7. Rock, rock, and roll into a pile. Roll.

Each section can be different lengths of time; however, the complete dance may only take about two or three minutes to perform.

II. An Environment Created by Ropes

Each student is provided with a piece of rope about four feet in length. The rope that I have used in this dance experience is from an Army parachute. It is very easy to manipulate into shapes on the floor or tie to furniture or other large equipment.

This lesson is focused on the different environments that can be created through changing the arrangements of the ropes. For example, ropes placed on the floor can become a space filled with all sizes of circles. These circles can be clouds that the students move between using slow and light floating movements, or puddles that they can jump and leap over. The ropes can also be connected together to form a road for different slow and quick traveling movements, or a road where the students change directions.

Students can also tie the ropes at different angles and levels to furniture or equipment to create an environment that has numerous spaces to move over, under, through, and around. This rope environment can become a spider web, an animal home, or an underwater city filled with seaweed and caves.

III. Color Environments

These environments are created by colored crepe paper streamers. In each corner of the room an environment will be designed using a different colored streamer (red, blue, green, yellow). The streamers will be on the floor in two of the corners; in the other two corners the streamers will be hanging from the wall or suspended on a string.

The first corner is the FIRE environment. The red streamers are placed on the floor in the corner spaced so students can move between them. The movement emphasis will be quick and small as in a flickery movement. As the students move between the streamers, they choose a streamer and explore how to move it using the flickery movement. A sequence can evolve with one student picking up the first streamer as the beginning flame, then touching other students who will pick up streamers and use the flickery movements they have explored. This sequence continues until all the students are moving with the streamers. The first student can then stop and slowly sink to the floor as if the flame was going out; the other students follow with the same movement until everyone is lying on the floor and only the streamers continue to flicker. Then slowly the streamers come to a stop.

The second environment uses yellow streamers to depict the SUN environment. The streamers are arranged in circles on the floor and the students are in groups of three or four. Together they lift the circle up (as in the rising of the sun), slowly travel across the space (as in the sun moving across the sky), and then slowly lower the circle to the floor (as in the setting of the sun). The movements emphasized are slow and light.

The third color of streamers is blue to depict the WATER environment. The streamers are in two-foot pieces taped to the wall at a variety of heights. The students will take the streamers off the wall and begin to move them in a curvy pathway high and low to demonstrate the movement of the water. The students individually explore making the streamer move in curves that are high, low, small, and large. Then students are organized into small groups; one student is designated as the leader, who begins to move a streamer using the movements created to represent the curvy movement of the water. The group follows and repeats the same movements as the leader. Each student takes a turn as the leader. The group can proceed to develop a sequence of movements as each group member contributes a favorite movement to form the sequence. The streamers are placed back on the wall at the end of the dance.

The fourth corner is filled with green streamers to represent the FOREST environment. The streamers are hung in long six- to eight-foot pieces from a string suspended across the corner in several different directions. The streamers hang from the string to the floor, with spaces between them through which the students can move. The students can create several different movement ideas in this environment. Some ideas include finding different ways to travel in the forest, using animal movements, or moving to demonstrate different emotions such as fright, excitement, or curiosity. The students can also make shapes with their bodies to express the shapes of different trees, becoming twisted, straight, or curved and using the streamers as the branches and leaves. Students can explore these ideas and develop a story about traveling through the forest and meeting different animals and trees.

IV. The Shadow Environment

This environment is created by using an overhead projector to project light on the wall. The room will need to be somewhat darkened for the light to be effective. When students stand facing the wall in front of the light, their shadows will be projected on the wall. Students can make different shapes with their bodies that will be mirrored in their shadows. Connecting their shadows to each other will create a group shape. This group shape can become a group portrait, a large animal, or a monster with many arms, heads, and legs. Objects such as geometric shapes, forks, a whiffle ball, paper doilies, or one's hand can be placed on the projector screen. These objects will show on the wall and students can create movements that interact or reflect the object. For example, when using letters or geometric shapes, the students can make the letter or geometric shape with their bodies. Paper cut-outs of snowflakes on the projector can inspire a dance about the falling snow.

Another idea is to place objects on the projector that cause shadows to appear on the wall forcing the students to move their own shadows over, under, and between the shadows of the objects, as if the characters are moving in a video game across the screen.

Theresa M. Purcell is a dance and physical education teacher at the Brunswick Acres School, South Brunswick Township Schools, Kendall Park, New Jersey.

ART

More than Movement: Scribbling Reassessed

Patricia Tarr

Parents and teachers often do not appreciate the unrecognizable marks and three-dimensional forms young children create when they begin to draw, paint, and work with other art materials. These beginnings in children's artistic expression are dismissed as "just scribbling," while the adult anxiously waits for the child to create recognizable people and objects. Art educators and researchers have done little to change these negative attitudes toward young children's scribbles because they have undertaken few investigations of the preschematic period of children's artistic development (Lowenfeld & Brittain, 1975; Matthews, 1984). The prevailing view, expressed by Heberholz and Hanson (1985), is that "the child at this stage is more fascinated with the kinesthetic process than by the marks he is making...and the size of the marks and movements are in relation to the size of the child's arm" (p. 55).

The purpose of this paper is to challenge the view that scribbling has value only as a precursor to later schematic or representational work, or is primarily of kinesthetic interest to the child, and to suggest that this first phase of artistic development is as complex a process as are the later phases of artistic expression. To this end the paper has three components: 1) suggestions as to why the literature has ignored the beginning mark-making period of children's art, 2) description of a perspective from which to consider the preschematic stage of development, and 3) anecdotal examples of two-year-olds' drawing and painting which illustrate the complexity of the art-making process.

Beginning Mark-Making Ignored

A number of possible reasons may have contributed to the lack of research interest in art-making by very young children. Art educators and early childhood educators occupy separate spheres at all educational levels, and Colbert (1984) noted a lack of communication between these two fields. In addition, art educators are most frequently concerned with teacher training and research directed toward children five years of age and older who attend school, rather than preschool-age children.

However, I believe a more basic reason for neglect of this area of artistic development lies rooted in attitudes toward children's preschematic art that are reflected in the language used to describe this period of art-making and that, in turn, influence the way the work is viewed (Matthews, 1984). I am not joining the debate over the artistic merit of drawings, paintings, collages and three-dimensional forms created by young preschoolers in relationship to adult art. I am drawing attention to the fact that adults place greater value on children's work once the work becomes representational than on the marks created by children working at the preschematic level. In this paper I will use the term "preschematic" to refer to the forms created by children before they draw recognizable representations and not as Lowenfeld and Brittain (1975) have used it to indicate work following the "scribble" or their first stage of artistic development.

Although Lowenfeld and Brittain found it unfortunate that adults have a negative view of the first marks children make, this is not surprising given that the most common term used to describe children's preschematic marking is "scribble," which Webster's Ninth New Collegiate Dictionary defines as, "to write hastily or carelessly, to fill or cover with careless or worthless writing; or to make meaningless marks." On a superficial level this definition may appear to be an accurate account of the markings by children under the age of three or four years. The viewer, not recognizing forms within the marks, interprets the marks to be meaningless, and consequently worthless. Implicit in this definition is the assumption that mark-making has representational or communicative intent. Hence, the act of creating marks is equated to the act of representation. This places the young child in a deficit position relative to this representational standard, or as Matthews has stated, the child is perceived to be "a 'failed realist'" (1984, p. 3).

Lack of value is reinforced further through the words used to describe the levels or stages of scribbles. Lowenfeld's first stage of artistic development, which he called "the scribble stage," was divided into three substages: "disordered," "controlled," and "named" (Lowenfeld & Brittain, 1975).

Other writers have used similar terms for the first substage: "irregular" (Herberholz & Hanson, 1985; Wilson & Wilson, 1982) or "random" (Brittain, 1979). These terms are intended to convey the idea that the marks the child makes may go in a variety of directions and have an inconsistent quality in pressure, width, length, and arrangement on the paper, yet the language used to describe these forms reinforces the notion that this activity lacks direction or purpose.

A lack of skill or mastery in the use of a particular tool or medium does not necessarily preclude purpose or intent as is implied in the words "random", "disordered," and "irregular." The child's purpose may be unclear to the viewer, or different from that of representation. In addition, Matthews (1984) has argued that representation needs to be redefined to include spatial, temporal, and action representations as well as the traditional figurative definition.

In North American culture, where trends toward standardization and regularization are exemplified in our consumer habits, elements which are disordered, irregular, and random seem to be valued less than those things which are predictable and ordered. So too, children's beginnings in art-making have been considered less important than those marks which are ordered or regularized into recognizable representations.

Kellogg (1970), stressing the child's innate aesthetic capacity, has described a "building block" relationship between children's first marks and later representational forms, in an attempt to understand or order these apparently random marks. However, other researchers have been unable to replicate Kellogg's results (Golomb, 1981; Golomb & Farmer, 1983), and Golomb (1981) has suggested that Kellogg may have imposed her own order on children's work.

Historically, researchers have favored the examination of the products children create and have placed little importance on the act of creation, or art-making process (Swann, 1985). This emphasis on the product removed from the creative process has also made it difficult to see children's visual formations as anything other than irregular marks or forms created during their sensory-motor level of development.

Presentation Not Representation

An alternate perspective, which does not impose an order on young children's drawings, may be introduced through a simple change of descriptive language. When Arnheim (1967) suggested that early marks should not be thought of "as representation but rather as presentation—that is they involve the exciting experience of bringing about something visible that was not there before" (p. 166), he introduced a term which eliminated the denigrating connotation of previous terms and placed a positive emphasis on these preschematic marks. This seemingly slight shift in language contains a major shift in attitude. Those marks which had meaning as a precursor to representation now have their own validity as an act of creation. Nor is this act of creation grounded in the view that early marking may be primarily related to kinesthetic pleasure the child receives as he or she marks, although it does not by definition exclude a kinesthetic aspect to the creative process.

Use of "presentation" also facilitates a shift in focus from the completed work, or item represented, to the process of creation. Directing attention to children actively engaged in "presentation" during the art-making process can illuminate the complexity of the process and accord children's beginnings in art a legitimate place in the development of artistic expression.

Video Episodes

In the remainder of this paper I will challenge some notions about children's beginnings in art, basing these challenges on examples of children's artistic behavior drawn from videotape recordings which I collected over six years as a researcher and preschool teacher at a university laboratory preschool. I have selected the following examples specifically to call into question the assumptions that body dynamics and the child's kinesthetic pleasure are the predominant influences on early mark-making, that the beginning "presentations" children create are random or disordered, and that children lack purpose in their work. The examples will demonstrate children making deliberate, conscious choices as they purposively strive to gain mastery of the materials.

Jennifer

In the first example, Jennifer, a small blonde child (about 2.5 years), is painting at an easel. Her right hand is on the tip of the brush handle. As she paints, she selects colors by systematically working down the tray of blue, green, red, and yellow paints and applying each in a linear pattern on the paper. She expands some of her lines into areas of color, but keeps her colors separate on the paper. This time as she moves down the paint tray with her hand touching each brush, she deliberately rejects the red and places her hand on the yellow brush. She turns away from her work to observe an event across the room. She turns back to her paper and applies yellow paint on top of an existing circular spot of yellow. She completes this action in a smooth, unhesitating manner.

This episode might be interpreted in several ways. It might be claimed that the placement of the yellow spot was coincidental. Or, it might be argued that placement of that particular mark was almost inevitable because that particular spot was at the apex of Jennifer's arm movement, due to the combined length of her arm and the brush and her position relative to the easel. However, if these interpretations are applied to each of the marks, they cannot account for placement of blue or other colors in several areas of the paper, nor do they explain why Jennifer reached up to apply a particular color in a particular empty place near the top of the paper. I suggest that placement of the yellow spot was a deliberate act on Jennifer's part, possibly triggered by the placement of the first yellow spot. Although this conclusion may appear to be conjectural on my part, a second episode will also demonstrate the care and visual attention Jennifer takes in her work.

In this sequence Jennifer is sitting at a large circular table with several other two-year-olds. Small aluminum pie tins containing moistened tempera paint blocks have been placed on the table along with water color brushes and 8-1/2" x 11" sheets of white paper. Jennifer, holding her brush at the tip of the handle, moves it clockwise around the paint container, creating a watery circle on the right side of her paper. She lifts the paint pan and places it on the left side of the paper. Holding her brush in her right hand, she makes a bright purple circle counterclockwise around the tin, going over the edge of her paper only where there is not room for the thickness of her brush mark on the page. As in the first incident, her motions are smooth and unhesitant. She focuses on her task as she paints. Singing from across the room draws Jennifer's attention away from her work and she watches the singer, brush poised over her paper. After about eight seconds she refocuses on her painting. She makes jabbing brush-dots around the perimeter of the circle on the right side of her paper. She comments, "I made (bubbles)" (unclear on tape). She continues making jab-dots with her brush until the circle is filled in, then she puts the brush down.

These two examples show a consistency in Jennifer's behavior with the paint. In both situations she is able to turn away from her work and resume painting with marking which is consistent with the work in progress. Matthews (1984) has suggested that consistency which occurs across children's work is due to the similar body dynamics which permits certain kinds of marking motions. To a certain extent her arm movements do contribute to the unity within each work. However, body dynamics do not completely account for similarities and differences in these two paintings. Smith (1983) has described how children construct fundamental art concepts of line, color, shape, representation, and expressiveness through the act of painting in what she calls a "kind of dialogue between the nature of the paint and the ever growing mind of the child" (p. 6). Jennifer seems to be developing her concepts of line and shape in these paintings. In addition, what Jennifer does in each painting appears to be partly influenced by marks she has made previously in that particular picture. Placement of the first yellow dot seems to influence placement of the second dot, and the watery quality of the first traced circle may have stimulated her to go over the shape with jab-dots.

Jennifer also demonstrates different purposes in each painting. In the first her interest in on the lines and areas of color she creates but in the second she has extended the concept of line to her interest in creating circles by painting around the tin, and then repeating the circle using variations of marks which she has mastered. Although it is apparent that she enjoys the kinesthetic component of making jab-dots with her brush, this does not override her visual sense of completion. There is no evidence apparent from the tape which suggests that an external factor contributed to Jennifer's decision to stop painting and she does not continue making her jab-dots beyond the bounds of the circular shape.

Jason

The third video segment focuses on Jason (2.2 years), also painting at an easel. He not only looks away from his painting but leaves it briefly and returns to continue to paint from one of his original lines on the paper.

Jason, wearing a solid colored, green shirt announces, "I want to paint," as he approaches the easel. Watching Sam paint, Jason walks to the unoccupied side of the easel. Standing on the right-hand side of the easel, left arm on his hip, he picks up a brush in his right hand and paints a green downward vertical mark on the right-hand side of his paper above the can of green paint. He enlarges the brush mark, ending in a circular line to the left, then walks to the other edge of the easel dragging his brush along the paper as he does so. He looks away, swings his arm on the paper, continuing to make a few marks as he looks across the room. He looks at the paper, marking and noticing that very little paint is being left on the paper. He examines the tip of the brush closely and replaces it in the green can. He moves back to the left side of the paper, looking at the cans of paint as he goes, and selects purple on the far left end of the paint tray. He makes a vertical stroke downward, roughly centered on his paper, curving the line to the right in a reverse "j" form. He paints over part of the line and makes a few brush jabs at the base of the curve, then walks around the easel to watch the teacher take the other child's painting off the easel. He goes to the adjacent table where the teacher is writing Sam's name on the paper. Jason sits down and manipulates scissors. He "suddenly" returns to the easel, picking up the purple brush, places it on the purple line, about one-third down, and makes a downward curving line. He dips the brush in the can, watches the paint drip from the end, then makes a sweeping line which crosses the vertical line at the junction of the two previous lines, sweeping the line in a curve up to the left corner of the paper. As he sweeps the brush upward, parts of the line are thicker and darker. He replaces the brush in the can and leaves.

It is possible that Jason's initial decision to paint was triggered by a teacher asking Sam if he had noticed a new color of paint on the easel. The teacher drew attention to the fact that this new color was also the same color as the playdough which Jason was using. Jason was aware of the painting on the other side of the easel as he stopped to observe both prior to his painting experience and during it. Whether he was influenced in his selection of colors by the other child or the teacher, we cannot tell from this video sequence. He did reject the other colors in favor of two: green and purple, the same color range Sam used. Nor do we know, without Jason's comments, whether green is a particular color preference of his as evidenced by his green shirt, or whether he selected the paints closest to the edges of the easel.

When he began painting, Jason's position at the easel determined the arrangement and placement of the green paint on the paper. However, body placement or body dynamics do not seem to account for the build-up of strokes on the center line, nor does it account for his return to the easel and continuation of marks along the center line. It appears as if his finger grip on the brush did not allow him to keep continuous pressure on the brush as he swung it upward. Only when he was making vertical lines was he able to keep a constant pressure on the brush. It is apparent from his rejection of the brush that had run out of paint and his painting over some lines that his primary intent is to create marks and lines in paint, rather than for the pleasure in moving his brush across the paper. Neither Jason nor Jennifer randomly selected colors from the array on the easel, but clearly rejected some in favor of others, even though they systematically moved along the easel to make their choice. Corcoran (1954) also found that there was a tendency for children to select paints by systematically working down the array, and Biehler (Lowenfeld & Brittain, 1975) found that children applied paint in relationship to the location of the color on the easel tray.

Jason, like Jennifer, was able to shift attention, then refocus on a work and retain a continuity and unity to the work. When he returned, his lines "finished" and connected to lines he had made previously. This would be less clear had he returned and begun to paint in any blank area on the paper.

Frederick

The care these two-year-olds took in making marks or creating visual formations was not limited to painting, but was a component of other typical preschool art activities as illustrated by this example of a young two-year-old engaged in creating one of his first collage pieces.

When the video camera first focuses on Frederick (2.3 years), he has just glued a single piece of yellow cellophane onto a sheet of green construction paper. He has also applied a strip of glue with a plastic glue spreader, about three inches from the cellophane. He carefully takes a second piece of yellow cellophane from the container on the table, unfolds it, peers at it intently, then carefully places it to the left of the glue strip. He spreads more glue about one inch away from the strip which is still visible, and chooses a black square. He puts this on the paper and carefully adjusts it to fit precisely between the two strips of glue on the paper. He drips and spreads glue in a patch adjacent to the black piece and leaves to explore the rocking boat, a new piece of equipment. Shortly, he returns to the table and picks up three pieces of collage material, dropping one as he does so. He returns this piece and another to the container, retaining one piece of yellow cellophane which he applies to the glue patch on the paper. He leaves the table.

Kate

In a second example of a child making deliberate choices while creating a collage, Kate (2.8 years) joins a group gluing at the art table.

Holding the glue spreader about eight inches from the table top, Kate, watching intently, drips glue onto the paper, moving her hand to create drippy glue lines and puddles. She comments, "Look at the lines," as she continues to make glue lines all over the paper. After dripping the glue for several minutes she selects a yellow circle from a container of small colored paper shapes. She continues to drip the glue, then places a purple piece on her paper. After dripping glue over the glued shapes, she takes a second yellow piece and deliberately places it over the purple one, obliterating the purple, then continues by choosing a third yellow shape.

As her picture progresses, Kate groups several purple pieces in an area. She places a piece of orange cellophane over the yellow shape which covers the first purple piece. She identifies the shapes as she selects them. She concludes her work by adding a deep pinkish-red rectangular shape so that it touches corners at an angle with the cellophane. Kate spent approximately 20 minutes on this collage. In total, there are about a dozen shapes visible on her paper, each carefully chosen and placed, and each covered with drizzles of glue. The configuration of the placement of the shapes is roughly circular with the two large pieces, the orange cellophane and red rectangle, in the center of this circular arrangement. The glue drips provide an added unity to the finished piece.

In these gluing sequences, both children show careful attention to the selection and placement of the collage pieces on their paper. The white glue forms a pattern on the paper which is incorporated into the configuration of the work, since the children do not yet realize the glue will become transparent when dry.

Conclusion

The children in each of these segments demonstrated care and attention to their work in ways which contradict the definition and usual description of children at the "scribbling" stage of artistic development. The examples suggest that young children are more visually attuned and deliberate in their mark-making than previously thought, yet these children cannot be considered precocious in terms of the visual forms which they created. They were not creating tadpole figures or other forms typical of a more advanced stage of expression. Perhaps previous notions and attitudes toward scribbling have encouraged viewers to focus on the frequency children look away from their work while drawing or painting and the obvious pleasure children display when they are enjoying the kinesthetic component of mark-making, with the consequence of overlooking the quiet, intense engagement, however brief, young children demonstrate as they make marks or select and arrange shapes on paper.

These video episodes also suggest that art-making for these two-year-olds involves complex factors both in the process of creation and in the resulting "presentation." Body dynamics and body position may play a role in determining the formation and location of marks, but cannot be used to account for the placement of all elements within a work. Color selection does not appear to be a random or even a purely mechanical process for these children, although it is not clear what prompts them to select specific colors as they work. Much further investigation would be needed to begin to determine how young children make such choices. Without additional investigation it is impossible to determine what role, if any, social interaction plays in the art-making process for them. However, their watching behavior indicates that they are very aware of the behaviors of others within their preschool environment, and it is naive to assume that this watching behavior plays no role in their artistic behavior, although what part it plays is unknown.

My purpose in this paper has been to challenge previous notions about children's preschematic art and not to make a case for a new theory of the first stage of artistic development based on a few examples. However, these examples do, I think, make a strong argument for the need for more detailed and systematic investigations of an area of children's artistic development that has been ignored and undervalued. At a time when more and more very young children are attending day care, preschool, and recreational art programs, art educators and researchers should provide teachers and parents with knowledge on which to base developmentally appropriate art programs and teaching strategies for children who are "just scribbling."

References

Arnheim, R. (1967). *Art and visual perception*. Berkeley: University of California Press.

Brittain, W. L. (1979). *Creativity, art and the young child*. New York: Macmillan.

Colbert, C. (1984). *Status of the visual arts in early education.* Art Education, 37 (4), 28-31.

Corcoran, A. (1954). Color usage in nursery school painting. *Child Development, 25* (2), 108-113.

Golomb, C. (Fall, 1981). Representation and reality: The origins and determinants of young children's drawings. *Review of Research in Visual Arts Education, 4,* 36-47.

Golomb, C., & Farmer, D. (1983). Children's graphic planning strategies and early principles of spatial organization in drawing. *Studies in Art Education, 24* (2), 86-100.

Herberholz, B., & Hanson, L. (1985). *Early childhood art* (3rd ed.). Dubuque, IA: Wm C. Brown.

Kellogg, R. (1970). *Analyzing children's art.* Palo Alto, CA: National Press Books.

Lowenfeld, V., & Brittain, W. L. (1975). *Creative and mental growth* (6th ed.). New York: Macmillan.

Matthews, J. (1984). Children drawing: Are young children really scribbling? *Early Child Development and Care, 18,* 1-39.

Swann, A. (1985). A naturalistic study of art making process in a preschool setting. Unpublished doctoral dissertation, Indiana University.

Smith, N. (1983). *Experience and art: Teaching children to paint.* New York: Teachers College Press.

Wilson, B., & Wilson, M. (1982). *Teaching children to draw: A guide for teachers and parents.* Englewood Cliffs, NJ: Prentice Hall.

Author's Note: Some of the video episodes mentioned in this article are included in the videotape "Beginnings in Art," presented by the author at the International Early Childhood Creative Arts Conference, Los Angeles, California. Funding for the videotape data collection from which these examples have been taken was provided by a Social Sciences and Humanities Research Council Grant. The author would also like to thank Ron MacGregor, head, Department of Visual and Performing Arts in Education, University of British Columbia, and Glen Dixon, director, The Child Study Centre, University of British Columbia; research assistants Jeanette Andrews and Lara Lackey; and camera operators Sheila Hall, Ray Hartley, David Rosenbaum, and Shawn Wilson for their support and assistance in this project.

Patricia Tarr is in the Department of Art, University of Calgary, Calgary, Alberta, Canada.

The Care and Feeding of Clay

Karen Neubert

Life is an art.... Every person is a special kind of artist and every activity is a special art. An artist creates out of the materials of the moment, never again to be duplicated. This is true of the painter, the musician, the dancer, the actor; the teacher; the scientist; the business man; the farmer—it is true of us all, whatever our work, that we are artists so long as we are alive to the concreteness of a moment and do not use it to some other purpose.

M. C. Richards, Centering

In Children, Painting and Clay workshops I advance the idea that clay can be a great benefit in the education of very young children. Clay is spoken of affectionately by many teachers. It is "good" for children. Clay enhances development of small motor muscle control and fosters self-expression. And yet, many people have a nagging memory of clouds of dust, hard gray globs, or slimy cold handfuls of the stuff. This discomforting vision may lead some teachers to "put clay out" and wait for the goodness to rise out of the clay without ever having to touch the icky stuff. This is communicated to the children and the clay. No conscious relationship is created, no passion generated for this friendly, venerable, ancient material of sculpture.

Clay is fun, inexpensive, nontoxic, and versatile. It is invaluable in teaching three-dimensional thinking and thinking-in-the-round, in the architectural and global sense. We present drawing, painting, and collage to our preschoolers but clay is often excluded. This leaves the atmosphere for full art expression ungrounded, unbalanced. Clay presents an opportunity for children to put their whole being into safe physical connection with the earth, and to gradually learn a sense of inner power from working with the material. It is possible to create a climate which demonstrates the potential use of clay and to model ways for it to evolve.

In my experience there is usually a place in one's school where clay can grow and take root. Maybe there will be a special corner under a tree. Find a sturdy table. Salvage a sink and some shelves or cupboards. An unused sandbox with easy access and minimum cleanup can be a permanent spot, out in the yard.

Clay lends itself to relaxation, stability, calmness and industry— all values we need in our lives. Its malleability allows us to form connections. We do not have to "make" anything to enjoy and learn clay lessons. The "things" come in their own time.

The Practice

As I introduce clay I say that clay comes in all colors, as many different colors as there are colors of earth. I tell the children that clay comes from stream beds and lakeshores. In southern California our clay varies from red to light brown, often found on the desert plains after a rain, or by a mountain stream. I talk about clay being safe, that flowers and vegetables come from the ground, too. I talk about volcanic changes, how the earth a long time ago made soft clay and how, when clay is cooked (fired), it becomes hard. People all over the world have used clay for thousands of years and have created homes from clay.

As I talk, I play with the clay, squishing and squeezing, rolling coils (worms) who ask the children, "How does your clay feel today?" ("Mine feels... cool" or "smooth" or "soft.") I demonstrate using the muscular pad of the closed hand and after a flurry of pounding and thumping, that energy will turn into lively conversation.

To illustrate, let me describe an experience I had with some 2 1/2 - 3 year-olds.

Twos and Threes Play with Clay

I arrived with a 25-pound bag of soft, tan clay (Amacco #5 low-fire), a few toothpicks in my smock pocket, and a wire tool for cutting the clay. I sat at a small table in the sun with room for four children. I cut four slabs of clay, laid them on the table and began to roll coils and balls which I gently pounded into slabs.

The children watched as the little coils "sat up" and "talked" to each other. Each child took up some clay and began to roll it. Soon, we were playing with "Waldo the Worm." From worms, they went on to balls and slabs. Later, I provided one toothpick to each child to use as a special drawing "pencil" (stylus) to put marks on the clay. I do not put out too many toothpicks, and I wait, or the children will not roll first, but simply stick picks in lumps.

What resulted in that hour was a complete set of coils, balls, and pancakes which became small faces. This series was done by Grant and Justine, a boy and a girl. When they were done, they were done. They left the table and went happily to other activities without a backward glance. We had fun that day, having a worm birthday party and adventures.

I saw this as an example of how playfully and gently young children could become aware of basic forms in clay sculpture. The coil, the ball, and the slab are all fundamental for further work. As children develop they will combine these forms into more complex and subtle forms.

Very young children can be gradually introduced to wooden clay tools as well as twigs, beverage stirrers, and small objects to put on clay, such as shells, pods, beads, etc. I avoid plastic and most metal tools. Plastic will snap and break, invisibly embedding in the clay where it can cut hands. Metal cookie cutters tend to draw the child into dough-like food-prep patterns, and spatulas should be reserved for use with the teacher, to transport a delicate landscape or complex of figures to a safe board.

With twos and threes the scribbling stage is paralleled in clay. The child takes a piece of clay and begins to "scribble" with it, dynamically interacting, by pinching, pulling, tearing, sticking together, pulling apart, stacking, carving, pounding, and rolling. If we allow a child to scribble freely she will learn to control her motions and to recognize the connection between the marks in the clay and her hand. "This is a great discovery for her, because at that time, unconsciously, she discovers for the first time she can master her movements." Now the child wants to practice, repeat, practice and repeat this thrilling discovery!

Fours and Fives Love Their Clay

By age four and five the practice has evolved into a beginning repertoire. There are favorite themes and children become very interested in establishing their identity. This is often when the practiced circle will sprout eyes, nose, mouth, ears, rays, limbs. Now children begin reacting to and describing the outer world in terms of their own identity. Universal themes appear. There are families (animals and humans), homes (rooms, furniture), space, school, city life (buses, cars, street lights), natural phenomena (flowers, volcanoes, caves, tunnels), friends and pets, food (cookies, pizzas), and wonderful amalgamations. "A rainbow going to a drinking fountain" is one of my favorites: a child struck by the wonder of a bubbling water fountain.

As the year unfolds, I introduce new tools slowly to allow time for the children to assimilate each one. Young children aged two to five can use coffee stirrers and popsicle sticks to cut, carve, dig, and stick into clay bodies. Garlic presses are an exception to the rule about metal tools. They are very popular, so plan to have one for every three children in the group. As the children learn to share, they cannot wait too long for their turn. Rollers are useful, at times, for making slabs. For this, and all clay play, children need ample seating space to use their arms freely.

A clay slab is an inviting surface for making marks and line drawings. Children enjoy drawing on the clay and a toothpick or wooden skewer works well. I tell how thousands of years ago people made shopping lists on clay tablets. I talk about the safe use of sharp objects and remind them that our clay tools are made from box wood trees. I feel the fewer implements, the better. We adults tend to get carried away by devices and techniques, and they should be used sparingly, when you sense a child could be freed by such an addition.

I introduce buttons, keys, computer parts, bottle tops, leather scraps, and pieces of costume jewelry for the children to press into slabs. As they learn about shapes, they also experience reverse-image, relief and impression, elements they will meet again in printmaking.

After mid-year, preschoolers begin to paint their clay creations and glue them to pieces of colored matboard recycled from local picture framers. The joy of using colors can be enhanced when children are allowed to tempera paint the clay objects they make. Most children do love to paint their clay from time to time. Some preschoolers and older children prefer not to put paint or glue on their clay. It seems most beautiful as it is. Painting or decorating one's sculpture is an esthetic choice and should be offered as an option. The unadorned surfaces of clay are sensuous and appear as an esthetic element in many cultures.

There are several options here: 1) Paint with plain tempera only, putting glue under the clay to attach it to a board; the clay surface is matte. 2) Paint with tempera to which glue has been added; the clay appears semi-glossy. (Our paint-glue recipe is one part white glue and three parts liquid tempera paint.) 3) Paint with white glue thinned with a little water to the consistency of heavy cream. 4) Leave the clay unpainted, but glue the bottom to a board. 5) Neither paint nor glue the piece, but secure it for the trip home in a styrofoam tray or container.

Soft bristle brushes work best with wide-mouth, nontipping containers which can be sealed with foil. The glue or paint brushes on thick over the rich warm surface of the clay and can appear suffocating to some children. If there is a concern, one can speak of the glue drying clear like a window pane or a see-through skin that protects it and makes it smooth. If possible, examples of clay that has been painted can be shown to the children.

What To Do With Children's Work

Children usually enjoy taking home their clay work the day it is created. Preschool and primary age children often work rapidly, finishing an art piece in a single session. Usually 15 minutes of warm up at the beginning and 15 minutes of clean up at the end leave a good half-hour for the children to create something.

On slower days the work can be stored until the next session. If there is a piece of work that is still in process, it can be stored inside a plastic bag and sealed. If airtight, the piece will stay soft for a week. Clay left on the shelf for several days and forgotten is pure process work and can safely go into the clay recycling bin for reconditioning.

Very young children, twos and threes, after a session of playing with clay, enjoy the ritual of putting away the still soft clay. Saying, "Good-bye, see you next time," to the clay can be as delicious as bringing it out to explore in the beginning.

Hot as a Volcano

In our area, California, clay is available in red, brown, grey, white, and grey-green. It is packed in plastic sacks, two 25-pound sacks to a box, 40 boxes to a ton. Twenty-five pounds costs about $5, or 100 pounds about $20. When a ton is ordered there is a substantial savings. Clay keeps well and can be stored air-tight, in a cool, protected place indefinitely. Order low fire clay, cone 04, cone 05, or cone 06 for best results in preschool and elementary school. The number designates a low-fire temperature.

To illustrate how clay can be cooked in its special oven, called a kiln, I tell children that the kiln gets as hot as a volcano inside. That heat makes the clay hard. Older children are pleased when something they have made goes through the fire. It is a mystery, a scientific event, an art that connects each child to the marvels of clay in ancient times as well as to modern ceramic microchips, water systems, and architecture.

Over the course of a year the children will turn out hundreds of pieces of work. I try to make certain that each child in the kindergarten and primary grades has one or two pieces fired. I found a local ceramicist who would fire our work for a small fee, but now we are happy to have our own kiln. A small electric kiln is relatively inexpensive to operate. Firing is an art, too, so that the artist, teacher, and children can participate in the transformation together.

Recycling

It's easy! Save those lumps and clods of dry clay, each color in its own pail, and one pail for mixed clay. (Variegated clay is a joy, and kiln-safe if you decide to fire, since you've ordered clay that will fire within the same temperature range.) When you have saved 25 pounds of dry clay, here's what you do:

Put the dry clay in a large burlap or canvas bag. You will need a large flat surface on which to work, a piece of canvas or a tarp to spread on the surface, a wooden or rubber mallet, and goggles to protect your eyes from stray bits of flying clay. You'll also need a plastic bucket with a lid in which to store the clay while it soaks.

Put the clay in the bag and take it to the flat area where you will work. A concrete slab, an area of the playground, or a solid table will work well. Spread your tarp, put the bag on the tarp and begin to strike the clay inside the bag with the mallet. Keep at it until the big lumps become small lumps. You may wish to have students assist you. (This is a good way for children—or adults—to vent steam.) In good weather you can let the children take turns wearing the goggles and smashing the clay.

Next, you sift the clay by pouring it out of the bag through coarse half-inch wire mesh into a plastic bucket. Put the big pieces back in the bag and continue to pound the bigger pieces until all the lumps are about the size of almonds. Keep crushing the clay until it is the size of small beans. Keep sifting it and collecting the small fine stuff in the bucket. And, remember to wear the goggles. Using a hand brush and dustpan, scoop up all the pulverized clay and put it in the bucket. Pour water into the bucket, just enough to cover it (like soaking beans). Put the lid on the bucket securely and let the clay soak for two or three days. How long it soaks will depend on the humidity and weather.

Pour off any extra water that wasn't absorbed during the days of soaking. Leave the cover off the bucket for a day and let the clay dry in the bucket until it feels like cooked oatmeal.

Conditioning the Clay

A surface for working the clay can readily be made. Use heavy duck canvas cloth to cover a table top; it should hang about six inches over the edge all around. Stretch the canvas tightly over the surface. With a staple gun, staple the canvas to the underside of the table. The table can be a permanent clay table—covered with a tarp when it rains, covered with newspaper for painting or collage. This can be reused daily by allowing it to dry in the sun and scraping it with a spatula and brushing the powder into your recycle bucket. (Any artist's supply store will have canvas, the kind used to paint paintings. Canvas lasts for years.)

Now, scoop the moist clay out of the bucket onto the clay table. If you have plaster bats they work well as a surface. (A "bat" is a slab of plaster that has been formed in a mold.) Like the canvas, the plaster absorbs excess water. You are ready to start getting the clay into shape.

Using your hands, knead the clay like bread dough. Work it until it has a firm, elastic, smooth consistency. The extra moisture will be gradually absorbed by the canvas or plaster surface. Use a rocking motion to homogenize the texture of the clay. Make grapefruit-size balls. Make a hole in the clay ball with your thumb and fill it with a little water.

Store the balls in an air-tight container with a lid. Five-gallon plastic buckets with handles are efficient and can be obtained from restaurants and school cafeterias. Keep the lid on to prevent the clay from drying out. (A damp towel over the clay is helpful, particularly during dry weather.)

Check your clay every few days and occasionally add 1/2 to 1 cup of water if the clay seems dry to the touch. Store the buckets of clay in an accessible, cool, protected spot.

Our studio has several 5-gallon plastic buckets with lids and handles for storing moist clays, dry clay, and mixed color clay and for warm-water hand-washing—an important and sensuous part of the process. (Clay should be washed off of hands and tools in buckets to prevent blobs of clay entering and blocking septic systems. The buckets of water can be used to water plants or poured down drains that have clay "traps" installed. These special screens can be taken out and cleaned from time to time.)

There are a few other items that a studio needs. Several clean, soft, older terry-cloth towels (paper towels feel too rough after a session with earthy clay) are for hand-drying. A dust pan, hand-broom, and brush will be useful during clean-up. A clay-cutting tool can be made with 20" telephone wire tied to two empty spools of thread. When you grip the spools, one in each hand, you loop the wire over the block of clay. Then, gently but firmly pull, as if pulling the reins of a pony, to cut a slab of clay. These items can be stored compactly in a box and brought out or left permanently in your "clay corner."

In Conclusion

The practice and process of clay, once established, can continue with a child for life. The role of the teacher is to inspire, guide, encourage, help discover, and be present to witness a child's unfolding development.

Viktor Lowenfeld wrote, "Whenever the child starts to express what she has perceived with her eyes or ears or with her hands or with her movements, she also has to find out how she can best organize what she has in her mind. This is always an unconscious process, but certainly the child who sees the whole paper (or piece of clay) before her and can utilize it, will distribute whatever she thinks of adequately. And this distribution, or harmonious organization of things, is most important, because it deals with the total integration of thinking, feeling and perceiving in life."

Suggested Reading

Centering. M.C. Richards.
Viktor Lowenfeld speaks on art and creativity. Viktor Lowenfeld.
Talking with the clay. The Art of Pueblo Pottery. Stephen Trimble
The living tradition of Maria Martinez. Susan Peterson.
Lucy M. Lewis: American Indian potter. Susan Peterson.
Finding one's way with clay. Paulus Berensohn.
When clay sings. Byrd Baylor.
Imagination: The key to human potential. Polly McVickar.
Art from many hands: Multicultural art projects. Jo Miles Schuman.
No more second hand art: Awakening the artist within. Peter London.
Art of the young child. Jane Cooper Bland.
Children's art. Miriam Lindstrom.
Doing art together. Muriel Siberstein-Storfer.
From a potter's perspective. Melanie Carr.
Sculptural beginnings: Helping children work with clay. Roberta Carasso.

Karen Neubert is a painter, living in Los Angeles. She has been an artist-in-residence for 20 years and won numerous grants and awards for her programs with young children.

Private Rituals and Public Performances: The Social Context of Early Childhood Arts

Christine M. Thompson

Introduction

Much existing research on young children's talk about their drawings focuses on the role of language in the transition from scribbling to representation. Yet language continues to guide and accompany drawing events throughout the early childhood years. When children make art in classroom settings, personal monologues enter the public domain where they are amplified and transformed in the company of others.

This paper describes patterns of personal and social speech demonstrated by children enrolled in seven early childhood art classes at a large midwestern university. The youngest children, at four, engaged in the uncensored and eclectic forms of egocentric speech characterized by Piaget (1974). Older children, in kindergarten, first, and second grades, favored the more specific, reflective mode of egocentric speech Vygotsky (1962) described. They spoke to themselves primarily when they encountered an impediment to action. This occurred, with increasing regularity, in response to teacher-directed activities in the first and second grades. Even among preschoolers, however, egocentric statements frequently evoked response from others: personal speech tended to be social in effect, if not in intention.

The distinctions between forms of language associated with voluntary and directed activities clarify the relationships between peer collaboration and structured teaching in early childhood art education. Informal, self-directed activities facilitate dialogue among children, encouraging mutual construction of meanings about art and the experiences it embodies. Formal lessons present challenges of a different order, requiring children to depart from customary ways of working and expanding the range of technique and imagery available for subsequent exploration. Voluntary and directed activities, complementary aspects of early art education, are attended by particular forms of personal and social speech which change in response to development and the social and ecological context of the classroom.

Interaction Among Children

Five-year-old Jacob had attracted an attentive audience. The boys who clustered around him at the drawing table watched and giggled as Jacob transformed his "big house" into the site of riotous calamity. "Here's the bathroom," Jacob announced as he drew. "The bathtub.

The man. He's in the bathtub. Look, guys." Blue marker gushed across the page as Jacob plunged his hapless protagonist further into the drink. The other boys remained transfixed, interrupting their own drawings to admire each ingenious twist in Jacob's plot. "And then his wife comes in the door. And here's the Kool-aid spilt on the floor," Jacob continued, bringing his domestic drama to its climax.

Jacob's completed drawing was densely layered, the house and its inhabitants submerged beneath successive waves of marker. The story enacted on the page was so thoroughly juxtaposed that its tranquil beginnings were impossible to detect. A chaotic tangle of incident, the drawing provided no entry to viewers who had missed the performance which brought it about.

As Dyson observed, "young children are symbol weavers. Their 'drawings' may be composed, not only of lines and colors, but of language as well" (1986, p. 381). Jacob's drawing was less an artifact than an event, a performance unfolding in time, in which speech and gesture, word and image, intertwined.

As Jacob's monologue suggests, children frequently address comments about their drawings to other members of the "child collective that arises in a day care or classroom" (Dyson, 1987, p. 3). Piaget (1974) described similar incidents as evidence of young children's intractable egocentrism. Even when a child seeks the attention of others, Piaget claimed, he "talks about himself just as he does when he soliloquizes, but with the added pleasure of feeling himself an object of interest to other people" (1974, p. 31). While the form of Jacob's speech fits this explanation, the spirit of his performance chafes at its limits. Jacob spoke, as artists do, of the image before him and the decisions he was making in its behalf. He relished this opportunity to amuse and edify his companions as he reflected on the progress of his drawing.

As young children gather in day care centers and classrooms, the personal monologues and kitchen table conversations we associate with early childhood art are amplified and transformed. The availability of other children as collaborators, witnesses, and critics presents a context for artistic exploration that can be both supportive and challenging. Young children must reckon with a variety of complicating factors when they draw in social settings: teachers' or caregivers' expectations, sharing of materials and space, rules of classroom decorum, the presence of other children. All of these factors must be considered as part of the changing cultural context of early childhood.

Children in Art Classrooms

One aspect of that increasingly complex situation—the interaction among children in art classrooms—has been the focus of my research for the past two years. The first year of this study was spent in four preschool-kindergarten classes sponsored by the art education program at the University of Illinois. As the children chattered their way through their weekly visits to "art school," I eavesdropped, recording comments and conversations that so often occur just beyond the earshot of adults. I was interested primarily in what children had to say, to themselves and to each other, as they participated in "voluntary" (Lark-Horovitz, Lewis, & Luca, 1973, p. 17) activities, when their choices of imagery and activity were limited only by the range of materials available. The social life of an early childhood classroom is at its height when each member is free to choose the focus and duration of his or her pursuits. It was only when the children gathered to tackle lessons orchestrated by their teachers that talk momentarily slowed.

I occasionally took advantage of these brief respites to visit other Saturday school classrooms. Emerging from the early childhood studio, the first and second grade classroom seemed an oasis of order and tranquility. Yet, I wondered why these children, not so much older than those I was studying, seemed so silent and self-contained as they worked. Had they learned, so quickly, to keep their thoughts to themselves? Something I had come to regard as essential was missing here. I set out, in the second year of the project, to determine its whereabouts.

Dyson observed how frequently "the stories of children's school lives—in fact, of our own school memories—are threaded with the `I' and the `we'. . .they are stories of children finding themselves among their peers" (1987, p. 4). For very young children, these stories may be simple vignettes. Undoubtedly, plots, characters, and settings acquire complexity and definition as children grow. Yet other children provide something more than a footnote to even the most rudimentary of these stories. Children interest, influence, and inform one another, even in the glancing encounters that characterize social life in preschools. Together, they improvise an informal curriculum, composed of knowledge few teachers would think to convey about topics selected by the children themselves.

Piaget's cautionary remarks prompted me to make careful note of the person to whom each recorded statement was addressed. There were times when it was impossible to specify an intended target, when a child solicited the attention of no one in particular or everyone in general. As Piaget might have predicted, these spontaneous eruptions occurred almost exclusively in the preschool-kindergarten classes.

Often, however, egocentric comments were interpreted as invitations to dialogue. When Tom mused to himself, "And the tornado's going to explode, 'cause I'm going to add a little explosion color," Hugh offered, "Here's my tornado." When Deanna advised herself, "I need pink. This is just a plain old girl," Grant responded, "It doesn't look plain, 'cause this leg's long and this leg's short." The children who initiated these exchanges did so unwittingly. They were surprised, and sometimes disgruntled, when others responded. Yet children routinely overheard and answered others' egocentric statements. Blissfully oblivious to the conventions that govern adult speech, the children entered without knocking and assumed they would be welcome.

The children communicated, succinctly and effectively, through actions as well as words. Piaget suggested that conversation requires, at the very least, "three consecutive remarks about the same subject. . .made by at least two interlocutors" (1974, p. 71). Measured by this standard, conversation was rare in the preschool-kindergarten classroom. Talking among themselves, children tended to abort their exchanges just shy of Piaget's three-turn minimum. A comment or question was often followed by a single sentence in response. Often the issue was decided in these brief verbal parries. "Wow, a shark," Luke observed, peeking at Paul's drawing on a neighboring easel. "It's not a shark. It's a whale," Paul replied. "She's my friend," Sabrina declared, draping an arm around Madison's shoulders. "We're both girls, right?" Madison added. What more was there to say?

Comments addressed by one child to another were often answered silently, with a smile or a shrug, or acknowledged as the children joined in a proposed activity. Many fragments of talk were social in intention, expressions of admiration or overtures toward friendship, received and reciprocated in action. "Hey, bud, do you want to sit with me?" Ethan accepted Carl's invitation with a grin. "Want to put some paste on your picture? I'm gonna put paste on my picture. I hope you like it," Madison chattered to a silent, busy, but clearly flattered companion.

Conversations were more sustained among kindergarten children, particularly when they worked in groups of three or more. Martin initiated a collaborative venture the morning after a dramatic storm: "I'm gonna make a tornado. . .a number of how many have been here. I've never been in a tornado, or probably I wasn't born." As Martin chalked spiralling marks and improbable numbers across the mural paper, Ben followed suit. "Look at _my_ tornado," he urged. Carl squealed, scribbling wildly, "Look at our tornado. Tornado! How do you erase that?"

These abrupt switches from past to present, from task-oriented to task-related talk, from word to action, were typical of children's conversations. The activity of the moment was the origin and focus of interaction, but also provided opportunity to exchange information about the world beyond the studio. Egocentric speech did occur, but seemed to be far more intermittent, and significant, than Piaget's (1974) theory implies. When the children withdrew for consultation with themselves, their retreats were strategic and purposeful. Vygotsky (1962) believed that young children lapse into egocentric musing when they encounter an impediment to their actions, a problem requiring thoughtful resolution. Young children give voice to this process of reflection. In doing so, they reveal the form and content of their thoughts to others, teachers and peers, who are free to overhear and to respond. This process of reflection—whether it occurs in conversation with teachers, peers, or the self—is fundamental to children's learning.

Changes in First and Second Graders

The balance between these various aspects of children's talk shifts appreciably as children reach the first and second grades. Although talking through a drawing was accepted practice among preschool children, these monologues fell abruptly from favor in the first and second grade classroom. Evan was the only child in his class of twenty who habitually provided play-by-play accounts of his drawings. Most children tolerated Evan's continuous banter, but some were unwilling to live and let live. As Evan huddled over his sketchbook, engaged in his customary vocal pursuits, Hans motioned Alan to Evan's table. The newcomers watched as Evan continued his drawing: "I'm gonna make a big triangular flower," he noted. "Oh, I guess I'll make a few petals." Hans and Alan launched a thinly disguised barrage of insult. Evan responded huffily, "So far, I'm doing quite well." When their teacher intervened, Hans and Alan reluctantly opened their sketchbooks and Evan resumed his monologue.

Following this visitation, Evan adopted the approved method of reserving these running commentaries until an adult could be recruited to listen to them. The effort to remain silent visibly taxed Evan's endurance. He continued to hum, squint, and sniffle at his work, occasionally blurting challenges into unresponsive air. Thinking hard about his drawings, Evan would have preferred to think out loud. Most of his peers had forsaken the practice, however. Like many things recently outgrown, its survival in others provoked disdain.

Occasional regressions were permissible in the first and second grade classes, but only when conditions were right. Egocentric statements were accepted when children tackled lessons directed by their teachers, when the challenges they faced were new and considerable. Sometimes, like younger versions of themselves, they answered one another's declarations. The children found the assignment of replicating Grant Wood's *American Gothic* difficult. "I can't even draw this," Lauren muttered. "It's hard," a nearby friend commiserated. "He's really bald," one child observed of Wood's farmer. "I put some hair on mine," Laura replied. Jean directed herself, "Oh, I make a face like this and draw two lines right there." Erik murmured, "The eraser is my best bud!"

Directed Teaching That Challenges Children

In both age groups, such reflective statements occurred most frequently in response to directed lessons. The talk surrounding voluntary activities was more relaxed and sociable. The rhythm of activities in these classrooms made distinctions between personal and social learning clear. Vygotsky (1978) maintained that all real learning occurs in advance of development: in a zone defined by the difference between what a child can accomplish unaided and what that child can do with the help of an adult or a more capable peer. Actions that a child can perform with guidance become, with practice, part of a repertoire of independent skills. This theory provides a strong argument for directed teaching which challenges children to depart from customary ways of working and expand the range of imagery and technique available to them. It also emphasizes the importance of the "unintentional helping" (Dyson, 1987) that occurs within communities of children.

Young children's art room conversations may alert teachers to concepts in the making, long before newly-constructed ideas appear on the drawing page. Equally, as children articulate, overhear, and respond to accounts of art in progress, they may discover new and intriguing ways to think about art and its place in their lives. Formal and informal learning experiences complement one another best in early childhood classrooms which provide ample opportunities for activity and for reflection, in both their personal and share forms.

References

Dyson, A. H. (1986). Transitions and tensions:Interrelationships between the drawing, talking, and dictating of young children. *Research in the Teaching of English*, 20, 379-409.

Dyson, A. H. (1987). *Unintentional helping in the primary grades: Writing in the children's world.* (Technical report no 2). Berkeley, CA: Center for the Study of Writing.

Lark-Horovitz, B., Lewis, H., & Luca, M. (1973). *Understanding children's art for better teaching* (2nd ed.). Columbus, OH: Charles E. Merrill Publishing.

Piaget, J. (1974). *The language and thought of the child* (Trans. M. Gabain). New York: New American Library.

Vygotsky, L. S. (1978). *Mind in society* (M. Cole, V. John-Steiner, S. Scribner, & E. Souberman, Eds.). Cambridge, MA: Harvard University Press.

Vygotsky, L. S. (1962). *Thought and language.* (Trans., Ed., E. Hanfmann & G. Vakar). Cambridge, MA: MIT Press.

Acknowledgment: Portions of this paper appear in a revised form in C. Thompson & S. Bales (1991), "Michael doesn't like my dinosaurs": Conversations in a preschool art class, Studies in Art Education (in press). The author wishes to thank the Center for Advanced Study at the University of Illinois at Urbana-Champaign for supporting this work.

Christine M. Thompson is a member of the faculty at the University of Illinois at Urbana-Champaign. She teaches graduate courses in children's artistic development and art methods courses for elementary and early childhood education majors, and supervises a practicum in teaching the arts to young children. Thompson recently completed a chapter on developmentally-appropriate art curriculum for a forthcoming publication of the National Association for the Education of Young Children and is the editor of an anthology on the visual arts in early childhood learning, to be published by the National Art Education Association late in 1991.

DANCE

Transforming Movement into Dance for Young Children

Susan W. Stinson

Dance comes in many forms, not all of them appropriate for young children. The kind of dance that is most appropriate for this age is most often referred to as *creative dance* or *creative movement*. It is an art form that is based on natural movement rather than movement of a particular style such as one might see in tap dance or ballet. But, of course, not all natural movement is *dance*. In our everyday lives we walk to a cabinet, reach up to get a box, or turn to hear someone talking, but it does not feel like dancing. Yet, a dance can be made of the same movements—walking, reaching, turning. What is it that makes movement *dance?*

For a moment, try pointing to an object in the room as though you were showing someone where it is. Now, point again, but this time with a difference: make the movement your arm performs more important than showing someone the object. This is what dance is about—making movement *itself* significant. (Otherwise, people would not bother to do it or watch it!)

How do we make movement significant? The first step is to *pay attention to it*. Most of our everyday movement is so well mastered that we no longer have any conscious awareness of what we are doing; we are "on automatic." In order to dance, we must sense ourselves just as completely as a baby taking its first tentative steps.

Perform the pointing movement again, trying to be fully aware. Notice if your arm moves all in one piece or if it moves sequentially (first the upper arm, then lower arm, then hand, then finger). Try it both ways and sense the difference. Does your arm feel tense or relaxed as it is pointing? Try doing it very quickly and then as though you have all the time in the world, and notice the difference. Now put your arm down and notice how it feels different from the other—you sense it more.

To dance is to discover a new world of sensory awareness. Awareness of movement is made possible by the kinesthetic sense, and it comes from the nerve endings in our joints and muscles. This sense tells us what our body is doing; it ordinarily works with the visual sense but even operates when our eyes are closed. Some degree of kinesthetic awareness is essential if we are to master skills with our bodies; the better developed it is, the more complicated the motor skills we are able to learn and perform. If the kinesthetic sense is acute, it even allows us to feel motion we see others doing; we can actually feel the tightness in a worried friend or feel stretch in our own bodies as we watch a basketball player reach toward the basket.

When I use the word "dance," then, I am referring not just to body movement, but to an inside awareness of the movement. However, dance as an art has to do not only with the body but also with the spirit, another dimension of the self. This does not mean that dance is always "expressing your feelings," but that dance is *magical*. This description has been so meaningful to young children who use it often—not in the sense of magic tricks, but in the sense of a magical state of being. Our magic comes from a calm, quiet place deep inside us, and each of us possesses it. We use our magic to transform *movement* into *dance*, and to transform ourselves from plain ordinary people into dancers.

Older dancers have spoken of this "magical" power of dance using other words, such as
"Transcendence...."
"I lose myself...."
"I feel like I'm in another world...."
"I *am* my dance...."
Probably all of us have experienced transcendent moments in our lives, times of total involvement when we feel deep connection, whether it is with movement, music, or even a sunset. It is difficult to find words to talk about these experiences, because the words often do not seem to make sense in a conventional way. Philosophers who study the arts refer to such experiences as "aesthetic." While an aesthetic experience has other characteristics as well, the sense of total involvement, connection, and transformation is essential. Interestingly, use of our kinesthetic awareness can help us find that kind of involvement in movement, because *body* and *spirit* are not completely separate; they meet in that special place inside each of us.

The mind is also important in dance—particularly in the kind of problem solving found in creative dance. However, the mind is also not separate from other aspects of the self. When children think *in* dance, the outcome is movement; when they think *about* dance, the outcome is often words. Their feelings affect what they do as well as what they say.

All teachers who believe it is important to help children go beyond *movement* to *dance* have their own ways to facilitate this transformation. I will be sharing some of the approaches I have found most helpful in my own work with young children.

In order for children to sense themselves moving and in stillness, I lead them in practicing the contrasts of making sound and making silence.

In response to a signal, make sound with your voice and/or body (e.g., slap your legs, pound the floor). To another signal, make silence—listen to the silence. What can you still hear when you make silence?

In response to a signal, move in place (e.g., wiggle) as much as you can without touching anyone. To another signal, make stillness—every part, even your eyes.

A freeze is when you make silence and stillness. A perfect freeze is very magical, especially when you freeze a movement right in the middle. While sitting, let your feet "run" on the floor; when you hear the signal to freeze, let your whole self freeze in the middle of the run; one or both of your feet will be in mid-air. Can you feel your muscles working to hold the freeze?

If children can appreciate and pay attention to the sensation of stillness, they are starting to use their kinesthetic sense. The kinesthetic sense can connect them to their special magic.

Shake your hands hard for several seconds, and then freeze them in mid-air. Can you still feel something going on inside—a little quiver, like something is alive? That aliveness is your magic. Can you use your magic to quiver your hands—as magically as a butterfly quivers its wings—and freeze. Can you still feel the quiver going on inside? That is your magic, and you need to use it to dance.

I have also found it helpful to contrast dance with other ways of moving. Again, the difference is not <u>what</u> movement is done, but how we attend to it. For young children, the idea of using their magic can help them attend to their own movement.

Select an everyday movement, such as standing up and sitting down. Try doing it so it feels "plain and ordinary"; then use your magic to push you up and pull you back down. Dancers sometimes use the words <u>rise</u> and <u>sink</u> to describe this. Add a surprise to your rise and sink—maybe a turn or a stretch, so it is your own rise and sink. Can you rise and sink <u>suddenly</u> without losing your magic?

Try using your magic to run in the dance space—and then freeze. A magic run is different from running on the playground. If you really use your magic, I won't be able to hear a sound as you run. You don't have to be tight and tense to run with magic; find a way to feel both free and magical when you run. Can you find another way to travel, and still keep it magical? Can you put in a surprise?

Make a dance with a beginning, a middle, and an end. The beginning is a magic rise, the middle is your own kind of magic traveling movement...then freeze. The ending is a magic sink. You may choose to put in a surprise at some point.

If you add music to the brief sequence above—especially music with a magical quality— it will seem even more magical. It also helps to make silence and stillness before the dance begins and after it ends.

Still another variation can introduce the important concept of "being your own teacher." Children are being their own teacher when they choose their own kind of traveling movement, telling themselves what to do. In addition, they can be their own teacher by telling themselves *when* to begin the magic rise, when to begin their own way to travel, and when to sink. Being their own teacher is empowering for children; it also helps make their dance their own.

Often children enter a dance session unable to find the calm quiet part of themselves; they may need to make sounds before they can make silence, moving very vigorously in order to release some excess energy. Sometimes I ask children to prepare for dance by running in circles around the room or standing up and sitting down as fast as they can, but to listen to their muscles. When their muscles let them know they are feeling tired, the children can be their own teachers by telling themselves to lie down on the floor, close their eyes, and relax. By listening to their own heartbeats and breathing, children can tell themselves when they are ready to sit up and find their magic dance energy. Because maintaining the concentration and focus of dance is tiring in its own way, other release times may be needed during dance class.

Understanding the concept of *shape* can also help children tune in to the inside. Usually we think of identifying shape by using our visual sense (what it looks like); to dancers, the idea of shape also involves the kinesthetic sense (what it feels like). To make a dance shape, you have to hold yourself up from the inside, using your bones and the strong, deep muscles inside. You can make shapes keeping all of your muscles strong, but you get tired easily from the tension involved. If you make yourself strong on the inside and soft on the outside, you can make shape after shape after shape. A stick figure made out of pipe cleaners is a good model: it is strong enough on the inside to hold whatever shape I make with it, but just soft enough to let me change the shape, and it is soft on the outside.

Themes Enlarge Dance Vocabulary

Once young children understand that they can make silence and stillness, make different shapes, and travel in different ways, they have enough material to begin working with themes that will enlarge their dance vocabulary. I like to use themes related to the world in which young children live, or imaginary worlds which they can enter readily—not only because it is usually more interesting to them to dance about things they care about, but because I believe that one important purpose for the arts is to help us feel connected with and make sense of the world we live in. Some themes have an additional advantage of calling forth a magical quality more readily; while I use a wide variety of themes with children, I particularly enjoy the magical quality evoked by themes that involve nature. I hope to inspire children to perceive the natural world with the sense of awe and wonder it deserves. Elsewhere (Stinson, 1988a, 1988b, 1990a, 1990b) I have described dance sessions using themes from the natural world, and I usually use them in demonstrations and workshops. However, even everyday work actions can inspire dance with a sense of magic, depending on how we approach them.

One favorite theme I have explored with young children involves movement derived from simple tools, such as a saw, hammer, screwdriver, and paintbrush. Usually these items may be found in the early childhood classroom; otherwise I bring in the tools to demonstrate. I ask the children to watch my arm bending and stretching while I demonstrate sawing and give them a chance to pantomime this basic action. Then we go beyond pantomime to explore other body parts that can bend and stretch, even how to travel from one place to another by bending and stretching. The next step is to make a "sawing dance," while we tell ourselves what part to bend and stretch and when to change from one part to another.

We follow a similar pattern to make a hammering dance, exploring different body parts that can "hammer" and different degrees of speed and force, from quick light tapping to slow strong pounding. Since we are dancers and not hammers, we are not limited to hammering down towards the floor, but can hammer the air as well. We make a hammering dance; each child is again his or her own teacher, determining which of the variations to use and when to change from one to another.

A screwdriver goes around and around in a repetitive turning action; a person using the screwdriver uses a twisting action. We explore different possibilities for twisting and turning before making our own twisting and turning dances.

In exploring the action of painting, we again can use all different body parts as "paintbrushes." We use different pathways as we paint the air, making circles, zigzags, spots, and other designs, both large and small. For the painting dance, all children can determine their own designs and imagine their favorite colors.

With each of these individual dances, we start and end with stillness and silence; accompaniment (recorded, sung, or played on simple instruments) for each dance helps support the movement qualities.

Sometimes we also talk about what we might make with all of these tools—in the case of young children, the construction is likely to be a wonderful "project" of different shapes and sizes of wood pieces put together. I am fortunate to have saved some of the projects my own children created at young ages and sometimes bring them in to show. They give us ideas for making very different body shapes; sometimes I am the "carpenter" and put all the pieces together by lifting each child (in his or her shape) and attaching them all together.

After several times of making "construction dances" with children, I eventually created a story to give the children a chance to review the individual dances and use their magic even more:

Once there was a poor housebuilder who worked all day in the hot sun (or the cold wind, depending upon the time of year) to build houses. She sawed the boards, hammered in the nails, screwed in the screws, and painted the final construction; each house was very different from any other house in town. As soon as she finished a house, she sold it to have enough money to buy food for her family and materials for the next house.

One day, she had just finished building a house when a big storm came and blew it down. The housebuilder was so sad that she sat down on a rock and cried.

While she was crying, something very magical happened. A group of elves came sneaking out and danced construction dances. First they did a sawing dance, then a hammering dance, then a twisting and turning dance to screw in the screws, then a painting dance. When they were finished with their dances, a wonderful new house with crazy shapes stood where the old one had blown down. It was just like magic.

The housebuilder stopped crying and thanked the elves—not just for rebuilding the house, but for teaching her about the magic of dancing. From that day on, she always danced while she did her work.

Before I have finished telling the story, the children are ready to dance the parts of the elves; I play the role of the hardworking housebuilder who learns about the magic of dance. The amazing thing is, each time I dance with young children, they remind me of this same truth—that each of us possesses our own magic which can transform what we see, what we do, and who we are.

Author's note: Portions of this article were adapted from my book, *Dance for Young Children: Finding the Magic in Movement,* published by the American Alliance for Health, Physical Education, Recreation and Dance in 1988.

References

Stinson, S.W. (1988). Creative dance for preschool children. *Journal of Physical Education, Recreation & Dance, 59,* 52-56.

Stinson, S.W. (1990a). Dance and the developing child. In W.J. Stinson (Ed.), *Moving and learning for the young child* (pp. 139-150). Reston, VA: AAHPERD.

Stinson, S.W. (July/August 1990b). Dance education in early childhood. *Design for Arts in Education, 91,* 34-41.

Susan W. Stinson teaches in the Department of Dance at the University of North Carolina at Greensboro. She has written extensively in the area of movement and dance education in early childhood.

Creative Dance for All Abilities

Margot E. Faught

Now, more than ever, we are evolving as a multicultural world. We can no longer compartmentalize or separate ourselves from the total picture, from the whole. We are approaching integration personally, within groups and globally. We are beginning to look at the education of the total child, the total person, and how to best accomplish that goal.

The arts as universal expressors/communicators provide valuable links internally and externally. The arts can bridge the gaps between the many facets of the whole, both individually and in group interaction. The arts can help connect the mind, body, and emotions, thus enhancing learning and development on many levels. Ultimately, we are providing options by opening channels and presenting more opportunities for enhanced learning. More and more, we know that barriers are transcended through the arts, encouraging communication that is not always in the traditional sense.

Creative dance, as other art forms, offers many avenues for expression. It provides movement experiences that promote motor skill development and general body awareness as well as basic learning skills such as listening, following directions, sequencing, and problem solving. Creative dance also encourages creativity, positive self-concept, individuality, cooperation, and compromise. The material presented here is basic and adaptable to varied ages and abilities.

We often approach "special needs" students with care, fear, and limitation in mind. As in any teaching, flexibility seems to be a critical factor. Certainly in teaching "regular" students in "regular" classrooms, we encourage each student to begin working from the current skill level and progress to the highest level possible. We do not teach homogeneous groups in any situation. We often approach special needs students with a different point of view, when, in fact, they are, as any population, in need of adaptability, challenge, and avenues for integration of the whole self into the whole group.

The curriculum presented here is material used in early elementary and preschool classes including varied special populations. I am currently using this material with preschoolers at Indianapolis Head Start and the Indiana School for the Deaf and elementary students at the Indiana School for the Blind. These projects are funded by Very Special Arts Indiana.

Three lessons are presented here. Each one could be scaled down or expanded upon, depending upon the length of the session and diverse needs of teachers and students. Within the sessions, basic elements of dance are informally explored. Cues for change of level, direction, tempo, and size and quality of movement are incorporated at various points throughout. A simple warm-up is done for each class with a focus on coordination, flexibility, stretching, and directionality, through isolations and total body movement. The warm-up is done in a circle or line formation. Recorded music and/or drum accompaniment are used throughout.

Sample Lessons

Lesson 1 - Shape and Motion

Part 1

A.   Introduction of shape by individual experimentation in creating frozen shapes with the body. Create shapes of objects such as a tree, rock, circle, square, etc., or more abstractly, a reaching shape, twisted shape, leaning shape, etc.

B.   Pick four shapes from class suggestions and establish a sequence by numbering the shapes: 1, 2, 3, 4. Practice the sequence both in and out of order.

Part 2

A.   Introduction of motion by using basic locomotor movements such as walking, jumping, skipping, hopping, etc.

B.   Pick four motions from class suggestions and establish a sequence by numbering the motions: 1, 2, 3, 4. Practice the sequence both in and out of order.

Part 3

Combine both shapes and motions in an alternating sequence. For example:

Shape 1, Motion 1
Shape 2, Motion 2
Shape 3, Motion 3
Shape 4, Motion 4

Part 4

Small groups perform any or all of the parts for each other.

Lesson 2 - Dance and Sculptures

Part 1

Everyone dances freeform to music or drum. When the sound stops, everyone creates an individual frozen shape.

Part 2

In a circle, each student individually dances to the middle of the circle and back out. For the second turn, students dance individually into the middle of the circle, make a frozen shape, then dance back to their original place.

Part 3

One at a time, students dance into the circle and make a frozen shape attaching to shapes already there, to form a group sculpture. Begin with small groups of four or five and end with the entire group in a sculpture.

Lesson 3 - Combinations

Part 1

Individuals create shapes. Choose four shapes from individual shapes for group sequence. Entire group learns the sequence using 8 counts for each shape, then 4 counts, then 2 counts.

Part 2

A.   Students walk forward, beginning on the right foot, for 8 counts; backward for 8 counts, beginning right; sideways to the right (step right, close left) for 8 counts; sideways to the left (step left, close right) for 8 counts.

B.   Reduce entire pattern to 4 counts, then 2 counts, then 1 count.

Part 3 - Combining Parts 1 and 2

A.   Walk forward 8 counts. Hold shape 1 for 8 counts.
Walk backward 8 counts. Hold shape 2 for 8 counts.
Walk sideways right 8 counts. Hold shape 3 for 8 counts.
Walk sideways left 8 counts. Hold shape 4 for 8 counts.

B.   Reduce entire pattern to 4 counts, then 2 counts.

Part 4

Combine Parts 1, 2, and 3, and perform in small groups.

As mentioned before, the material in these sample lessons could actually be divided into multiple lessons depending upon the adaptations needed for a particular group. Each is process-oriented with potential for a performance product. As Margaret H'Doubler wrote: "To release and foster creativity is one of education's biggest challenges."

Resources

Effeldt, L. (1967). *A primer for choreographers.* Palo Alto: Mayfield Publishing Co.

H'Doubler, M. (1966). *Dance: A creative art experience.* Madison: The University of Wisconsin Press.

Joyce, M. (1973). *First steps in teaching creative dance.* Palo Alto: National Press Books.

Lockhart, A., & Pease, E. (1977). *Modern dance: Building and teaching lessons.* Dubuque: Wm. C. Brown Co., Publishers.

Murray, R.L. (1975). *Dance in elementary education* (3rd ed.). New York: Harper & Row.

Margot E. Faught is a dance/movement specialist in Indianapolis, Indiana.

Creative Dance for the Primary Child: A Progressive Approach

Vicki Faden Nicholes

Children are full of spontaneous creativity. To watch them at play is to marvel at imaginations in full drive. That instinctive seeking of discovery and that drive to move and explore make children natural participants in creative dance. The potential joy children find in dance, however, is determined by the quality of their learning experiences. Children must be instilled with fundamental tools and age-appropriate components of dance elements (body articulation, time, space, energy, and motion) that will allow them to make richer movement choices (see Appendix A[1]). Just as they must be taught developmentally appropriate movement skills and progressions, they must become part of a progressive learning experience that offers appropriate challenges in movement creativity.[2]

In presenting creative dance as a significant educational medium at the primary level, process must become a prime emphasis. The process of movement exploration, in fact, should receive more attention than the product (Laban, 1963, pp. 11-12). I suggest four levels of teacher-student interaction that give emphasis to that process, and thereby assist children in more fully discovering the joy of expression through movement.[3]

Level One

Level One emphasizes awareness, exploration, and discovery. The teacher assists students in the following endeavors:

1. Becoming familiar with the body instrument (parts and whole) and exploring the potential for movement.

2. Experiencing the fundamental elements of dance: body articulation, time, space, energy, and motion.

3. Becoming aware of various stimuli (kinesthetic, visual, auditory, tactile, olfactory, gustatory, affective, and cognitive [curricular]), and the body's ability to respond to a given stimulus.

4. Identifying an internal motivation to search for new possibilities.

5. Developing skills in listening, concentrating, and committing to a guided exploration learning experience.

6. Sensing the joy of motion while experiencing movement in a non-threatening environment.

Level One is a teacher-dependent experience with guided exploration of single movement tasks being the primary teaching approach. The teacher continually feeds students with helpful information or "tools": action words, spatial qualifiers, and effort qualifiers that will expand their movement vocabulary and stimulate innovative movement choices (see Appendix B) . The teacher also provides students with a variety of learning experiences in movement exploration and decision making that will allow them to experience the dance elements, thereby confidently advancing to Level Two. Selection of thematic material must be within their understanding if movement responses are to come, as they should, solely from the children (Russell, 1958, p. 54-55). Any theme outside their grasp will result more in teacher demonstration, which defeats the purpose of the experience.

Throughout interaction with the children, the teacher should deliver appropriately timed verbal cues that are simple and specific; must see the children as they work through each problem; look for "dead spaces" that reflect inhibitions or lack of understanding; and provide further motivation and movement qualifiers. This feeding, observation of response, secondary input, and enhanced response becomes a cycle or a "learning loop" (Sheffield, 1988); successfully applied, it will eliminate confusion and self-conscious decision making and result in more committed exploration of movement concepts.

Level One Example

Theme: Connecting partner shapes and transitions.

Objectives: Experience spatial and motional factors; develop body awareness, partner awareness, and cooperative skills.

Preliminary Work: The teacher guides the children through an exploration of a variety of shapes (twisted, tilted, pointed, up-side-down, etc.) and then asks the children to select a partner they can work well with, and proceeds with the following specific teaching cues.

Teaching Cues: "See if you and your partner can create exciting crooked shapes that connect to each other." Allow time for children to respond. "Look how spread out this connected shape is, and how narrow this one is. Here's one that is a tricky balancing connected shape." By describing what is seen, the teacher helps the children learn why their selected shapes are interesting and how they contrast the others. Comments on performance and commitment are also helpful in this learning stage. "Jenny and Cindy, I can tell that you have terrific focus and concentration. Your connected shape hasn't even wiggled!" The teacher continues to guide the children through an exploration of different kinds of connecting shapes, then proceeds to the next stage of the activity. "Wouldn't it be neat if we could make the transitions between our shapes as interesting as the shapes themselves? What is a transition?" The teacher allows for responses, and demonstrates the word to assist if necessary. "Can you move in very slow motion into a tilted connecting shape? Great! Now try it very quickly. Yes! Wow, Michael, you did that so quickly and kept your balance the whole time!"

Additional Teaching Suggestions: The teacher continues to give students a variety of action words, energy qualifiers, and spatial qualifiers to explore, and acknowledges the varieties of interpretations. As students begin to feel comfortable with the experience, they can advance to Level Two.

While there are no real "right" or "wrong" solutions to a movement task, there are definitely stronger solutions than others. If a student's response lacks interest, commitment, or risk taking, consider the following:

1. Provide other movement qualifiers that can be more easily understood or identified with.

2. Commend a student who has shown involvement and produced a response of even the slightest interest. This will elevate the confidence of one while encouraging others to participate and helping them expand their visualization of possible solutions.

3. Move with the students. Seeing the teacher move provides a great deal of motivation, and subtly assists students in broadening their own imaginative thinking.

4. Demonstrate a "weak" solution and have the students play the part of the teacher by suggesting temporal, spatial, or effort qualifiers that can make the shape or transition more interesting.

5. Contrast a weak solution with a strong solution. Have the children tell which is better and why.

6. Evaluate your movement qualifiers. Do they elicit responses that require commitment and risk taking?

7. Reconsider your overall theme. Is it too sophisticated for this particular population? If so, alter or simplify your idea.

It is natural and practical to spend more time at Level One than at the other stages in the primary grades. Level One provides the tools and necessary experience for developing problem solving skills while exploring a wide variety of movement stimuli. Students who are relatively young, learning disabled, or mentally handicapped need a single task approach. Teachers in tune with student needs and development will know when to take a child on to Level Two, where more lengthy and challenging movement problems can be introduced.

Level Two

Level Two emphasizes internalization and application of the tools for expression. The teacher assists students in the following endeavors:

1. Learning to take initiative in discovering feelings, ideas, and experiences to express through movement.

2. Developing skills in self-direction.

3. Developing divergent thinking skills, and discovering a variety of solutions to a given movement problem.

4. Learning to organize movement material, and thereby learning fundamentals of composition.

5. Beginning to comprehend and internalize the dance elements, which will enhance expressive capabilities.

Level Two is a teacher-student interdependent experience. The teacher gives the students a movement problem (a combination of movement tasks) to solve, and offers guidance and feedback as needed. The children are then given the chance to play with and practice using the tools they were exposed to in Level One. Movement problems should be specific enough to provide a comprehensible framework from which to work, yet open-ended enough to stimulate divergent thinking and physical response. It is through experiencing the problem solving process that students begin to internalize the dance elements and compositional skills that will allow their movement expression to mature. Here they start to see what does and does not work in the interpretation, through movement, of their thoughts and feelings.

Level Two Example

Theme: Connecting partner shapes and transitions.

Objectives: Experiencing, understanding, and internalizing spatial and motional factors; developing skill in problem solving.

Teaching Cues: "When you hear the music, begin working with your partner and create an action word transition into a connecting shape." Basic terms such as "action word," "transition," and "connecting shape" should have been introduced in Level One. "Keep the shapes and transitions going, and freeze when the music stops."

Additional Teaching Suggestions: If students seem to struggle, and movement choices become repetitive or stagnant, revert back to Level One and suggest more qualifiers to guide the students through the variety of movement choices available to them. Acknowledge committed effort, and point out exciting discoveries.

It is important that students be encouraged to explore a variety of solutions to a given movement problem. As they do this, they will begin to expand their movement vocabulary and be ready to advance to Level Three.

Level Three

Level Three emphasizes selecting and developing ideas. Students apply the skills necessary to give clearer form to an idea through movement. The teacher assists students in the following endeavors:

1. Developing convergent thinking skills, and learning to select and develop one solution among the many explored.
2. Developing skills in perceiving stimuli and using fundamental dance elements along with aesthetic judgment to respond to that stimuli through dance.
3. Increasing ability to manipulate the dance elements, and learning how that process enhances expressive capabilities.
4. Recognizing a developmental process in creating a dance composition.
5. Learning commitment to an idea.
6. Developing aesthetic perception and open-mindedness that allow creative activity to evolve.
7. Beginning to participate in evaluation.

Level Three is teacher-initiated and student-directed. The teacher provides the students with a movement stimulus and leaves the development up to them. However, the teacher maintains a supportive role and provides feedback when necessary. While Level Two relies primarily on improvisation, Level Three emphasizes form and the development of selected ideas. Level Three also challenges the students to repeat and perform what has been practiced.

This stage is the most sophisticated of the first three levels and should not be presented too early or, in most cases, to grades K-2. If students have not developed necessary problem solving skills, this level can potentially frustrate rather than foster creativity. Students should have a good grasp of the dance elements and their components and be able to explore and incorporate them as they support a given theme. Careful selection and presentation of a compositional stimulus is also a must. Well-defined, thematically appropriate compositional problems enable students to focus more on the excitement of process and to overcome their self-consciousness. Students who actively progress as participants and observers in Levels One and Two find self-expression at Level Three comfortable and encouraging.

Level Three Example

Theme: Connecting partner shapes and transitions.

Objectives: Enhance skill in selecting and developing the best ideas from the many explored; develop a sense of composition by selecting a beginning, middle and end; learn to remember sequences of movement; develop a heightened sense of performance quality and commitment to an idea.

Teaching Cues: "Working with your partner, create a short dance that has three dependent and connecting shapes, and an action word transition between each shape."

Additional Teaching Suggestions: The teacher should instill the importance of cultivating shapes and transitions. The amount of teacher input at this point, however, should be highly selective and only rendered if the students need clarification. The teacher may, if needed, specify the compositional challenge by suggesting that 1) each connecting shape occur at a different point in the room, 2) the shapes themselves move, or 3) the transitions encompass many actions such as spinning, jumping, rolling, freezing, etc.

Level Four

A creative experience that emphasizes self-initiation and refinement. The teacher assists students in the following endeavors:

1. Being willing to exercise initiative and self-direction in the creative process.
2. Adding refinement to the fundamentals of composition.
3. Developing performance skills.
4. Developing good judgment in evaluating creative work and in modifying that work according to need.

Level Four is student-initiated and student-directed. Students generate and develop their own ideas. The teacher, however, provides feedback and guidance when needed. Level Four belongs to the students who have shown a mature willingness and ability to commit to an idea for an extended period of time. The past involvement of students in the stages of awareness, exploration, discovery, internalization, application, selection, and development will also determine their readiness for Level Four.

Because creative activity at Level Four is student generated and directed, there can exist an underlying fear of failure, since students are putting themselves and their ideas on display. The teacher, then, has a highly significant role as one who establishes a comfortable, nonthreatening, noncompetitive environment that fosters creative work. The teacher must help students realize that success does not come solely from work produced, but from what has been given to the total creative process.

We see, then, with each progressive level of creative dance activity the changing role the teacher assumes in nurturing a student's natural creative instincts. The position in Level One as initiator and guider becomes less dominant with each advancing level, although expertise remains available through feedback. Students, in turn, become increasingly independent in initiating, directing, and evaluating their own creative activity. Process becomes the key to that successful independence, which in turn opens a door to greater enrichment. While students can seek and explore on their own, independent of teacher input, they must be guided and taught fundamental principles if they are to give significant form to worthwhile ideas. Taught how to shape their thoughts and creative instincts through quality guidance in a process-oriented learning environment, they will discover broader avenues of expression through dance.

Appendix A

ELEMENTS OF DANCE [4]

Body Articulation

A. Working in isolated parts.

  1. Upper body: head, neck, chest, upper spine, shoulders, arms, hands, and fingers
  2. Lower body: lower back, pelvis, lower abdomen, legs, feet, and toes
  3. Right side vs. left side
  4. Upper body vs. lower body
  5. Trunk vs. limbs

B. Working as a synergistic whole.

C. Initiating movement with various body parts.

D. Supporting weight with various body parts.

E. Leading movement with various body parts.

F. Assuming different body positions: standing, sitting, kneeling, crouching, etc.

G. Assuming different body relationships (to own body, to another individual, to a group): mirroring, conceptual mirroring, shadowing, echoing, contrasting, linking, touching, lifting, etc.

Time

A. Metric Rhythm.

    1. Meter
        a. duple 2/4, 4/4
        b. triple 3/4, 6/8
        c. mixed meter (advanced))
        d. accumulative (advanced)
        e. decumulative (advanced)
        f. resultant (advanced)

    2. Accent
        a. predictable down beat
        b. random
        c. syncopated (advanced)

    3. Tempo
        a. fast
        b. slow
        c. increase
        d. decrease

B. Breath Rhythm (nonmetrical): personal timing and use of irregular fasts, slows, and pauses.

C. Occupational Rhythm: the rhythm of exertion and recovery identified by Laban and found in such working actions as sawing, chopping, pulling a rope, hammering, digging, sewing, etc.

Space

A. Shape (the body's design in space): linear, rounded, twisted, bent, pointed, symmetrical, asymmetrical, etc.

B. Negative Space (unoccupied space surrounding the body or between body parts).

    1. Two-dimensional space created by the placement of the body parts.
    2. Volume or the three-dimensional space created by the shaping of body parts.

C. Shape Factors (motional shaping of space versus still shape [advanced]).

1. Shape-flow: body-oriented growing and shrinking that promotes a flow of shape changes in the body.

2. Directional Movement: spoking (an outward reaching of the limbs away from the torso) and arcing (a flat arc-like movement).

3. Shaping: constant muscular/joint adaptation to the volume or three dimensionality of space.

D. Personal Space (kinesphere) or range: near, middle, or far "reach" space.

E. Focus/Graining: with eyes, body parts, or whole body.

F. Levels: low, medium, high.

G. Directions: forward, backward, sideways, up, down.

H. Spatial Relationships: near, far, over, under, beside, in front of, behind, surrounding, meeting, parting, weaving, etc.

I. Extension of the Body (adding a prop or costume).

J. Planes (advanced): vertical (door); sagittal (wheel); and horizontal (table).

K. Spatial Tensions and Countertensions (advanced).

1. Dimensions

    a. forward/backward (sagittal dimension)
    b. left side/right side (horizontal dimension)
    c. up/down (vertical dimension)

2. Diameters (two dimensionality) combining two dimensions to create any of the following:
    a. in the vertical plane (high/low plus side/side)
        left side high to right side low
        left side low to right side high
    b. in the horizontal plane (side/side plus front/back)
        left forward middle to right backward middle
        left backward middle to right forward middle
    c. in the sagittal plane (front/back plus high/low)
        forward high to backward low
        forward low to backward high

3. Diagonals: combining the three dimensions to create any of the following:

     a. left forward high to right backward low
     b. right forward high to left backward low
     c. left forward low to right backward high
     d. right forward low to left backward high

L. Pathways.

    1. Floor pathways (straight, curved, zig-zag, spiraling).
    2. Air patterns: upper body motional designs in space; space writing.

Energy/Effort

A. Qualities of Movement.

    1. Smooth Flow: a smooth, even release of energy. Flow may be free or bound.
    2. Percussive: a great deal of sudden force resulting in a momentary stop.
    3. Suspended: defying gravity in an "effortless" movement; a potential release of energy.
    4. Collapsing: a release of tension (energy), and giving in to gravity.
    5. Pendular: a suspension, a collapse, and a follow-through along the path of an arc, with a momentary suspension before repetition.
    6. Explosive: a sudden burst of energy.
    7. Impulse: a sudden surge of energy followed by free or bound flow.
    8. Vibratory: a release of energy in short sporadic bursts.

B. Effort Actions.

    1. Pressing: a strong, direct, sustained action such as pulling or pushing.
    2. Flicking: a light, indirect, sudden action such as quivering or pushing.
    3. Slashing: a strong, indirect, sudden action such as throwing or flinging.
    4. Dabbing: a light, direct, sudden action such as darting or pinching.
    5. Wringing: a strong, indirect, sustained action such as twisting or squirming.
    6. Gliding: a light, direct, sustained action such as brushing or stroking.
    7. Punching: a strong, direct, sudden action such as shoving or lunging.
    8. Floating: a light, indirect, sustained action such as hovering or flying.

Motion

A. Axial Movements: bending, stretching, twisting, pushing, pulling, shaking, etc.

B. Locomotor Movements (traveling through space).
1. Walking
2. Running
3. Hopping
4. Jumping
5. Leaping
6. Skipping
7. Galloping
8. Sliding
9. Nonpedal (rolling, crawling, slithering, etc.)

C. Combining Locomotor and Axial Movements simultaneously (e.g., running while spoking the arms).

D. Locomotor and Axial Movement Sequences (e.g., slide-freeze-bend-twist-fall-roll-jump up-shake).

E. Falls (all directions; from standing, kneeling, or sitting).

Appendix B

Action Words (the "what")

arch	balance	bend	bounce	brush	burst	catch
chop	climb	collapse	connect	crawl	cringe	crinkle
crumble	crush	curl	dangle	dash	dodge	drag
droop	envelop	explode	fall	flap	flick	flip
float	flop	fly	fold	freeze	gallop	glide
grasp	hang	hop	hover	inflate	intertwine	jerk
jiggle	jump	kick	kneel	lean	leap	lift
lunge	melt	ooze	perch	pierce	pivot	point
press	pull	quiver	reach	rebound	repel	revolve
ricochet	ripple	rock	roll	rotate	run	scatter
scamper	scoop	scoot	scratch	shake	shatter	shiver
shrink	shrivel	sink	skid	slide	slip	slither
soar	spin	spiral	splash	spread	spring	squirm
squeeze	stagger	stir	stretch	struggle	suspend	sway
swing	swivel	tap	thrust	tilt	tiptoe	topple
toss	trace	trip	tumble	turn	twirl	twitch
uncurl	vibrate	walk	weave	whip	wiggle	wind
wither	wobble	wring				

Spatial Qualifiers (the "where")

angled	around	away	backward	beside
between	circling	curving	diagonally	far
forward	high	inside	low	narrow
near	off	on	outside	over
sideways	spiraling	through	towards	under
wide	zig-zag			

Effort Qualifiers (the "how")

abruptly	carefully	droopy	explosively	firmly
heavily	jerkily	lightly	loudly	percussively
prickly	quickly	quietly	softly	sloppily
slowly	smoothly	sporadically	vivaciously	

Appendix C

LESSON PLAN PROGRESSIONS

Movement Theme I: Exploring poetry through movement.

Objectives: Identify and explore the movement potential of words and their images by manipulating a scarf; transfer the quality of the scarf to the body.

Equipment: Light-weight scarf for each child; poem: "I Can Be Many Things"; tape player; a light and airy "new age" musical selection.

Age: Levels One and Two/K-2; Levels One through Four/2-6 (for Levels One and Two, age-appropriate poetry and props should be selected).

Level One

1. Ask the children to share something they like to imagine.

2. Give the children scarves. Challenge them to use their imaginations and explore different things the scarf can become. Let them observe each other and guess how they see the scarves being used.

3. Explore the following poem by manipulating the scarves. Use a light and airy new age musical selection as background accompaniment.

I Can Be Many Things

I can be many things, many things, you'll see:
A soft summer breeze,
A falling leaf,
Or a fiery blaze.

A battling sword,
A bird of grace,
A ball to toss,
A hiding place.

And a hat I'll be on your head to rest.
What kind of something can you be? Let's see.

Vicki Nicholes

As you introduce each new phrase, qualify the exploration to assure that the children experience the greatest possible number of movement choices:

"How can you move your whole body with your scarf to blow like a summer breeze? How would you move if that breeze became a stronger wind? Show me how that wind can take you jumping and spinning in the air. Let that wind become a soft breeze again that slowly spins you down to the ground and back up again."

Each phrase, then, is specifically explored in terms of its time, space, energy, and motion potential. After two or three phrases are explored, go back and add these together so the children can internalize the concepts and get a sense of sequence. At the completion of the exploration, add music and speak the poem in its entirety. Even at this point, specific movement qualifiers may be needed if students have hesitant moments.

Level Two

As you read aloud the poem "I Can Be Many Things," have the children use a scarf and explore on their own each word and image. They choose which and how many body actions, spatial, energy, and time factors they want to explore. Their experience at Level One should allow this Level Two experience to occur with little teacher input.

Level Three

Share a selected number of children's poems with the students. Assign them to work in small groups and choose one of the poems to explore. They must determine which words have the most action potential, how they want to explore and develop the words, and how to connect them into a meaningful whole.

Level Four

Have the students write their own poetry and explore it through movement.

Movement Theme II: Pictures and their properties.

Objectives: Use visual stimuli as a way of eliciting creative movement responses; identify elements seen in pictures such as size, shape, texture, color, etc.; transfer the properties of pictures into movement patterns, shapes, or locomotor progressions.

Equipment: Paintings, photographs, or pictures from magazines; a variety of magazines that can be cut up; construction paper; scissors; glue; tape player; a lively new age musical selection.

Age: Early childhood and older.

Level One

1. Show the students a painting, photograph, or a picture from a magazine. Ask them to identify sizes, shapes, colors, textures, etc., that they see.

2. Explore the selected properties of the picture through movement. Add music.

3. Display, one at a time, three other pictures, all of which have contrasting elements. Explore, through movement, each additional picture. Perform all four "picture" dances using different music for each. Each dance should include differing movement qualities, shapes, locomotor actions, and spatial patterns that can be easily distinguished from each other, just as the pictures can be distinguished from each other.

Suggested paintings/photographs:

Photo: a snowy scene.
Properties: cold; slippery; white; imprints in the snow made by people or other objects.
Movement Associations: shivering; sliding; negative space shapes to represent snow flakes; space writing to represent imprints in the snow.

Photo: a scene showing pine trees.
Properties: sticky, thick, slow moving sap.
Movement Associations: slow moving motions; slow dripping actions; bound flow motions that stick to another person and pull away; group shapes that stick to each other creating large empty spaces for flowing water (a child performing flowing, swirling actions)

to rush through each of the created holes and disconnect the sticking shapes as it passes through.

Painting: Starry Night by Vincent Van Gogh.
Properties: sleeping village; pointed church steeple; towering cypress trees; swirling sky; golden moon; waves from the stars.
Movement Associations: reclining shapes; pointed shapes that grow into towers; towers created by two or more children together; waving actions; swirling actions.

Level Two

Show the children a painting. Ask them to identify, as a group, three interesting elements of the painting and their shape/motion possibilities. Have the class explore, on their own, shapes and motions of the three identified elements in the painting. Add music, and indicate when to perform each of the three element interpretations.

Level Three

Design space maps. Bring magazines for the students to cut up. Also provide scissors, glue, and a piece of construction paper for each child. Instruct the children to cut out five pictures they find with interesting shape and motion possibilities. Have them arrange and glue the pictures onto the paper. The paper will represent the dance space of the room they are in. Indicate that where they paste each picture determines the location in the room that they perform the elements of that picture. Instruct the students to draw a floor pattern (straight lines, scallops, zig-zags, etc.) to connect each picture. Let the children develop dance movements that are associated with each picture. Challenge them to progress through the floor patterns of their space map by developing a property of each picture into a locomotor movement. Give assistance when needed. Let the children show each other their maps and then perform the map dances, one or two students at a time.

Level Four

Have the students base a composition on something visual (a photo, painting, sculpture, nature observation, etc.).

Endnotes

1. Laban identifies eight basic movement themes as age-appropriate for primary children (p. 29-33). These themes coincide with the fundamental dance elements presented in Appendix A.
2. This creative movement teaching model for physical educators utilizing levels of progression had its inception in 1988 in a cooperative project with Fran Cleland, assistant professor of physical education

at the University of New Hampshire. The progressive approach to teaching creative movement I introduce here is a model I have since developed for the dance specialist.

3. See appendix C for full lesson plans that illustrate the four levels of creative involvement.

4. Adapted from Rudolf Laban's effort-shape and space harmony factors and Shirley Ririe's Movement Chart (p. 31-33). Shape factors, developed by Laban's protege Warren Lamb, are explained by Cecily Dell in *A Primer for Movement Description* (p. 44-58). For space harmony factors, see Dell, *Space Harmony*.

5. All components designated as advanced are more suitable for students beyond primary age.

References

Dell, C. (1977). *A primer for movement description: Using effort-shape and supplementary concepts* (2nd ed.). New York: Dance Notation Bureau.

Dell, C. (Rev. A. Crow & I. Bartenieff). (1977). *Space harmony: Basic terms*. New York: Dance Notation Bureau.

Laban, R. (1963). *Modern educational dance* (2nd ed.) London: Macdonald.

National Dance Association. (1988). *Dance curricula guidelines for K-12*. Reston, VA: AAHPERD.

Ririe, S. *Dance for children*. Course manual. Salt Lake City: University of Utah.

Ritson, R. J. (1986). Creative dance: A systematic approach to teaching children. *Journal of Physical Education, Recreation and Dance, 57,* 67-72, 78.

Russell, J. (1958). *Modern dance in education*. London: Macdonald.

Sheffield, K. B. (1988). Feedback in modern dance: The development, presentation, and application of a model which illustrates the function of feedback in learning, performing, and teaching modern dance." M.A. thesis. Brigham Young University.

Tucker, J. L., & Kline, R.L. (Eds.). (n.d.). *Dance: A Maryland curricular framework.* Baltimore: Maryland State Depart of Education.

Weiler, V., et al. (1988). *A guide to curricular planning in dance*. Madison: Wisconsin Department of Public Instruction.

Vicki Faden Nicholes is an instructor of dance at Brigham Young University-Hawaii in Laie, Hawaii.

Imagery Use in Children's Dance

Lynnette Young Overby

Mental imagery is a very useful technique for teaching dance to young children. It is an important means of reinforcing their movement vocabulary and expanding their skill development, retention, and creative development. Imagery contributes to the development of skill by eliciting specific qualities of movement. Creativity is developed through the exploration of images. Imagery enhances the child's memory for movement by attaching meaningfulness to the movement.

Imagery and the Developing Child

Learning theorists and imagery theorists are in agreement that mental imagery should be an integral component in the learning and development of young children. Mental imagery processes and verbal symbolism appear in young children at about 1 1/2 years of age, as they move from the sensorimotor stage to the preoperational stage (Wadsworth, 1979). As the child develops, mediating responses like mental imagery can influence the child's behavior (Piaget & Inhelder, 1971). Research evidence indicates that imagery may operate to promote learning and memory in children as young as preschool and kindergarten age (Pavio, 1971).

Imagery and Movement

Research focused on the effectiveness of imagery in the acquisition and performance of motor skill learning has demonstrated the power of imagery as a facilitator of learning in adult subjects (Feltz & Landers, 1983). Fewer studies have utilized young children, and none to my knowledge focus on the metaphorical imagery used most often by creative dance teachers. However, the anecdotal reports of dance teachers would certainly attest to the power of imagery used with young children. A survey of dance teachers indicated that imagery is used to a great extent during improvisational activities (Overby, 1990).

Movement imagery involves components of imagery ability and imagery use. Imagery ability refers to certain general traits which may be developed with imagery use. Kinesthetic imagery and visual imagery are two movement imagery abilities. Kinesthetic imagery involves imagining what a movement feels like. An example of a kinesthetic imagery teaching cue would be to have a child move slowly as if moving through deep water. An example of a visual imagery cue would be to have the children imagine seeing a movement sequence performed perfectly in their mind's eye. In a recent study, Fishburne (1990) reported that both kinesthetic and visual movement imagery increase with age.

Indirect Imagery Use

Imagery use is dictated by the objective of the teaching/learning situation. Unstructured dance classes like creative children's dance classes utilize indirect imagery, defined as a metaphorical image, indirectly related to a specific movement (Dimondstein, 1971; Studd, 1983). An indirect image involves relating some external object or idea, intended to enhance the quality of movement. An example of an indirect image would be to ask the child to "imagine ice cream melting in the hot sun as you move slowly from standing to a lying down position."

Direct Imagery Use

When the objective of the dance teaching is to learn a structured dance, e.g., folk, square, or choreographed movement sequence, the child's memory may be enhanced by the use of direct imagery. Direct imagery involves imagining and mentally rehearsing a specific movement or movement sequence. The large majority of research studies of mental practice imagery have incorporated direct imagery. Many positive results have been reported. As many teachers in the public schools have to prepare children for assembly programs, PTA programs, and community functions, the use of direct imagery could have a positive effect on the child's memory and self-confidence.

Guidelines for the Use of Imagery with Young Children

Imagery Use in Unstructured Dance Forms

Children's dance literature is rich with examples of imagery use because it is an integral part of the dance teacher's pedagogy. However, if not utilized properly, imagery may be detrimental to the ultimate objective of dance education, which is expression through bodily movement.

Several authors of children's dance books and articles have written about the use of indirect metaphorical imagery (Dimondstein, 1971; Joyce, 1983; Murray, 1975; Purcell, 1990; Stinson, 1988). All agree that the development, exploration, and learning of movement must be the primary focus of imagery use with young children. Imagery should be used as a helper in increasing the movement vocabulary of the child.

Dimondstein refers to the metaphoric nature of imagery:

Although imagery frequently takes its sources from nature, the sense of focusing on certain attributes or features of the metaphoric power of dance is that it shapes nature's forms into movement forms. Thus, when children are released from inhibiting instructions, such as move like a frog or move as the poem says, they are freed from literal mimetics to engage in the metaphoric process. (p. 220)

Ruth Murray provides some examples of imagery that may either grow out of or elicit movement.

"The movement you are doing is heavy and slow. Does it remind you of anything?" or "I'm thinking of something that is floppy and loose." "Can you think of something, too, and let us guess what you are by the way you move?" or "Can you move like something scary? Is it huge and strong, soft and slinky, twisted, jerky, stiff, crawly?" (p. 96)

Mary Joyce provides the following examples of three phases in the use of metaphorical imagery.

1. Images that lead to movement: "Make your back round like an orange." 2. Images that arise from movement: "What else do you know that is round?" 3. Images as a basis for movement: "What kind of movement might an orange do?" (p. 23)

Sue Stinson gives examples of the appropriate use of imagery with preschool children:

Even when I work with animals as thematic material, I do not ordinarily ask children to pretend to be any animal—or, for that matter, to be the wind or a melting candle, either. This is not only because it is limiting (there are many ways to jump besides the way a rabbit jumps) but because dance should help us see beyond movement that is ordinary and expected."

In order for images to work with young children they must be related to events and experiences of the particular child. Images must be a part of the child's background and experiences. Objects, feelings, and/or events cannot be used metaphorically unless the child has had sufficient experience with the images. Children must "see, hear, touch, smell and it is through these faculties that experiences and impressions are transformed in movement to create images in dance" (Dimondstein, 1975, p. 222). Images should be discussed in terms of their characteristics and relationship to movement (Purcell, 1990).

An appropriate use of imagery would be to ask the children to dance about things such as happiness, horses, machines, or witches. The children will begin to use pantomime and movement will be secondary to acting out the "things." The images should help the movement to develop. For example, "skip and jump as if you are happy," or "gallop, like a horse," or "vibrate your arms and legs like washing machines." The use of indirect imagery as a teaching tool for children's dance appears to proceed in the following manner:

1. Providing activities which encourage children to develop an awareness and sensitivity to sensory phenomena around them.

2. Discussing specific images of objects, feelings, and/or events in terms of their characteristics and relationship to movement.

3. Exploring specific images through movement.

4. Structuring the movement exploration into a dance.

Examples of Metaphorical Imagery

Indirect imagery can be used to explore dance movements, use the qualities of an object, and inspire dance movements (Purcell, 1990).

1. *Objective:* Use qualities of an object to enhance the kinesthetic and visual awareness of maintaining a strong shape.
Image: Living sculpture (Joyce, 1983, pp. 89-91)
You are going to be living sculpture. Do you know what a sculpture is? I am going to unveil all these new works of art, and we shall watch the latest masterpieces of living sculpture. Take a low shape now and imagine yourself covered with a black cloth. As the music starts, imagine I am unveiling you for the first time, and begin to move slowly with muscles up through space. When you have moved to a high level, then slowly return to a low level. Do as many movements as you can between high and low. Then hold your low shape until everyone finishes.

2. *Objective:* Use of a mirror image to inspire the execution of sustained movement.
Image: Mirrors
Look at the person next to you. If that person is looking at you, go to that person. Now face your partner and let us imagine that we are looking in a mirror. We will perform slow sustained movement. One of you must become the leader. Now let us begin with arm movement; now add torso movement; now change levels. Let your partner lead now. We should be able to tell who is leading and who is following. *Extensions:* Add music and have children stand still at the beginning and fade music as they come to a still, ending position.

3. *Objective:* Basic jump—exploring dance movements.
Image: Feel as though you are being lifted by a string that extends from the spine through the head. Push away from the floor (Hawkins, 1964).

4. *Objective:* Heavy movement—using the qualities of the object.
Image: Clay
Change into many different shapes, while maintaining the heavy quality and connection of clay (Weiner & Lidstone, 1969, pp. 41-42).

Imagery Use in Structured Dance Forms

Children may be given relaxation training and imagery training to enhance their use of imagery for mental practice. In this type of imagery use, the children would be directed to form a mental image of a specific movement sequence, floor pattern, or body position. For this type of imagery to work, the children should have physically practiced the movement. They will be unable to utilize direct imagery if they are not familiar with seeing and experiencing the movement.

Children could be given specific times to use direct imagery. For example, children could be directed to use imagery before they go to sleep at night, before and after a rehearsal, and when they are ill and unable to physically practice.

Children could be directed to watch a particular movement sequence then spend a few seconds imagining the sequence. If performed to music, the music should be played while they imagine moving through the different parts of the dance. Mental practice does not take the place of physical practice, but can be an effective complement. The following imagery training sequence could prove helpful in the child's ability to utilize direct imagery.

1. Have children relax.
2. Have children practice utilizing all of the senses and emotions as they imagine specific people and objects from their environment.
3. Have children practice imagining specific movements.

Young children age three to eight are developmentally able to utilize imagery in their learning experiences. Mental imagery in children's dance can be used to enhance creative expressions, explore dance movements, and inspire dance movements. In structured dance forms, imagery can enhance memory and self-confidence.

Imagery can capture the child's interest and stimulate the child to think and feel. Imagery is the catalyst that makes possible the bridging of movement-as-function and movement-as-expression so that the child is not merely imagining but feeling experiencing, if even for a moment, that exhilaration of being one and the same time both the creator and the creation, the shaper and shaped (Weiner & Lidstone, 1969, p. 97).

Images that Work

The participants in the workshop shared examples of images that work well for them and their students.

Objective: To improve posture, a slouched back
Image: Banana back—let's pull up and eliminate the banana back
Contributor: Candy Brown, The Studio of Dance, Olathe, Kansas

Objective: Arm placement, second position
Image: Hugging a huge teddy bear—so large you can't get your arms half way around
Contributor: Judy Herridge, physical education consultant, Surrey School District, British Columbia

Objective: Use turnout

Image: Draw a happy face on the inside surface of the heel. When you tendo front, you can see the happy face; to the side, the teacher can see the happy face; to the back, the happy face is looking at the floor.

Contributor: Dianne Homan, Portland, Oregon

Objective: Develop imaginative ways to respond to an environment

Image: You are making your way through an area of jello which is neck deep.

Contributor: Robert Lee Kidd, III, Eisenhower Elementary School, Norman, Oklahoma

Objective: Releve

Image: Stand high on your toes and reach for the stars. Stars are all over the sky. Touch as many as you can.

Contributor: Carol Kay Harsell, founder, Kinderdance International, Melbourne Beach, Florida

Objective: To make a circle

Image: Blow up a big, beautiful balloon. Children select color and design, hold hands, and breathe deeply as they walk backwards to expand the circle.

Contributor: Starr Edwards, Kinderdance Franchises, Long Beach, California

References

Dimondstein, G. (1971). *Children dance in the classroom.* New York: Macmillan Company.

Feltz, D.L., & Landers, D.M. (1983). The effects of mental practice on motor skill learning and performance: A meta-analysis. *Journal of Sport Psychology, 5,* 25-57.

Fishburne, G.J. (1990, October). Imagery, movement and children: What do we know? Paper presented at annual conference of the Canadian Society of Psychomotor Learning and Sport Psychology, Windsor, Ontario.

Hawkins, A.M. (1964). *Creating through dance.* Englewood Cliffs, NJ: Prentice Hall.

Joyce, M. (1973). *First steps in teaching creative dance.* Palo Alto, CA: National Press Books.

Murray, R.L. (1975). *Dance in elementary education.* New York: Harper and Row.

Overby, L.Y. (1990). The use of imagery by dance teachers: Development and implementation of two research instruments. *Journal of Physical Education, Recreation and Dance, 61*(9), 24-27.

Pavio, A. (1971). *Imagery and verbal processes*. New York: Holt, Reinhart and Winston.

Piaget, J., & Inhelder, B. (1971). *Mental imagery in the child*. New York: Basic Books.

Purcell, T. (1990) The use of imagery in children's dance—making it work. *Journal of Physical Education, Recreation and Dance, 61*(9), 22-23.

Stinson, S. (1988). *Dance for young children: Finding the magic in movement*. Reston, VA: AAHPERD.

Wadsworth, B.J. (1979). *Piaget's theory of cognitive development*. New York: Longman, Inc.

Wiener, J., & Lidstone, J. (1969). *Creative movement for children*. New York: Van Nostrand Reinhold Company.

Lynette Young Overby is assistant professor in the Department of Physical Education and Exercise Sciences at Michigan State University. She was formerly director of the Center for Imagery and Motor Behavior at Howard University in Washington, D.C. She is chair of the Research Committee of the National Dance Association. Her research interest is primarily focused on the relationship of imagery to motor behavior.

Motor Creativity and Self-Concept in Young Learning Disabled Boys

Omar Holguin and Claudine Sherrill

Learning disabled students are a specific group of handicapped individuals who have negative self-perceptions (Kistner, Haskett, White, & Robbins, 1987; Sherrill & Pyfer, 1985). Recognizing and utilizing learning disabled individuals' creativity can help to overcome this perception, or self-concept. Several researchers (Jaben, Treffinger, Whelan, Hudson, Stainback, & Stainback, 1982; Paget, 1979; Sherrill, 1986, Hellison, 1973; Schatz & Buckmaster, 1984) have suggested examining the relationship between creativity and measures of the affective domain, particularly self-concept. However, in contrast with these researchers, Harter (1988) does not believe that creativity is related to self-concept.

Method

Subjects

Subjects were 7- and 8-year-old boys ($\underline{M}$ = 7.96 years, $\underline{SD}$ = .54) from six public school systems located in the Dallas-Denton-Ft. Worth metroplex. These children had IQs within one standard deviation (i. e., 15 or 16 points) of the normative mean (i. e., 100 points) as measured by several IQ tests, and had no other handicapping conditions, such as emotional disturbances or physical impairments. IQ scores ranged from 85 to 118. Random samples of thirty 7-year-olds and thirty 8-year-olds were drawn from a pool of 86 learning disabled boys, ages 7 and 8 years. A preliminary check for outliers revealed that one subject had scores too extreme to be included in the sample and this necessitated an adjustment of the sample sizes to 29 for each age group (Wynne, 1982).

Instruments

The Torrance Test of Thinking Creatively in Action and Movement provided measures of motor creativity and yielded separate scores for fluency, originality, imagination, and total motor creativity. These scores were derived from four activities. The first, third, and fourth activities were scored for fluency and originality, and the second activity was scored for imagination. Fluency was defined as the ability to produce alternative ways of moving. Originality was defined as the ability to move in novel, unique, or unusual ways. Imagination was the ability to pretend and assume unaccustomed roles. The fluency, originality, and imagination were standardized and combined for total motor creativity as described in the test manual (Torrance, 1981).

This test was individually administered. For the first activity the child was asked to run or walk across the room in as many ways as possible. The second activity included six pretend situations. For example, the child was asked to pretend being a snake crawling in the grass. The third activity required that the child demonstrate all the ways to put a paper cup in a trash can. For the fourth activity the child played with and found different uses for a paper cup.

The Torrance Test of Thinking Creatively in Action and Movement (TCAM) has been evaluated for its psychometric properties with various groups of children. Content validity is reported by Torrance (1981) and supported by test reviewers (Mitchell, 1985). With nonhandicapped children as subjects research on criterion validity has yielded significant correlation coefficients between the TCAM and several measures: (a) .58 with a Piagetian measure of divergent problem solving (Reisman, Floyd, & Torrance, 1981), (b) .51 with a motor creativity videotaped protocol (Bonatis, 1986), and (c) .40 and .46 with three measures of humor (Erickson, 1977). For young learning disabled boys the TCAM is an age-related measure, $r = -.40$, total motor creativity and age in months (Holguin & Sherrill, 1990a). Various researchers (Jay, 1987; Lubin & Sherrill, 1980; Warger & Kleman, 1986) have concluded that using various creativity programs (e.g., guided movement exploration, dance, and creative dramatics) scores from the Torrance Test of Thinking Creatively in Action and Movement improved for various groups of disabled children (e.g., preschool handicapped, prekindergarten deaf, and severely behaviorally disordered children), which gives this instrument predictive validity. Test-retest reliability studies of preschool children with intervals of 1 to 14 days between testing have resulted in coefficients of .95 (Lubin, 1979) and .84 (Torrance, 1981).

Reliability coefficients from studies with young learning disabled boys were .89 for test-retest reliability and .79 for internal consistency reliability (Holguin & Sherrill, 1989). The Torrance Test of Thinking Creatively in Action and Movement has been shown to be an administratively feasible tool for measuring motor creativity in young learning disabled boys in terms of time (Holguin & Sherrill, 1989).

The Pictorial Scale of Perceived Competence and Acceptance (Pictorial Scale) was designed to be a developmentally appropriate measure of self-concept in young children (Harter & Pike, 1984). Separate scores for academic self-concept and physical self-concept are provided by this instrument, in addition to the children's perceptions of maternal and peer acceptance.

This instrument was administered individually to each child by an examiner who used pictures to elicit responses concerning feelings of self-concept and no writing, speaking, or reading was required from the child in the testing process. Writing, speaking, and reading have often proven difficult for both the young child and learning disabled child. Reseachers have demonstrated that the Pictorial Scale is a valid and reliable measure of self-concept for both the young nondisabled child and learning disabled child (Harter & Pike, 1984; Holguin & Sherrill, 1990b).

Data Collection and Treatment

All testing was conducted indoors at the subjects' own schools. The motor creativity and self-concept tests were administered first to equal numbers of 7- and 8-year-olds to prevent order effects.

Before analyzing the data for relationships between variables a pair of preliminary steps were taken: Certain statistical assumptions had to be met and tests for significant differences were applied to see if the two age groups could be combined into one sample (Tabachnick & Fidell, 1989). An outlier was found which violated one of the assumptions so the subject was eliminated from the sample of 7-year-olds. To maintain equal sample sizes for the tests for significant differences a subject was randomly eliminated from the 8-year-old sample.

To see if the two age groups could be combined into one sample, tests for significant differences were applied. Hotelling's T^2 (which were converted to F values) and a series of univariate t tests (with the Bonferroni technique) were used in the examination for group differences. The Hotelling's T^2 analysis indicated no significant differences across the motor creativity values, $F(3, 54) = 2.16$, $p = .10$, and across the self-concept values, $F(2, 55) = .59$, $p = .56$. No significant differences were found among the t tests at the .05 level of significance: (a) fluency, $t = 0.47$; (b) originality, $t = -0.32$; (c) imagination, $t = 0.54$; (d) academic self-concept, $t = -0.61$; and (e) physical self-concept, $t = -1.08$.

Because no significant differences were found between the age groups across the motor creativity and self-concept variables, the subjects were placed into one sample of 7- and 8-year-old learning disabled boys ($N = 58$) which was ready for the examination of relationships between the motor creativity and self-concept variables.

Results and Discussion

The Pearson product correlation technique was used to determine relationships between the motor creativity and self-concept variables. Coefficients between the two sets of variables ranged from -.08 to .15, but none of the values were significant at the .05 level. These findings contradict the position held by many researchers (Jaben et al., 1982; Paget, 1979; Sherrill, 1986, Hellison, 1973; Schatz & Buckmaster, 1984), but this study's findings support Harter's (1988) belief that creativity and self-concept are not related.

Replication of this study with young learning disabled boys and other populations of young children is necessary before any definitive conclusions can be made about the relationship between creativity and self-concept.

Another suggestion for further study is to examine the relationship between motor creativity and motivation orientation (Moustakas, 1967; Silon & Harter, 1985).

References

Bonatis, G. (1986). *The TWU motor creativity rating scale: A validation study.* Unpublished master's thesis, Texas Woman's University, Denton.

Erickson, J. G. (1977). A study of the verbal productive humor of preschool children. *Dissertation Abstracts International,* 38A, 5999. (University Microfilms Order No. 70-03984)

Harter, S. (1988). Issues in the assessment of the self-concept of children and adolescents. In La Greca (Ed.), *Childhood assessment: Through the eyes of a child.* Boston: Allyn & Bacon.

Harter, S., & Pike, R. (1984). The pictorial scale of perceived competence and social acceptance for young children. *Child Development, 55,* 1969-1982.

Hellison, D. R. (1973). *Humanistic physical education.* Englewood Cliffs, NJ: Prentice-Hall.

Holguin, O., & Sherrill, C. (1989). Use of a motor creativity test with young learning disabled boys. *Perceptual and Motor Skills, 69,* 1315-1318.

Holguin, O., & Sherrill, C. (1990a). Correlates between age and the Torrance test of thinking creatively in action and movement in young learning disabled boys. Unpublished manuscript. Austin, TX: Austin Independent School District.

Holguin, O., & Sherrill, C. (1990b). Use of a pictorial scale of perceived competence and acceptance with learning disabled boys. *Perceptual and Motor Skills, 70,* 1235-1238.

Jaben, T. W., Treffinger, D. J., Whelan, R. J., Hudson, F. G., Stainback, S. B., & Stainback, W. (1982). Impact of instruction on learning disabled students' creative thinking. *Psychology in the Schools, 19,* 371-373.

Jay, D. M. (1987). Effects of a dance program on the creativity and movement behavior of preschool handicapped children. Unpublished doctoral dissertation, Texas Woman's University, Denton.

Kistner, J., Haskett, M., White, K., & Robbins, F. (1987). Perceived competence and self-worth of learning disabled and normally achieving students. *Learning Disability Quarterly, 10,* 258-266.

Lubin, E. (1979). Motor creativity of preschool deaf children. *Dissertation Abstracts International,* 40A, 154. (University Microfilms Order No. 79-15879).

Lubin, E., & Sherrill, C. (1980). Motor creativity of preschool deaf children. *American Annals of the Deaf, 125,* 460-466.

Moustakas, C. E. (1967). *Creativity and conformity.* New York: Van Nostrand Reinhold.

Mitchell, J. V. (Ed.). (1985). *The ninth mental measurements yearbook.* Lincoln, NE: University of Nebraska Press.

Paget, K. D. (1979). Creativity and its correlates in emotionally disturbed preschool children. *Psychological Reports, 44,* 595-598.

Reisman, F. K., Floyd, B., & Torrance, E. P. (1981). Performance on Torrance's thinking creatively in action and movement as a predictor of cognitive development of young children. *The Creative Child and Adult Quarterly, 6,* 205-209, 233.

Schatz, E. M., & Buckmaster, L. R. (1984). Development of an instrument to measure self-actualizing growth in pre-adolescents. *Journal of Creative Behavior, 18,* 263-272.

Sherrill, C. (1986). Fostering creativity in handicapped children. *Adapted Physical Activity Quarterly, 3,* 236-249.

Sherrill, C., & Pyfer, J. (1985). Learning disabled students in physical education. *Adapted Physical Activity Quarterly, 2,* 283-291.

Silon, E. L., & Harter, S. (1985). Assessment of perceived competence, motivation orientation, and anxiety in segregated and mainstreamed educable mentally retarded children. *Journal of Educational Psychology, 77,* 217-230.

Tabachnick, B. G., & Fidell, L. S. (1989). *Using multivariate statistics* (2nd ed.). New York: Harper & Row.

Torrance, E. P. (1981). *Thinking creatively in action and movement.* Bensenville, IL: Scholastic Testing Service.

Warger, C. L., & Kleman, D. (1986). Developing positive self-concepts in institutionalized children with severe behavior disorders. *Child Welfare, 65,* 165-176.

Wynne, J. D. (1982). *Learning statistics: A common-sense approach.* New York: Macmillan Publishing.

Omar Holguin teaches adapted physical education for the early childhood classes in the Austin Independent School District, Texas, and serves as the secretary of the Adapted Physical Education Section for the Texas Association for Health, Physical Education, Recreation, and Dance. He has coauthored several articles on motor creativity, self-concept, aerobic dance, and disabled children.

Claudine Sherrill is professor of kinesiology at Texas Woman's University. Her research has included creative arts for the severely handicapped, the affective domain in disabled children, and socialization of disabled athletes into sports.

DRAMA

Integrating Drama & Sign Language
A Multisensory Approach to Learning for Children with Special Needs

Victoria Brown

Between the ages of two and six most children are well on their way to communicating needs, solving problems and establishing truths verbally. However, for some young children with disabilities such as mental retardation, aphasia, autism and other learning disorders, the process for acquiring aural/oral language is impaired. These children rely heavily on visual/gestural modes of communication. The following discussion addresses the use of sign language and drama activities with these children as a multisensory approach to learning. Examples of activities are given along with descriptions of techniques for developing drama/sign activities for this special population.

Drama and Language Acquisition

An increasing number of studies have been conducted that link the use of drama with language acquisition in children. The few that have focused on children with disabilities indicate enhanced language acquisition (Adamson, 1981; Saltz, & Johnson, 1977). One reason cited for this is that drama activities can create a language experience that the child participates in first hand. Additionally, the visual and physical elements of drama communicate to these children in a language they can understand.

Sign Language and Language Acquisition

An increasing number of studies have also been conducted that examine the use of sign language with children who have disabilities affecting language development. Most of these studies have revealed significant improvement in language acquisition when sign language is incorporated into the curriculum (Carr & Kologinsky, 1983; Daniloff, Noll, Fristoe, & Lloyd, 1982; Konstantareas, 1984). These studies indicate not only that a method of communication is established through sign language, but that for many children this visual language often initiated or enhanced oral language as well (Acosta, 1981; Grinnell, Detamore, & Lipke, 1976).

Reasons cited for this success include the following:

1. Sign language makes fewer information processing demands than a spoken language (Konstantareas, Oxman, & Webster, 1978).

2. The visual/spatial modes of sign are considered to be primarily functions of the brain's right hemisphere, whereas many of the disabilities mentioned here involve damage to the left hemisphere.

3. Signs used in conjunction with speech provide multiple sensory cues simultaneously (Grinnell et al., 1976).

Sign language is a symbol system, as is spoken or written language. Yet many signs visually represent an idea making it easier for young children to learn and recall.

Combining Drama and Sign Language

In tandem, sign language and drama-related activities create a highly stimulating atmosphere for language acquisition. By gesturing or signing what is being verbally discussed while at the same time dramatizing the action of the discussion, the learner is provided with optimum sensory cues. The signs represent the spoken word visually and kinesthetically. The dramatization presents the action visually, aurally, and physically. Together they have the possibility of creating a multiple imprint on that learner's memory (Brown, 1988).

In a study of a Head Start program (Brown, 1988), 60 children participated in activities combining drama and sign for 30 minutes a day throughout the school year. The teacher-directed activities resulted in significantly higher scores for children in the drama/sign group on the Head Start Measures-Language Scale than for those 60 children in the control group.

A series of activities has been developed by the author tailored for young children who are language delayed or who have disabilities affecting language acquisition. These activities integrate the dramatic element of sign language with the visual/ gestural element of drama. They are goal-oriented activities, 25 to 35 minutes in length, guided by a teacher, that involve the children as active participants and incorporate one or more of the following techniques: role play, mime, story dramatization, and improvisation.

Adapting Drama for Children with Special Needs

The drama teacher will need to make major adaptations in preparing and leading drama activities for children with special needs. The following techniques are recommended:

1. Use pictures to visually represent new vocabulary and concepts.

2. Break the drama lesson up into a series of short segments.
3. Use repetition to reinforce new language and concepts.
4. Allow children to imitate as a starting point.
5. Sequence the activities, building from the simple to more complex.
6. Begin the activities with warm ups and end with a closing.
7. Introduce techniques to maintain focus and control.

Pictures

To assure optimum learning, every effort is made to provide a multisensory experience for the children. Pictures provide concrete visual information for introducing characters, new vocabulary, and other concepts such as size and color. In one story dramatization about a giraffe, the children are shown a picture of a giraffe that is referred to when describing specific features such as the long neck and legs: "Look at the giraffe's long neck. Can you stretch your neck and make it long like a giraffe? How can you make your legs look really long like Lance." Pictures may show concepts or ideas that the children will be acting out such as a picture of the giraffe eating leaves off a tree or a witch stirring her brew. Simple drawings can be made by the instructor, before each lesson.

Breaking-up Activities

Young children, particularly children with special needs, often have a short attention span. Though drama and sign language help to maintain interest, frequent breaks are necessary to regroup. An activity may be 15 to 35 minutes in length but should be made up of a series of short activities that build on one another. For example, there are six short segments in the following drama lesson on autumn leaves: 1) The children are shown a real leaf or a leaf cut out from tissue paper that will float slowly to the ground. They are then asked to copy the movement of this leaf with their hand. First one hand floats gently to the ground then both hands. 2) A picture of a tree with colored leaves falling is shown. Children are asked to make a tree with one hand and let their other hand be the leaf on the tree. Then all leaves can fall off the hand/tree to the ground. 3) The teacher becomes a tree and children gather around and make their hands leaves on the teacher's arms/branches. As the branches sway, the children's hand/leaves fall slowly to the ground. 4) The teacher assists the children in making their whole bodies look like leaves. They are encouraged to make different shaped leaves then asked to make their body/leaves fall slowly to the ground. 5) Next the children move around the room in their leaf shapes slowly with soft music. The music represents the wind. When they hear the music stop they fall gently to the ground. 6) When all the "leaves" have fallen, the teacher rakes them up into a large pile with an imaginary rake. "Now it's time for all the leaves to become very quiet and go to sleep. Leaves, can you find a nice place on the ground for your long winter nap?" When all the leaves are quiet the activity has ended. Each segment is just a few minutes long. Changing levels and type of action keeps children involved and interested.

Repetition

Repetition is important for reinforcing concepts. Additionally, as the children become more comfortable with the movement or dialogue being repeated, they gain self confidence. This can be done with a sequence of events that is repeated or with an activity that is repeated three or four times on different days. In the above activity representation of "falling leaves" is repeated three different ways. A sequence of three works well.

In one drama activity a giraffe named Lance makes three attempts to be special. He tries to climb a tree like a squirrel, fly like a bird, and swim like a fish. The children use signs to dramatize each of these three efforts. The children also become Lance three times in the activity, first limping with a stubbed toe, then with a sore neck, then sneezing with a terrible cold, all resulting from his failed attempts. By the third series of giraffe mishaps, the children are usually quite enthusiastic and their dialogue is much more spontaneous than at the beginning of the lesson.

Imitation

In drama, creativity is always encouraged, but young children tend to imitate the teacher as well as their peers. Imitation is a safe place for a beginning, especially for those too shy to participate on their own. Eventually children should be encouraged to show the teacher a different way of dancing like a giraffe, or making their bodies look like a leaf. Teachers can verbally recognize children who show something new or different.

Sequencing

Segments within the activity should be carefully sequenced, starting with the simple and building to more complex and creative ideas. In "Autumn Leaves" the children begin by copying the movement of the falling leaf with their hands. At the end they must create their own leaf using their entire body and follow the music with their movement. A follow-up drama might involve acting out a story about a tree (e.g., The Fir Tree Who Wanted Leaves) and incorporating many of the actions from the previous activity.

The sequence of another activity called "Butterflies and Elephants" is as follows: First the children make a butterfly with their hands and practice moving it gently through the air. Then they become butterflies and fly gently around the room looking for an imaginary flower to sit on. The same sequence is repeated with a heavy elephant. The children are brought back into a circle to hear the elephant's heavy footsteps (demonstrated with fists as the elephant's stomping feet). They then become elephants and stomp heavily around an imaginary jungle. Perhaps they drink or bathe in a river.

Next, the children are divided into two groups, light butterflies and heavy elephants, and interact in some way that incorporates dialogue and problem solving. For example, the elephants are too big and heavy to scratch an itch behind their ears and the butterflies must think of a way to help.

Warm-up and Closing

A warm-up introduces the children to the activity and can also be used as a physical warm-up. When stories are dramatized a warm-up may include introducing the characters, or signs to be used in the story. If the main character is an animal, the children might become that animal and act out the associated movement and sounds. In "Elephants and Butterflies," the children might prepare for the activity by moving different body parts as if they were very heavy or light. They are also shown pictures of the animals for discussion. As a closing, they come to the circle and are transformed back into children. Then they discuss the activity and what they enjoyed best. Reading a poem or singing a song works nicely as a closing too. A closing should provide for a cooling down period and time for discussion and review.

Maintaining Control and Focus

Teachers of special needs children often avoid trying drama for fear of losing control of the class. Children do need a certain amount of freedom within a drama activity but limits can easily be established. A circle formation serves as a "home base." When the children become overexcited they can be brought back to home base and continue the activity on another level. Birds looking for food can be brought back to their nest for a nap, or squirrels racing around, are called back to their tree to bury the acorns they've found.

One clever Head Start teacher places masking tape Xs around the circle, one for each child. When the children become overexcited in the activity, they are told to sit on their X. This becomes a game for the children and a good control device for the teacher. Choose a sign or develop a signal for the group that they must remember, such as clapping hands three times or flashing the lights. When the children see or hear that signal they must stop and look at the teacher for directions. Directions (such as "freeze,","stop," or "sit on your X") can be given vocally or in sign. Children often think of signs in this context as a secret code and want to be the first to respond.

Incorporating Sign Language

In the drama activities, children alternate between using signs and using their bodies to dramatize stories and simple problem solving situations. Four basic methods by which sign language is incorporated into a drama activity are as follows:

1. Signs are used in conjunction with speech to clarify new vocabulary.
2. Signs are used to create or define a character in the drama activity.
3. Signs are transformed into puppets or objects to be used in the drama activity.
4. Signs are used to illustrate a concept or action within the drama activity.

Using Signs in Conjunction with Speech

Accompanying speech with signs provides children with multiple sensory cues: visual, aural, and kinesthetic. It is not necessary to sign every word being spoken; rather, only the key nouns and verbs are signed to reinforce main ideas. Each activity might incorporate five or six new signs that can be reviewed as an introduction to the activity. Children seem to respond best to signs that visually represent an object or action. If the standard sign is too abstract, the teacher can create a gesture that better represents the word. For example: one commonly used sign for "dog" involves slapping the thigh twice with one hand. However, using two hands on top of one's head to represent the dog's floppy ears creates a clearer image of the dog and children enjoy playing along.

Creating Characters with Signs

Hand shapes are often used in sign language to represent the main features of a person or animal. This idea works well for introducing or describing the main characters in the drama activity. An animal's ears, eyes, nose, tail, paws, and body shape can all be described with gestures, as can its spots, stripes, and feathers. A witch's long nose, tall hat, crooked smile, long finger nails, and witch's brew can also be signed or gestured by the children.

As the children add on each new feature with their hands, they "become" the character, creating a voice to match. This is analogous to putting on pieces of a costume: "Alright witches, let's put on our tall black hats. Let me see your long nose, your long fingernails...."

Transforming Signs into Puppets

In addition to becoming a character in a story or drama activity by adding on features, children can use their hands to represent characters. The index finger can represent a person or the hands can be shaped in various ways to represent different animals (e.g., turtle, butterfly, or fish). The children are then free to control the movement or voice of that character.

As is true with puppets, a great deal more language is often drawn from the child when he/she is actually speaking as the character. Movement and dialogue can be initiated by such questions as: "Can you make your bird sit in the nest?" or "What do you think the bird said when she saw the broken eggs? Show me." The children often become very involved with a character that they've created themselves and ideas for action or dialogue occur spontaneously.

Illustrating the Concept or Action with Signs

By using one hand to sign a tree and the other hand to sign a leaf the teacher can demonstrate the concept of autumn, as well as the gentle movement of the falling leaf. Prepositions are clearly illustrated in sign language. Once the children understand the concept from the teacher's demonstration, they can join in the activity by moving their own hands: "Can you show me the boy standing in front of the car?" or "Make the boy tip toe around the tree."

Comprehension is increased by reinforcing a concept with drama. Children can create a turtle with their hands, moving it slowly across the floor, then become the turtle and scoot off to find a bug in the grass or a puddle in which to swim.

Opposites are also easily demonstrated in sign, then reinforced with drama as in "Light Butterflies and Heavy Elephants." Signs for opposites such as happy and sad or soft and hard are illustrated clearly in sign language. These ideas are then brought to life by dramatizing a related short story.

Adapting Activities for Children with Physical Disabilities

The activities described above were developed to assist children who are language delayed or who have disabilities affecting language development. However, the use of sign language in these activities provides a wonderful method for involving children who cannot physically participate in the action. While some children become frogs hopping from log to lily pad, other children may carry out the action with a puppet-frog and environment created from signs and gestures.

Give children in wheelchairs a special role by using the chair as an integral part of the activity. Wheelchairs make great spaceships and train engines. Children with limited movement can be given the role of the tree in the middle that the other children's hand/leaves fall from, or the Indian chief who must call back the braves from a hunt.

Conclusion

Teachers who have used drama/sign activities in the classroom have noted growth not only in language acquisition but also improved self esteem, social awareness, fine and gross motor development, and creativity. It is hoped that this discussion will provide motivation for further investigation. Teachers should consider exploring other forms of visual and/or physical communication, including mime, gesture dance, and the visual arts. The objective is to create a multisensory learning experience that children can enjoy.

In considering possible applications of a multisensory approach to learning, perhaps we should follow the advice of one Head Start child who participated in a drama/sign program throughout the school year. This four year old summed it up in her response to the question "What do we use our eyes for?" Although she answered the question with silence upon entering the program, her answer at the end of the school year was: "We close them and use our imaginations."

References

Acosta, L. K. (1981). Instructor use of total communication: Effects of preschool Down's syndrome children's vocabulary acquisition and attempted verbalizations. Dissertation, University of Iowa.

Adamson, D. (1981). Dramatization of children's literature and visual perceptual kinesthetic intervention for disadvantaged beginning readers. Dissertation, Northwestern State University of Louisiana.

Brown, V. L. (1988). Integrating drama and sign language: A multisensory approach to language acquisition and its effects on disadvantaged preschool children. Unpublished raw data.

Carr, E.G., & Kologinsky, E. (1983). Acquisition of sign language by autistic children II: Spontaneity and generalization effects. *Journal of Applied Behavior Analysis,* 16 (3), 297-314.

Daniloff, J. K., Noll, J. D., Fristoe, M., & Lloyd, L.L. (1982). Gesture recognition in patients with aphasia. *Journal of Speech and Hearing Disorders,* 47, 43-49.

Grinnell, M.G., Detamore, K.L., & Lipke, B.A. (1976). Sign it successful: Manual English encourages expressive communication. *Teaching Exceptional Children,* 8, 123-124.

Konstantareas, M.M. (1984). Sign language as a communication prosthesis with language-impaired children. *Journal of Autism and Developmental Disorders,* 14 (1), 9-25.

Konstantareas, M. M., Oxman, J., & Webster, D. C. (1978). Iconicity: Effects on the acquisition of sign language by autistic and other severely dysfunctional children. In P. Siple (Ed.), *Understanding language through sign language research* (pp. 213-237). New York: Academic Press.

Saltz, E., & Johnson, J. (1977). Training disadvantaged preschoolers on various fantasy activities: Effects on cognitive functioning and impulse control. *Child Development,* 48, 367-380.

Victoria Brown is an associate professor of theatre arts at Gallaudet University in Washington, D.C., and a drama specialist for the Wolf Trap Institute for Early Learning Through the Arts in Vienna, Virginia. Portions of this article were first published in the Fall 1988 issue of *Teaching Exceptional Children*, and are reprinted here with permission.

Section III

Model Programs

The Interrelated ARTS Program: Making Arts Connections with the Basics

Betty Weincek and Ann Richardson

The Interrelated ARTS program in the Montgomery County (Md.) Public Schools involves children as participants in art, music, dance, and drama. The art forms are used as channels for learning. The Interrelated ARTS teacher goes to the classroom to work with students on objectives in the curriculum, in language arts, social studies, science, or mathematics. The objectives in these academic subjects are taught through use of the art form. Consequently, a lesson may involve art and mathematics: the symmetry of a natural form; music and social studies: songs from the Caribbean; dance and science: flow of electrons; or drama and language arts: creating a narrative. The connections between content areas and the arts are limitless. Once begun, associations are apparent in numerous areas and the methods for instruction in the classroom are multiplied.

Theory Supporting the Program

Instruction through the arts is based upon the work of Howard Gardner in Project Zero at Harvard University. His theory of multiple intelligences (Gardner, 1985) supports use of the arts as methods for teaching students who may not be motivated by an approach which is primarily verbal. By engaging students in the arts and offering participation in learning through dance, music, art, or drama, the teacher is able to expand the number of routes for classroom instruction.

Gardner's theory of multiple intelligences suggests some obvious linkages with the arts. The first two areas, verbal/sequential and quantitative/mathematical intelligences, comprise the greatest part of the school day, even for early childhood once reading is begun. Beyond these two time-tested standards reminiscent of the "3 Rs," Gardner identifies five other intelligences: musical; visual and spatial, which correlates with art; physical and kinesthetic, which is evidenced by dance; and knowledge about self and knowledge about others, which reflect the observation, internalization, and interpretation of behavior found in drama. Each art form is a method for reaching students and enhancing the classroom experience.

For the classroom teacher, observation of the students' intelligences offers a profile of preferences and abilities that can be used to develop a plan for instruction. The arts are both a part of the content learned and the process for learning. For the classroom teacher who is visited by the Interrelated ARTS teacher, this means a new tool for observing students and an adaptive method for teaching.

The Interrelated ARTS teacher offers a demonstration of the lesson by teaching the students, then, upon departure, leaves a written lesson plan. Classroom teachers acquire skills through modeling, observation, and participation and through reflection upon the experience, the plan, and expectations or outcomes.

Organization of the Program

There are 12 teachers of Interrelated ARTS, three in each of the four art forms: visual art, music, dance, and drama. They work in teams of four, representing all four art forms. At the elementary school, Interrelated ARTS teachers confer with classroom teachers concerning the objectives in the regular curriculum that the teachers plan to use. The Interrelated ARTS teacher suggests an approach to an objective through the arts and designs an appropriate lesson to teach the students. The classroom teacher remains with the class and participates in the lesson. Time for scheduling, conferring, and planning is built into the programs—it is vital to success.

School Participation

Schools participating in the program are self-selected. They ask to have the Interrelated ARTS teachers come to the school. The principal must sign an agreement stating that the arts will be central to study in the school and that all of the teachers will participate. Prior to beginning Interrelated ARTS in a school, the team of teachers involved offers a comprehensive half-day workshop and arranges for scheduling with teachers.

Each teacher in the school receives a semester of drama, of dance, of music, and of art or two years of services, 24-28 lessons involving the four art forms in learning the basics. Through the program, they learn to develop their own arts-centered lessons.

Curriculum/Multiculturalism

The lessons taught, in plan form, make up a resource for reference to the curriculum. Although they must frequently suit specific needs, there are some lessons that can be used repeatedly. One such lesson involves the use of an African banner that symbolizes attributes of the personality or lifestyle of the students who develop it. Another example is a chant or rap that explains traffic signs and, hopefully, improves safety practices. Throughout the collection of lesson plans, multicultural themes are evident. They are not just references to another nationality; they involve understanding the culture through participation in some aspect of it. Cross-cultural understanding is promoted through discussion of similarities and differences.

Several factors influence the development of Interrelated ARTS lessons. The process involves the arts, using one or more of the art forms as a method for learning. Content is established by the curricular objective in a basic subject that is being met, knowledge about the art form(s) used to teach, and the multi-cultural emphasis of the lesson. The products and/or outcomes should show achievement of the objectives, objectives which may be multiple or "layered," involving the basic subject area, the art form, and the multi-cultural emphasis. Evaluation of the lesson may be achieved through an appropriate use of the art form or a performance or product that shows understanding of the lesson. The arts become an integral part of the curriculum.

Evaluation of the Program

Evaluation is accomplished through use of an evaluation form after a team has spent two years in a school. An exit meeting is held in order to summarize the accomplishments and offer suggestions for continuing development of lesson plans involving the arts.

Other Services Offered by Interrelated ARTS

The Interrelated ARTS teachers offer seminars called ABCs, Arts in the Basic Curriculum, for elementary schools throughout the system. They center on a variety of themes. A few examples follow. "Pump and Jump" involves dance and the science of health; "Shadows" relates Indonesian shadow puppets and studies of light; "Ellis Island" is a full dramatization of the immigrant experience; "Harlem Renaissance" involves the flowering of the arts during the 1920s and 30s in Harlem.

DARTS (Developing Arts and Reading Techniques and Strategies) is a series of four lessons for second-graders from Chapter 1 schools in which Interrelated ARTS strategies in all four art forms are used to start children writing journals and following narratives.

The Arts Resource Center is the source of instructional support packages developed by Interrelated ARTS for use in the schools. Packages containing artifacts and instructional materials for classroom use are available to elementary teachers throughout the system who may borrow them for two weeks to use with students. Topics cover a wide range of subjects, from primary language arts to the environment to international cultures. Recently developed instructional support packages include: "Central America," "Harlem Renaissance," "The Arts of the Caribbean," "The Jack Tales," and, in progress, "The Arts of Southeast Asia."

Examples

The Interrelated ARTS program involves students in the arts as a learning process. It extends the invitation to the child to participate in the arts and engages the imagination to find new ways to solve problems and to learn. Basic subjects are taught through strategies involving the arts and activities that offer opportunities for individual solutions as well as cooperative efforts. Use of the arts is a catalyst for learning. The lessons that follow are examples of instruction through dance.

The lessons presented here are extensions of one or more of the basic objectives in the reading and language arts curriculum of Montgomery County Public Schools. Each of the three dance lessons uses a narrative for its structure.

The reading component of the first, *Ten Bears in a Bed*, stresses word and number sequencing and auditory memory skills. The dance segment stresses individual student interpretation of action words and learning to read simplified dance notation.

Dance Away is a story about a rabbit and his problems and how he solves his problem with a dance. In reading, the students deal with the concept of conflict/resolution in narrative form. The dance is created by the students using the structure of Rabbit's song. Some social dance history is introduced by teaching the "Bunny Hop" as a follow-up activity after creating an original "rabbit dance."

Ragtime Tumpie is a biography of dancer Josephine Baker. In this book she relates how she learned the "two-step" from her father and used it to win her first dance contest. After reading the book, the students learn the two-step as well as other popular social dances of the 1920s. These dances, which have become part of our cultural social history, were introduced in our society during the Harlem Renaissance and Josephine Baker was an important dancer of that historic period.

TITLE: TEN BEARS IN MY BED

OBJECTIVES:
> Reading/language arts: Students will develop ability to interpret creatively using dance/movement. Students will listen and read for a purpose.
> Math: Students will subtract "one less than."
> Dance: Students will perform certain locomotor movements.
> Students will create original movements to accompany certain vocabulary.

GRADE LEVEL: Primary (pre-K - 3)

MATERIALS: *Ten Bears in My Bed,* a book by Stan Mack. Paper teddy bear cutouts, music, yarn at least 20 feet long, chart paper.

PROCEDURES:
1. Review the song "Roll Over."
2. Read and discuss the book *Ten Bears in My Bed,* by Stan Mack. Pay particular attention to the ten movement vocabulary words in the story.
3. On chart paper, list all ten ways the bears left the bed.

4. As you list the words on the paper, add the dance movement symbols that accompany the words.

TO PERFORM THE DANCE:
1. Using the yarn, lay out the outline of a rectangular bed.
2. Pass out the paper bears with the words and symbols printed on them. Have those students get in the bed and create a "teddy bear" shape.
3. Either to music or as the remainder of the class sings "Roll Over," or both, each student should leave the bed in the manner written or shown in symbol on his/her paper bear.
4. Repeat song and dance until all students have had a chance to perform.
5. Variation: Use blank bears for students who create their own movements to leave the bed.

MOVEMENT VOCABULARY:

FLEW   GALLOPED   SKATED

ROARED   CHUGGED   JUMPED

BOUNCED   PEDALED   TOOTLED   RUMBLED

EVALUATION:
Decide if real bears could move these ways. Why? Why not? Decide who and what could move in each of the ways listed.

EXTENSION:
Read the book *Ten in the Bed,* by Penny Dale. In discussion, compare and/or contrast this book to Stan Mack's book. Use another art form to interpret this book.

This lesson was originally conceived by Nancy Harris, dance instructor, Interrelated ARTS Program.

SUBJECT: DANCE AWAY!

OBJECTIVES:
    Reading/Language Arts: Develop sight vocabulary
                                 Develop understanding of word meaning
                                 Develop ability to listen for a purpose
                                 Develop ability to interpret creatively
                                 Develop understanding of conflict/resolution
    Dance: Recall a given movement phrase
                                 Interpret a movement phrase in various dynamics, levels,
                                      rhythms

GRADE LEVELS: Primary

MATERIALS: Book: *Dance Away*, by George Shannon, music: Bunny Hop or some other upbeat piece, written chart

PROCEDURE:

1. Read the book *Dance Away*.
2. Discuss why Rabbit liked to dance
3. Have students define Rabbit's problem.
    Have students analyze how Rabbit solved his problem with a dance.
4. Read, line by line, Rabbit's dancing song.
5. Have individual students interpret Rabbit's dance phrase with their own moves.
6. Teach all to the entire class.
7. Perform complete dance to music.
8. Teach the "Bunny Hop" to the students. Compare the two dances.

POSSIBLE QUESTIONS: Do we usually use a dance to solve a problem? Why?
                                  How exactly did Rabbit save his friends?
                                  Why did Rabbit like to dance so much?
                                  Why did Rabbit's friends hide from him?

EXTENSION:

Create an experience story or journal story in which Rabbit uses this movement phrase
    to solve another conflict.
Create a celebration dance that could be performed by Rabbit and his friends.

DANCE AWAY! (THE SONG)

Left two three kick
Right two three kick   Actual performance of
Left skip Right skip   the steps to be interpreted
Turn around!   by the students.

SUBJECT: RAGTIME TUMPIE —A STORY ABOUT THE DANCER, JOSEPHINE BAKER

OBJECTIVES:

Social Studies: Learn about the different contributions of Afro-Americans to American culture

Dance: Learn the "two-step," "Charleston," and "Black Bottom" dance steps of the 1920s; the "Electric Slide" dance steps of the 1980s

LEVEL: Primary

MATERIALS: Book: *Ragtime Tumpie* , by Alan Schroeder, ragtime music on tape or record, optional music: "The Electric Slide"

PROCEDURE:

1. Read and discuss the book *Ragtime Tumpie*.
2. Explain Josephine Baker's contributions to the fields of dance and theatre.
3. Learn the "two-step," the "Charleston," and the "Black Bottom" steps.
4. Create a dance phrase or combination using all three dance steps.

IF THERE IS TIME AND INTEREST:

5. Teach the class the contemporary dance, "The Electric Slide."

EVALUATION:

Compare the dance steps of the 1920s to dance steps of today, particularly "The Electric Slide."

ELABORATION:

Contact grandparents and, if possible, great-grandparents and have them give oral history anecdotes about doing these dance steps.

Betty Weincek is a dance instructor in the Interrelated ARTS Program of the Montgomery County, Maryland, Public Schools, Silver Spring.

Ann Richardson is the coordinator for the Interrelated ARTS Program.

The Wolf Trap Institute

Early Learning Through the Arts Project

Miriam C. Flaherty

The Wolf Trap Institute is an education program of the Wolf Trap Foundation for the Performing Arts, the United States' first and only national park for the performing arts and an internationally-renowned cultural center located near Washington, DC in Vienna, Virginia.

Founded in 1981 under a grant from the Head Start Bureau of the US Department of Health and Human Services, the Institute's Early Learning Through the Arts project places professional performing artists in classroom residencies working with children between the ages of three and five years old, their teachers, and parents. The goal of this unique partnership is not to teach children how to perform, but rather to incorporate the arts into their lives and education. The goal of the Institute is to train early childhood professionals in the use of performing arts techniques which help young children learn. Under the leadership of Institute-trained performing artists, drama, music, and dance become powerful teaching strategies capable of helping the children learn the important life skills and academic skills that serve as part of the foundation for all future learning.

Through active participation in Institute residencies, young children learn by doing. For example: they demonstrate their ability to identify numbers and colors by interacting with a puppet that "eats red 7s" (and other colored numbers!); children who may be frightened of health care workers are reassured and encouraged in a song to brush and floss; through dance, the children are taught movements which demonstrate opposites such as big/small, high/low, and fast/slow; children increase proficiency in spoken English by becoming involved in African folk tales told with accompanying gestures and American sign language. Throughout a Wolf Trap Institute residency, the children enjoy the success of individual accomplishments. Group problem solving activities challenge their creativity and imaginations and bring the children, and often their teachers and parents, to richer understandings of their artistic, cultural, and ethnic heritage.

Regional Programs

In addition to the program serving the Washington, DC/Maryland/Virginia areas, the Wolf Trap Institute's Early Learning Through the Arts project has been replicated in urban, suburban, and rural communities in Arizona, California, Michigan, and Tennessee. In these states, local professional dancers, musicians, actors, and other performing artists have joined with community arts agencies and early childhood professionals to form regional programs that follow the Wolf Trap Institute model.

Programmatic Highlights

Classroom Residencies

The centerpiece of all Institute programs is the classroom residency in which the Institute artist and early childhood educator work together to translate instructional goals into performing arts activities designed to meet the objectives and needs of the teacher and class. By observing and participating in the artist's activities with the children, the teacher gains the experience and confidence needed to integrate the arts into the ongoing curriculum. Residencies are available for one-week and seven-week periods of time.

Curriculum Materials

Each teacher participating in an Institute classroom residency receives a three-volume set of drama, music, and movement activities developed by Institute artists and refined through years of partnerships with early childhood educators. The materials have been acclaimed for their many applications with young children and their adherence to age and developmentally appropriate practices.

Performing Arts Training Workshops: Artsplay!

The Wolf Trap Institute offers participatory workshops designed to train teachers, parents, and arts professionals in performing arts activities that help children learn. Institute Master Artists drawn from all of the Wolf Trap Regional Programs conduct workshops that focus on their particular art forms and demonstrate the use of the arts to teach designated skills and concepts important to preschool children. Sponsors can choose from a variety of different workshops, such as "Singable Songs for Non-Singers," "Using Gestures and Drama for Language Development," "Themes and Variations: Creative Movement to Build Cognitive Skills," and "Songs and Stories about Science and Nature." Communities in nearly every state and many foreign countries have sponsored Wolf Trap workshops. Artsplay!, a training series of combined workshops, is presented at The Barns of Wolf Trap and may be offered as professional development and continuing education to sponsoring organizations around the country.

Field Trips

The Institute presents music, drama, and dance presentations for classes of preschool children, their teachers, and parents. Institute artists perform material specially created and arranged to give three, four- and five-year-olds their first introduction to live performance. In the Washington, DC area, The Barns of Wolf Trap hosts the Institute's field trips; Regional Wolf Trap Institute programs present field trips on professional stages within their communities.

The Wolf Trap Institute has emerged through its local and regional programs as a national leader in the field of arts-in-education. Institute artists have been showcased at leading conferences sponsored by organizations including: National Association for the Education of Young Children, Head Start, and the American Alliance for Theatre Education. The Institute's methodology and curriculum have been the basis for scholarly research. These collaborations have led to the identification of specific skills and objectives that are achieved by the participating children in Wolf Trap Institute Programs:

-foster group awareness and social competence
-increase gross and fine motor coordination
-increase motivation and enthusiasm for learning
-improve ability to concentrate and observe
-foster individual artistic creativity
-improve self awareness and build self-confidence
-increase expressive and receptive language skills
-develop conceptual and abstract thinking skills

The national program is now the subject of a three-year study conducted by Project Zero of Harvard University's Graduate School of Education. Research by Victoria Brown (see pages 172-179) and activities by Wolf Trap artists Lenore Blank Kelner and John Taylor (see following pages, 194-204) illustrate the impact of the Wolf Trap Institute's program and methodology.

Miriam C. Flaherty is director of the Wolf Trap Institute for Early Learning Through the Arts and is responsible for the overall administration of the Institute's national and six regional programs, including program development management, content, and expansion. She has served as associate director of National Programs for Very Special Arts and organized a symposium at Princeton University addressing the role of the arts in early childhood education for children with special needs.

Storybuilding and Dramatization/Role Playing

Lenore Blank Kelner

Activity: Clara The Complainer
Adapted by Lenore Blank Kelner from the book *The Tale of Meshka the Kvetch,* by Carol Chapman, N.Y.; Button Children's Book, 1980.

Materials: a shawl
                 a scarf

Procedure: This story asks children to use their problem-solving skills to help Clara with her dilemma. Problem-solving may be difficult for the children at first, but allowing them the opportunity to think independently is important.

Developing creativity is a process. Don't be discouraged if the first time you try the story, Clara's questions aren't answered. The more you allow the children to use their imaginations, the sooner they will learn problem-solving and critical thinking.

Note: you can change the character of Clara to fit any ethnic background. You can alter her homeland to one that may be more appropriate to your children; that's why the Russian names and allusions are in brackets. One teacher in a Head Start center in Washington, D.C. made Clara a Caribbean woman and turned her potatoes into yams, which she carried on her head.

Once you have done the story with the children they can discuss who everyone pretended to be and what things they complain about. The children can also draw or paint any of the images they saw in their imaginations while you were doing the story. Read Meshka the Kvetch to the children. You can then compare the two versions and discuss their differences.

Story Key: 1. _____Underlined words are words that the children need to remember and repeat.
2. [   ] Bracketed words are ethnic words that can be replaced depending on the country in which you locate the story.
3. (   ) indicate directions and suggestions for the storyteller.

Script: Ahhhhhhhh, hello, my name is Clara. Can you say my name with me? CLARA. Good! And as you can tell by my accent, I come from another country. I come from [Russia], that is right. And I came here today to tell you my story, so that what happened to me in [Russia] should never ever happen to you.

You see in [Russia] I was not known as Clara; I was known as Clara the Complainer, that is right. Now, what is complaining? Who here can tell me? And who here complains? Let me see hands. What kind of things do you complain about? (If the children don't supply you with solid answers to these questions, you can suggest some typical complaints, for example, "Who here makes a face when they have to eat something they don't like"; "Who cries all the time when they can't get their own way"; "Who whines when they have to pick up their toys?") Ahhhh, I see then I am in the right place. That is why I am here, to tell you my story so that what happened to me in [Russia] should never happen to you.

You see in [Russia] every morning when I woke up, I would say the same thing. I would get up and look at my small tiny house that my husband built before he died, may he rest in peace. The house was all right but so small that I would shake my head and say 'Ahhhhhhggggggg, this house is too small. It is so small, it is like a matchbox.' (As you say matchbox clap your hands together once.) Can you say that word with me? Matchbox (clap!) Good.

Then I would go and wake up my son. My son was so lazy, he never did anything to help me in the house. He never set the table or took out the garbage. Nothing! All he did was sit on his bed and read, read, read, his books. So every morning I would say 'Fooooooeey, my son is so lazy — so lazy he is nothing but a pickle.' Can you say that word with me? Pickle. Good.

So what could I do? I had to make a living for me and Pickle. So after breakfast I would go to the village and sell [potatoes] to the villagers. Every day I would take a sack of [potatoes] (pantomime a sack of [potatoes]) and walk all the way to the village. But I had to walk so far, so far, that my feet would swell up and get so fat. Every morning I would say, 'Oooooooohhhhhh, my feet are so fat, they are like watermelons.' Say that with me. Watermelons. And then I'd say, 'Ahhhhhhhhggggggggg, these [potatoes] are so heavy, they are like bricks on my back.' Say that, too. Bricks on my back.

And that is how I lived every day, complaining about my house, my son, my feet and my [potatoes.] I would take my [potatoes] to the village and some nice villagers would ask me how I was feeling. Will you now pretend to be the villagers in my town? Someone here, ask me how I am. Let me see here, who will ask me? Ahh, Miss Blue T-Shirt! (Rename child, when called upon according to something they are wearing. The children love it and it gives them new identities as they become characters in the story.)

So, Miss Blue T-Shirt, how are you today? Would you like to buy some [potatoes]? Do you have any [rubles]? Do you have anything to ask me? (Child should ask you how you are. If the child doesn't, ad lib with something like, 'I'm sure you'd like to know how I am so I will tell you.')

Ohhhhh, Miss Blue T-Shirt, I am not good, I am terrible. Because I have a house that is so small, it is like a what? (The class will respond with matchbox.) That is right, let us say it together with the clap. Matchbox (clap)! And Miss Blue T-Shirt, I have a son, he is so lazy he is nothing but a what? (the class will respond with <u>pickle</u>.) Good, a <u>pickle</u>. and look at my feet. They are so fat, they are just like <u>watermelons</u> (pause for the class to fill in <u>watermelons</u>). <u>Watermelons</u>, yes. And my [potatoes] are so heavy, they are like <u>bricks on my back</u> (the class fills in bricks on my back). Yes, <u>bricks on my back</u>.

And then this Miss Blue T-Shirt and all the other villagers would be so sick of hearing me complain, that they would all shake their heads four times and say: 'Oh no, it's Clara the Complainer.' Let us all do that together.

(Repeat this process 2 to 3 times with different children. Have them ask you how you are. Repeat the sequence. Have them all say, "Oh, no, it's Clara the Complainer." You will be able to feel when the attention of the children fades. Stop while they are still with you.)

And so, life went on like this for years and years until one day something terrible happened to me.

I got up one morning , just like every morning, and started to make breakfast for me and <u>Pickle</u>. As I was stirring the hot water in the pot, all of a sudden (make a terrible face) my tongue started to itch like mad! I could not stop my tongue from itching. I didn't know what to do. It was driving my crazy. So I thought I'd go and have <u>Pickle</u> take a look in there and see what was going on.

So I ran to his room, but he was not there! (slowly) Instead, on his bed were all of his books and a huge <u>GIANT PICKLE</u>!!! MY SON HAD TURNED INTO A <u>PICKLE</u>!!! Ohh, my gosh! What could I do? My son! My son!!! Meanwhile my tongue was itching like mad.

I had to get some help. So I ran out of the house. Just as I turned around to shut the door, my house shrank!!! My house became this small (show the children). MY HOUSE HAD TURNED INTO A <u>MATCHBOX</u>!!! Ohh, my gosh! I picked up my [potatoes] and ran to the town for help. But when I got to the middle of the village, I couldn't run anymore because MY FEET HAD TURNED INTO <u>WATERMELONS</u>!!! I couldn't stand because MY [POTATOES] HAD TURNED INTO <u>BRICKS</u>!!! and I was stuck in the middle of the town looking like a nut. (Stand hunched over and twisted.)

Suddenly, an old man, a wise man from our village, came up to ask me what had happened. Well, I told him how my house had turned into a <u>matchbox</u>. And that my son had turned into a <u>pickle</u>. And look at my feet! They are <u>watermelons</u>. And my [potatoes] are <u>bricks</u>. (Children will fill in the words). And he said, 'Clara, did your tongue itch this morning?'

'Why, yes, sir. Yes, and it is still itching like crazy right now.'

'Ohhhhhh, Clara, you have the Curse of the Wicked Itch. It comes from complaining too much. If you do not think of the good things in your life, you will be stuck like this forever.'

Stuck like this forever!!! No, thank you. But how could I think of good things? I had been complaining for years! So I turned to the villagers who had gathered around me, and I said, 'Villagers, help me please! I know I have made you sick of me by complaining, but I need your help. If I don't think of good things, I will be stuck like this forever! But I don't know where to begin. Tell me, what can I say good about my house? It is small; I cannot tell you it isn't. Help me.' (See if the children can think of a positive statement for each complaint. If they have trouble, you can offer suggestions like, "My house does keep me and

Pickle warm in the winter. That is not so bad, is it?" Then go through the list of complaints again. See if they can think of something good to say about each topic of Clara's complaining.)

Oh, all of this is true, and you know what? I do like coming to the village every day and talking to you, and seeing your smiling faces. And I do love to see the sun come up every morning.

And just as I said that I love to see the sun every morning, I could stand up. And my [potatoes] were no longer <u>bricks</u>. And my feet were no longer <u>watermelons</u>. So I ran home and, Ohhh, I was so happy, because my house . . . my house was no longer a <u>matchbox</u>. And then there was just one more thing, my son. And I made a promise on that day that, if my son was well and back in his bed, I would never ever call him <u>Pickle</u> again. So I peeked into his room and sure enough, there he was. And guess what he was doing? (Let the children answer you.) That is right, he was reading a book. and I said, '[Ivan], for that was his real name, [Ivan] you keep reading and grow up to be a smart boy.'

So that is my story. I hope you enjoyed it. And I also hope you will think about me so that what happened to me in [Russia] should never ever happen to any of you. I never want any of you to get the Curse of the Wicked Itch. So how many of you will think about me today at lunch, if you have something you don't like? And how many of you will think of me when you are playing with friends and don't get to play with the toy you want? I hope you will.

Well, I must go now. Goodbye.

Lenore Blank Kelner is a professional actress, director, writer, and educator. Since 1981, she has directed her own educational theatre company, InterAct Story Theater, which performs in schools, museums, libraries, and theatres all over the United States. She serves the Wolf Trap Institute as an artist-in-residence in the classroom as well as the coordinator of the Baltimore Wolf Trap program.

RHYTHM, CHANTS, AND SPACE GAMES: MOVEMENT FOR MEMORY

John Taylor

Moving in Place, Dancing Through Space

In dance, a primary consideration is how the children move in relation to the space around them. Are they moving in place (axial movement) or through space (locomotive movement)? These basic terms of creative movement are guideposts in a movement vocabulary.

Axial movement involves moving on, around, or along an axis. An axis is a straight line that passes through a body. In this case, the axis is the child's spine. Moving in place helps a child improve fine and gross motor control and coordination.

Locomotive movement involves moving from one place to another. Moving from place to place helps the children to understand their relationship to the space around themselves and others, and to explore qualities of motion, shapes and patterns.

Activity: Your Own Chair

Materials: Chairs for yourself and everyone in the class

Procedure: This activity uses a chair to help the children establish and recall a short sequence of movements.

Arrange the children and their chairs so that you are visible to all.

```
                chair           chair
        chair           chair           chair
    chair           chair           chair           chair

                        Teacher
```

Sit in your chair. Tell them that this is Position Number One. Have them sit in their chairs. Ask them what number this position is.

[I'm sitting in my chair. This is Position Number One. Show me Number One with your chairs. John, can you show me Number One? Letitia, can you show me Number One? Let's all clap for John and Letitia.]

Stand up in front of your chair. Tell them that this is Position Number Two. Have them stand up in front of their chairs. Ask them what number this position is. Ask them to show you Number One and then Number Two. Clap for the children who perform the sequence correctly.

[I'm standing up in front of my chair. This is Position Number Two. Show me Number Two with your chairs. Michele, can you show me Number Two? Who can show me Number One? Who can show me Number One and then Number Two?]

Stand beside your chair. Tell the children that this is Position Number Three. Have them stand beside their chairs. Ask them as a group to show you Positions One, Two, and Three. Choose several individuals to show you the positions.

[I'm standing beside my chair. This is Position Number Three. Show me Number Three with your chairs. Aisha, can you show me Number Three? Who can show me Number One? Who can show me Number One and then Number Two? Who can show me Number One, Number Two and then Number Three?]

Stand behind your chair. Tell them that this is Position Number Four. Have them stand behind their chairs. Ask them as a group and individually to show you Positions Number One, Two, Three and Four.

[I'm standing behind my chair. This is Position Number Four. Show me Number Four with your chairs. Terence, can you show me Number Four? Who can show me Number One? Number One and then Number Two? Number One, Number Two, and Number Three? Who can show me all four positions?]

Activity: Furniture Maze

Materials: One large chair, one table, one stand-up coat rack, two small chairs

Procedure: This formation game uses pieces of classroom furniture. In the game, the children are asked to remember not only a sequence of movements, but spatial relationships as well.

[I'm going to show you a secret way to get through this line of furniture. Watch carefully.] Line up the furniture as illustrated.

X	X	X	XX
large	table	coat	two
chair		rack	small
			chairs

Sit in the large chair. Explain that this is Movement Number One. [I'm sitting in the chair. This is Movement Number One. Who can show me Number One? Good.] Crawl under the table from the chair. Explain that crawling from the chair to the table is Movement Number Two. [Now I'm crawling under the table. This is Movement Number Two. Who can show me Number One? Let's give him a hand. Now can you show me Number Two?] Hop from the table around the coat rack as Movement Number Three. [Movement Number Three is hopping around the coat rack. Who can show me Number One? And then Number Two? And now Number Three? Let's all clap for Terry.] Walk to the space between the two small chairs and explain that this is Movement Number Four. [Okay, Terry, you can do Number Four with me. Number Four is walking between the chairs. Can you do that with me?]

As you demonstrate the sequence, ask individual children to describe each number for you. Always have the class applaud for the children who demonstrate a number or a sequence of numbers correctly.

When you have demonstrated the individual movements in the sequence, ask for a volunteer to do all four movements. [Who can show me Numbers One, Two, Three, and Four? Who can show me the secret way to move through the line of furniture?]

If a child does a movement incorrectly, ask the class to help recall it. Always have the child repeat the sequence before sitting down, even if you have to join in. [That's almost right, Gene, but not quite. Why don't we go through the line of furniture together?] Moving through the furniture with you as a partner will prepare the child for the next trip into the maze.

Variation: Use the same furniture, but change the styles of traveling and the action associated with each piece of furniture. For example:

Movement #1: Stand behind the chair.
Movement #2: Slide between the legs of the table.
Movement #3: Jump beside the coat rack.
Movement #4: Stoop in front of the two chairs.

Activity: 8 . . . 9 . . . 10, Let's Do It Again

Materials: Objects in the classroom

Procedure: This activity is similar to "Furniture Maze." Instead of focusing the children's concentration on a row of objects, however, it challenges them to remember a sequence of actions done all around them.

Introduce the children to this action sequence by doing it yourself. Start with two or three actions. As you repeat the activity, build up to seven or eight actions. Count off the numbers as you do each task.

Action #1: Touch the fire extinguisher.
Action #2: Walk around the desk.
Action #3: Skip to the trash can.
Action #4: Lift the box on the shelf.
Action #5: Draw on the blackboard.
Action #6: Hop to the piano.
Action #7: Touch the potted plant in the window.
Then say, "Eight, nine, ten; Let's do it again."

Ask for a volunteer to go through the sequence. Give the numbers with the instructions. Then ask if someone can do it without the instructions. Call out the numbers. If a child has a problem remembering something in the sequence, ask for assistance from the other children. Add two or three actions each time you do it. You can go as high as you judge feasible for the children. In one Washington, DC, Head Start class of four-year-olds, the children were able to do a series of ten commands without being prompted by the directions or the numbers. It took them only three sessions to reach that point. The teacher had presented the activity as a game. The children enjoyed the challenge of remembering what came next.

This sequencing game can evolve over the course of a day, several days, or several weeks. You can begin the series in the morning, add a few more tasks before lunch, and finish up your list in the afternoon. Or you can spread it out over a longer period of time. Its success depends on the interest of the children, and the time available to you.

Activity: A Space Game—Beside, Behind, and Between Your Friends

Materials: One sheet of construction paper for every child in the class, with his or her name on it

Procedure: Before beginning this activity, make a map placing the children in your class in the simple configuration as illustrated. An X represents the spot where each child will stand. Write each child's name under an X.

```
X    X    X    X    X
  X    X    X    X    X
X    X    X    X    X
  X    X    X    X    X
```

In a large open space, place pieces of construction paper corresponding to the X's in your map. [(Chant as you put the pieces of paper on the ground.) "Space, space all around. Space, space on the ground. And here is my space to be found." This is your space. (Repeat this chant for every child as you put the pieces of paper on the ground.)] Line up the children so that each stands facing you, toes on the edge of a piece of paper. Explain that each child has his or her own space. It belongs to no one else. Ask the children to look at their spaces (the pieces of paper), to point to and touch their spaces, and to put a foot on their spaces. [Look at your space. Point to your space. Touch your space.] When the children are lined up, ask them to look around. They should note who is in front of them, behind them, and beside them on each side. [Look around you. Look in front of you. Who is beside you? Who is on the other side of you? Who is behind you? What is above your head? Look at your space again.]

Activity: Shapes on the Floor

Materials: Masking tape, wrapping paper, ribbon, string, or some type of material that can be used to make large shapes on the floor

Procedure: This activity is designed to help the children learn shapes. Start with circles. Show them a drawing of a circle. Have the children draw the shape with you in the air. Then draw the circle in the air again. [(Chant as the children draw). "Draw a circle in the air. Continue that line, as you stare."] Make a circle on the floor, using masking tape. Have the children follow as you walk around the masking tape. [All of the boys draw circles while the girls watch. Now all of the girls draw circles while the boys watch. Who has the color red on today? Everyone with red on, draw your circles in the air.] Now take up the masking tape. Walk around the same circle again. Now have all the children make their own imaginary circles on the floor. Make sure the circles are spread apart from each other. [(Chant) "Draw the circle round and round. Put that circle on the ground. Make it big and make it round. Put that circle on the ground."]

Direct two or three children to come and shake your hand, and then go back to their spaces. Remind them to look and see who is beside them, behind them, and in front of them so that they will recognize their space later. [Connie, can you come up and shake my hand and then go back to your space? Before you leave your space, look at it again. Look around you. Look in front of you. Who is beside you? Who is on the other side of you? Who is behind you? What is above your head? Look at your space again.]

Repeat this process until all the children have come to the front, shaken your hand, and gone back to their spaces. When a child goes back to a different spot, correct the error by naming the persons who are standing beside, in front, and between the child in the correct space.

Seat three or four children in the chairs behind you and pick up their pieces of paper. Then ask them to go back without the aid of the paper to the exact spot where they had been standing. Correct their errors by pointing out their relationships to their friends.

Repeat this process until everyone has completed the task. Remove all of the pieces of paper and ask the entire class to leave their spaces, go sit down in the chairs behind you, and then return to where they had been standing. [Now, when I say "Go," everyone sit down in these chairs, and then go back to your space. Slowly. Ready? "Go." (Chant after a child succeeds in finding his or her space.) "Hip, Hip, Hip, Hooray. We have found our space today."]

You will probably repeat this activity several times before all the children succeed in recalling their spaces. Use your map every time you play this game.

Variation: When the children can locate their own spaces, switch the spaces of two or three of them. Call them from their spaces, shake their hands and then send them to a friend's space near their own. This variation should be tried with four- and five-year-old children. It is slightly confusing for three-year-olds.

Activity: Patterns on the Floor

Materials: Masking tape or drawings of the four basic shapes used in the previous activity: circle, square, diamond, and heart

Procedure: Once the children have mastered "Shapes on the Floor" and have made shapes with their hands, arms, and whole bodies, you can use the shapes as the basis for developing movement patterns on the floor.

First, trace a large circle on the floor with masking tape. Inside the circle, trace a square. The circle should be about four feet across; the square should fit just inside it. [(Chant as the children draw.) "Make it big and make it round. Draw that circle on the ground. Square, square on the floor. Two lines here and two lines more."]

Pick two or three lines in the pattern and march on them, using a drum to keep a steady rhythm. Ask the children to follow your path. Explain that this is the secret path out of the pattern. Stress the importance of staying in line and remembering the exact path. [Look at these shapes on the floor. What is inside the circle? A square, that's right. I'm going to see if I can find my way through the shapes. This is the way through. I'll show you the pattern through the shapes.]

Variation: After you have laid masking tape in a circle shape on the floor, have the children stand on the sides of the circle. Direct the children to walk around the circle, stepping only on the masking tape. After you and the children have walked on the shape a few times, stand on the tape again. Now have the children step backwards off the tape. Count the number of steps you take. Start with four or five steps. Now have the children close their eyes and walk back to the masking tape with their eyes closed, counting the steps. [Let's move backward five steps from our circle. Slowly. 1 . . . 2 . . . 3 . . . 4 . . . 5. Now come forward five steps. See if you can move back to the tape. Good! You have made the circle again!] Have them open their eyes and see how close they came to standing on the masking tape. Repeat the activity using more steps. Have the children walk inside the circle toward its center using tiny steps. Ask them to close their eyes and walk backwards to the masking tape. See how close they come to re-forming the circle shape. [Can you take five tiny steps forward with your eyes closed? Can you make your circle again by taking five tiny steps backward with your eyes closed?] This variation will develop their awareness of spatial relationships.

Variation: Try this activity with a square, a diamond, and a heart shape. [(Chant as the children draw.) "Square, square in the air. Two lines here and two lines there. Draw your square on the floor. Two lines here and two lines more."]

Ask for a volunteer to trace the secret pattern alone. Use a soft drum beat to provide a rhythm for the child's march through the pattern. The drum will focus the children's attention on the game, but the child need not march in time. If the child wanders off the path, use a bell or other sound to signal that a new volunteer must take up the challenge. [Can you follow my pattern through the shapes? Let's march through the shapes. Daniel, can you show the way through the shapes while we watch?]

When the children are able to follow you through three-line patterns, change your direction by marching forward, then backward. As they master memorizing three-line patterns, add lines to make the pattern more intricate.

Variation: Use colored tape, string, or ribbon to make the pattern on the floor, and vary the colors of the pathways as shown. March through the yellow path several times with the children. Then ask for a volunteer to do it alone.

Define different pathways with other symbols, shapes, or pictures.

John Taylor, a movement specialist, is associate director of the Columbia Dance Theater. Taylor has worked for the Wold Trap Institute since 1981, conducting artist residencies and teacher and parent training workshops, with over 200 workshops presented across the United States.

The Arts:
The Key to Exemplary Programs

Gwen Brickett, Donna Bull, and Ken Sedgewick

The overall purpose of this presentation is to consider those characteristics of an exemplary classroom for three- to eight-year-olds and provide an evaluation instrument in relation to these findings for the teacher's own use in program evaluation. It focuses on research being done to identify a more effective way of preparing early primary teachers.

The Early Primary Project

Background

In September 1985, the Faculty of Education at Queen's University introduced its Early Primary Pilot Project. The project provided an opportunity for specialization at the early primary level for selected B.Ed. students. During the pilot phase two evaluations were carried out to determine the effectiveness of this teacher education program.[1] The evaluation included an observation instrument designed by teachers and faculty. It identified the characteristics of exemplary classrooms based on Ontario Ministry Guidelines, literature, research, and area classrooms which closely reflected attributes outlined therein. Findings showed that the program in the practicum classroom (including the influence of the classroom teacher) was the single most powerful factor in the development of the student teacher.

During the second year of the project, a program evaluation was conducted to ascertain whether the project students were more able to articulate and implement the knowledge and skills of the primary-junior guidelines as a result of their experiences. Results of this evaluation, based on observation of project students and a control group indicated that the project provided a more effective way of preparing early primary teachers than the regular training program.

In order to confirm the results of the first program evaluation, a follow-up evaluation was conducted of project students in their first year of teaching. All project teachers teaching in Canada and working in a position that included responsibility for both program and a classroom environment were included in the study. Data collection included classroom observation and an interview. In addition, most of the principals of the first year teachers were interviewed. From the Data Analyses and Results, questions two and five are highlighted here.

Data Analyses and Results

Question Two. How important are the associate and the classroom to the regular development of the teacher?

Regression analysis was used to estimate the impact of the associate and the classroom on the first year teacher's behavior with a "global" classroom measure used as the basis of the comparison between project and nonproject classrooms. The regression equation used this measure of the first year classroom as the criterion variable and the same measure obtained during the two rounds of practice teaching as the predictors. About 54% of the variability in the classroom established by the first year teachers was accounted for by the experience they gained in their practice teaching. This affirms the importance of the practice teaching component.

The classroom and the associate were critical influences in the training of the student teacher. When a teacher had had significant experience in a classroom during teacher preparation that was congruent with Ministry guidelines, that teacher was more likely to have the knowledge and confidence to set up such an experiential classroom during the first year of teaching.

The first year teachers implemented to a significant degree the characteristics of the experiential classroom described in the first report. Such a classroom asks the pupil to develop the skills of cooperation and accept the responsibility of independence while providing an atmosphere of care and acceptance and the opportunity to feel successful and creative.

Question Five. Which classroom characteristics are the ones most likely to produce a positive learning environment?

The characteristics which produced the classrooms most congruent to the Ministry guidelines in the original study were monitored in the classrooms of the first year teachers to see if they were implementing them in their own classrooms. Regression analysis was used to examine the impact of the various combinations of factors.

In both models, the criterion variables were the global class measure. In the first model the predictor variables were: a caring and accepting teacher; the use of the arts to foster imagination; the opportunity to acquire the social skills of group work; opportunities for pupils to plan their own learning; and decisions of curriculum based on student needs. This model accounted for 84% of the variability in the classroom measure.

The second model replaced curriculum decisions based on student need and the use of the arts with the presence of hands-on learning materials and opportunities for success for each student; this model accounted for 88% of the variability in the classroom measure.

Once again, it was noted that the characteristics that help to explain the variability in a successful experiential classroom revolve around the principles of learner independence, learner cooperation, and learner security. The descriptive statistics indicated that the project teachers were establishing such classroom environments to a greater degree than the comparison teachers.

Because of the interest expressed by associate teachers, student teachers, and administrators, the original criteria instrument was refined for use by teachers in the Self-Evaluation Questionnaire.[2] The instrument being presented here derives from the foregoing, emphasizing the criterion which fosters creative thinking. More specifically the factors include: the use of the arts to foster imagination, opportunities to acquire the social skills of group work, and the opportunity for pupils to plan their own learning.

The analysis of the characteristics of these exemplary classrooms showed that the arts played a significant role. The teacher's role in developing a program became a major focus because of the emphasis on the process of creative problem-solving rather than on product-oriented learning. The evaluation instrument focused on the teacher's ability to inspire young children to explore, respond creatively, think divergently, share with others, and enjoy the security gained from achievement. The arts in the teacher's program provided an avenue for these forms of development. Analysis of the exemplary programs provided essential data in writing the questionnaire.

We are sharing this instrument with you in the firm belief that self-evaluation with its potential for professional growth will lead to stronger programs, programs which use the arts as key components to provide young children with quality educational experiences.

SELF-EVALUATION QUESTIONNAIRE FOR TEACHERS

KEY

1. Are the arts seen as an integral part of the pupils' development?

1	2	3	4
No	some	considerable	abundantly

Comments _____

_____

2. Does the teacher accept play as an essential part of learning by providing an environment which supports this assumption?

1	2	3	4
No	some	considerable	abundantly

Comments _____

_____

3. Does the teacher listen, observe, and intervene through relevant questions designed to accept and extend pupil responses as well as provide vocabulary as related to texture, qualities, shapes, and color relationships as appropriate?

1	2	3	4
No	some	considerable	abundantly

Comments _____

_____

LEARNING ENVIRONMENT

4. Does the classroom environment foster growth and development in the arts through support for pupils to use their imagination, explore the innerself, and respond to their environment with all senses?

1	2	3	4
No	some	considerable	abundantly

Comments _____

_____

5. Is the learning environment one in which the teacher shows care and acceptance of all children with their wide variations in ability, physique, and personality?

1	2	3	4
No	some	considerable	abundantly

Comments _____

_____

PROGRAM AND PUPIL EXPERIENCE

6. Are pupils in the classroom encouraged to explore drama in spontaneous play such as movement to sound, mime, speech, music both song and instrument, physical education, visual art, etc.?

1	2	3	4
No	some	considerable	abundantly

Comments _____

_____

7. Is the program in environmental studies and the classroom environment generally designed to help pupils see, understand, and evaluate relationships with the environment? e.g., relationships among people, relationships among things, relationships between people and things, relationships of the child to people and things.

1	2	3	4
No	some	considerable	abundantly

Comments _____

_____

8. Are there opportunities for pupils to participate in the planning of their daily or weekly activities as well as make decisions about the sequence in which they will do activities?

1	2	3	4
No	some	considerable	abundantly

Comments _____

_____

9. Are there opportunities for pupils to work alone, work in a small group, work in a large group, and participate in pupil-teacher conferences?

1	2	3	4
No	some	considerable	abundantly

Comments _____

_____

10. Do learning experiences provide opportunities for pupils to develop a personal set of values through problem solving? e.g., group discussion, one to one with adults and peers, identifying alternatives, consequences (if ... then), following instructions, acting independently, feeling successful, etc.

1	2	3	4
No	some	considerable	abundantly

Comments _____

_____

11. Do learning experiences provide opportunities for pupils to acquire social skills required to work in a group? e.g., courtesy to peers and adults, obtaining and returning materials needed, sharing, taking turns, working cooperatively to complete a task, working independently to complete a task, etc.

1	2	3	4
No	some	considerable	abundantly

Comments _____

_____

12. Does the classroom program provide opportunities for each pupil to experience success?

1	2	3	4
No	some	considerable	abundantly

Comments _____

_____

13. Do learning experiences over time and in a variety of settings provide opportunities for pupils to acquire knowledge and express their learning in symbols, numerals and words as well as express themselves through music, movement, paint, poetry, and drama?

1	2	3	4
No	some	considerable	abundantly

Comments _____

_____

14. Do the teaching/learning experiences provide opportunities for the pupils to learn skills through direct instruction according to individual needs?

1	2	3	4

No   some   considerable   abundantly

Comments _____

_____

15. Do learning experiences provide opportunities for students to practice/reinforce skills both in a variety of situations and in relevant situations?

1	2	3	4

No   some   considerable   abundantly

Comments _____

_____

16. Does the program provide opportunities for pupils to learn from each other? e.g., sharing time.

1	2	3	4

No   some   considerable   abundantly

Comments _____

_____

17. Does the program provide opportunities for individuals from the community to visit the classroom in order to share their experiences? e.g., career, music, art, poetry, drama, travel, etc.

1	2	3	4

No   some   considerable   abundantly

Comments _____

_____

18. Are there opportunities daily for pupils to record or express their learning with three dimensional materials? e.g., blocks, cardboard boxes, bottletops, corks, cubes, cups, jars, cuisenaire rods, macaroni, pebbles, plasticene, unifix, etc.

1	2	3	4
No	some	considerable	abundantly

Comments _____

_____

LEARNING MATERIALS

19. Do the concrete learning materials provide opportunities for the pupils to explore and manipulate objects familiar to children?

1	2	3	4
No	some	considerable	abundantly

Comments _____

_____

20. Is there variety in the classroom's concrete materials that accommodates each pupil's stage of development? e.g., physical, social, emotional, intellectual, etc.

1	2	3	4
No	some	considerable	abundantly

Comments _____

_____

21. Do the learning materials provide opportunities for experiences in qualitative relationships? e.g., texture, colour, sound, shapes, etc.

1	2	3	4
No	some	considerable	abundantly

Comments _____

_____

22. Do the learning materials provide opportunities for experiences in quantitative relationships? e.g., number, length, size, mass, etc.

1	2	3	4
No	some	considerable	abundantly

Comments _____

23. Do the learning materials provide opportunities for the pupils to play, observe similarities and differences, classify, order, question, think, experiment, estimate, test, and communicate learning?

1	2	3	4
No	some	considerable	abundantly

Comments _____

ASSESSMENT

24. Does the teacher model self-assessment support as well as teach the skills of self-assessment to the pupils?

1	2	3	4
No	some	considerable	abundantly

Comments _____

25. Are the pupils' experiences recorded in a variety of ways by both pupils and teacher as a record of progress? e.g., daily charts, teacher daily chart, weekly charts by teacher or pupils, file folders, teacher anecdotal records, etc.

1	2	3	4
No	some	considerable	abundantly

Comments _____

Endnotes

[1] The Report on the Evaluation of the Early Primary Pilot Project, 1986 and Follow-Up Evaluation, 1987. Brickett et al., Faculty of Education, Queen's University.

[2] Self-Evaluation Questionnaire for Teachers, Frank Fowler, Faculty of Education, Queen's University.

Gwen Brickett, Donna Bull, and Ken Sedgewick are members of the Faculty of Education, Queen's University, Kingston, Ontario, Canada.

Section IV

MULTICULTURAL/INTERNATIONAL

Multicultural Principles for Head Start Programs

E. Dollie Wolverton

Effective Head Start programming requires understanding, respect, and responsiveness to the cultures of all people but particularly to those of enrolled children and families. Since its inception in 1965, Head Start has recognized the importance of nurturing the self-esteem of each child and family in the program. Head Start Program Performance Standards stress the importance of enhancing the sense of dignity and self-worth of each child and his/her family. Head Start grantees seek to develop approaches which support this humanizing goal.

Children and their families come to Head Start rooted in a culture which gives them meaning and direction. The same statement is true of the staff and administrators who work in Head Start programs. This culture is a set of rules that governs their "world," organizes their physical and social interactions, and shapes their understanding and perceptions of behavior and ideas. This world is a milieu, a context, in which people actively live, develop, and interact. Head Start staff need to be helped to understand culture as functioning through their own basic core beliefs and values. Because the child's culture and family provide the foundation upon which the child's social competence is developed, Head Start staff must be sensitive to the role culture plays in child development.

Our hope is for each Head Start child to become a world citizen through multicultural programming. For each parent and staff member to grow is also our goal. The Head Start program goals are the foundation for this set of principles. These principles have been developed to guide Head Start grantees in meeting these goals.

Section 1304.1-3 of the Head Start Program Performance Standards (45 CFR-1304) states:

(a) The Head Start Program is based on the premise that all children share certain needs, and that children of low-income families, in particular, can benefit from a comprehensive developmental program to meet those needs. The Head Start Program approach is based on the philosophy that:

(1) A child can benefit most from a comprehensive, interdisciplinary program to foster development and remedy problems as expressed in a broad range of services, and that

(2) The child's entire family, as well as the community, must be involved. The program should maximize the strengths and unique experiences of each child. The family, which is perceived as the principal influence on the child's development, must be a direct participant in the program. Local communities are allowed latitude in developing creative program designs so long as the basic goals, objectives, and standards of a comprehensive program are adhered to.

(b) The overall goal of the Head Start program is to bring about a greater degree of social competence in children of low-income families. By social competence is meant the child's everyday effectiveness in dealing with both present environment and later responsibilities in school and life. Social competence takes into account the interrelatedness of cognitive and intellectual development, physical and mental health, nutritional needs, and other factors that enable a developmental approach to helping children achieve social competence. To the accomplishment of this goal, Head Start objectives and performance standards provide for:

(1) The improvement of the child's health and physical abilities, including appropriate steps to correct present physical and mental problems, and to enhance every child's access to an adequate diet. The improvement of the family's attitude toward future health care and physical abilities.

(2) The encouragement of self-confidence, spontaneity, curiosity, and self-discipline which will assist in the development of the child's social and emotional health.

(3) The enhancement of the child's mental processes and skills with particular attention to conceptual and communications skills.

(4) The establishment of patterns and high expectations for success in the child which will create a climate of confidence for present and future learning efforts and overall development.

(5) An increase in the ability of the child and the family to relate to each other and to others.

(6) The enhancement of the sense of dignity and self-worth within the child and his/her family.

As the entire Head Start community implements these principles in policies, procedures, and practices, the development of social competence in children will be supported while the critical role of the family will be acknowledged, reinforced, and enhanced. As a result, the child, the family, and the Head Start staff become participants in a larger community.

Multicultural or culturally diverse programming celebrates individual differences. The cultural, racial, and ethnic composition of the Head Start community is becoming increasingly diverse as Head Start reflects the demographic changes in America. To be successful the Head Start community must understand and commit to appropriate multicultural programming which builds upon each child's culture and helps the child accept the many differences among individuals and eventually deal effectively with other cultures. Children enrolling in Head Start now will interact in the future, if not today, with others unlike themselves in this diverse society.

Head Start grantees must address issues of cultural relevance and diversity if they are to help children achieve social competence and reach their full potential. Cultural relevance supports each child's background as an integral part of the child. Since children are part of all who care for them, the significant people in their lives must be respected and nurtured by all who work with cultural issues. Culturally relevant programming in all Head Start components and services incorporates approaches that validate and build upon the culture and strengths of the enrolled children and their families. Such efforts require that policies, practices, and personal philosophies be examined for bias. This examination process is continuous and central to program development and evaluation.

The following principles form the framework for multicultural programming. They can serve as steps or structure by which participants can examine the task and develop strategies with which they personally and organizationally can reach the goal of helping children reach their full potential.

PRINCIPLES SUPPORTING THE FRAMEWORK FOR MULTICULTURAL PROGRAMMING

1. **Every individual is rooted in culture.**

2. **The cultural groups represented in the communities and families of each Head Start program are the primary sources for culturally relevant programming.**

3. **Culturally relevant and diverse programming requires learning accurate information about the culture of different groups and discarding stereotypes.**

4. **Addressing cultural relevance in making curriculum choices is a necessary, developmentally appropriate practice.**

5. **Every individual has the right to maintain his or her own identity while acquiring the skills required to function in our diverse society.**

6. **Effective programs for children with limited English speaking ability require continued development of the primary language while the acquisition of English is facilitated.**

7. Culturally relevant programming requires staff who reflect the community and families served.

8. Multicultural programming for children enables children to develop an awareness of, respect for, and appreciation of individual cultural differences. It is beneficial to all children.

9. Culturally relevant and diverse programming examines and challenges institutional and personal biases.

10. Culturally relevant and diverse programming and practices are incorporated in all components and services.

E. Dollie Wolverton is chief, Educational Services Bureau, Head Start Bureau, Office of Human Development Services, U.S. Department of Health and Human Services, Washington, D.C.

Weaving the Cultural Mosaic
Using the Arts in Teaching African-American Children

Marvin V. Curtis

African-American children face a public school culture that tends to embrace the values of the dominant Caucasian culture while routinely excluding theirs. While the dominant culture has attempted to include African-American culture in the classroom by focusing on once-a-year Black History Month celebrations, these have failed to provide the meaningful, ongoing educational experiences that African-American students need. This is reflected in the drop-out rates for African-American students, particularly males, as high as 72% in New York City,[1] 48% in California,[2] and 17% nationwide.[3]

A possible solution is for schools to "modify the educational environment in order to make it more consistent with the culture of ethnic minority youth. If this is done, students will experience academic gains in schools."[4] By doing this, schools will go one step further by providing all students with opportunities to become familiar with other races and cultures. This will help young people develop ethnic literacy and become more sophisticated about other cultures. This could be achieved most readily by focusing on multiethnic arts education programs.

For African-American students, those arts education programs should include African-American music and folklore. African-American music is a cultural link for Black youth by being a "crucial component in the life stream of the Black community. It is a potent social, political, and religious force."[5] African-American folklore provides a "resource for educating children about other people's cultural heritage, since it is the primary source of cultural knowledge."[6] In addition, African-American folklore facilitates "the interpretation of fantasy [that] is important in the development of children and is closely related to the development of creative thought and cognitive ability."[7]

The combination of music and folklore, especially in a dramatic form, can provide a way for students to "explore the meaning of social and personal experience as reflected in drama [because they] focus on familiar situations and conflicts."[8] In addition, using drama in this way may "teach all children...how to bring their own human worlds into a literary framework for criticism and appreciation."[9] It is important to explore the correlation between music and folklore related to the culture of the African-American child.

The Cultural Life of African-American Students

Even though they grow up in the same country, African-American children are nurtured in a different environment from many other children, one of interdependent human relationships. African-American students are descendants of the various West African tribes captured during the American slave experience. Although they were not born in Africa or exposed to slavery, many of these children come to school having been exposed to aspects of African-American culture and approach "the school environment with a sense of emotional vitality and resilience, unique survival skills, suspicion about the future, and their own style of communicating, interacting with others, processing information, and synthesizing his or her thoughts."[10] A child learns to work cooperatively with others and contributes toward the survival of the group. This group usually involves a large nuclear family and may be extended to include grandparents, aunts, uncles, cousins, and other members of the church and community. This idea is related to African child rearing practices known as the "care syndrome" or the tradition of "the African is his brother's keeper."[11]

Involvement in this kind of society has as a benefit growth and development through the arts, religion, industry, and philosophy. In African folklore, animals were used to represent human characters. The lion, while strong and powerful, was not too bright; the elephant was ponderous and slow; the hyena possessed brute force but was rather stupid; and the leopard was untrustworthy and vicious, but often tricked in spite of his cunning. Smaller animals such as the tortoise, hare, and spider were regarded as tricksters and were "able to turn any situation, old or new, to their advantage."[12]

The Africans involved in American slave life kept similar animal characterization codes to talk about their conditions. The hare (Brer Rabbit) usually represented the slave, who outwitted the master (Mr. Bear or Mr. Lion). The coded language also created characters such as John Henry and High John, the Conqueror, who were involved in a struggle against the master. In the folktale *The People Could Fly,* the word "flying" was used by African-Americans to explain slave escapes. This use of coded language in African-American folklore was a way of addressing the wrongs of oppression in favor of the oppressed.

The folktale tradition was not encompassed in written texts, but used the oral tradition. This oral tradition, the verbal passing down of folklore, music, and other aspects of African life, continued into African-American culture and manifested itself in the style of African-American worship. African-American preachers are known as great storytellers, using their voices in spoken dialogue and chant to create a rich speaking style similar to the African oral tradition. They are known for interweaving words of unusual length with shorter words in a rhythm pattern that creates spaces for a congregation to respond with "Thank you Lord," "Amen," "That's right!" "Hallelujah," or "Thank You Jesus." It is evidenced in the way many Black children tell stories or recite poetry by talking with their hands and bodies. Many Black children, who find it difficult to write their thoughts on paper, can perform them in a folktale style of acting. These students are likely to respond well in learning situations where this ability is praised by teachers and peers.

Using folklore in the classroom will help teachers better understand their students and help educate all children about the cultures of other people. Studying folklore helps students draw their own conclusions about what another culture is like from the picture presented in literature. Folktales can help children face difficult situations by providing alternative answers to problems.

For African-American children, use of folklore corresponds with the imagery and symbolic language found in African-American life. Many tales:

     (1) express the social values of African-Americans;

     (2) give insight into how African-Americans dealt with slavery;

     (3) contain other aspects of African-American culture.

The idea of connecting the past and present is important for all children. It counteracts ideas that:

     (1) Africans and African-Americans have no cultural past;

     (2) slavery saved the African people by introducing them to
           civilization;

     (3) Africans learned everything from Anglo culture.

As Edward Swope said,"It is from past experiences and future expectations that one derives meaning from the present."

Using folklore in the classroom "can do much to change negative attitudes...these can serve as wholesome instructional materials and aid in the teaching of English composition."[13] Using an extended reading unit on folktales that are familiar and also less familiar will expose children to the cultural ties within their African heritage and the African-American experience.

Music

African-American music is a product of African culture which incorporates polyrhythms, coded messages, and dance. African-American music (spirituals, work songs, gospels, jazz, rock and roll, soul, rhythm and blues, and rap) historically included dual coded messages within its lyrics. For example, spirituals used Biblical characters and the image of Jesus to represent freedom and liberation in the struggle against slavery. In today's society, the message is no longer hidden, but has become a part of the history of the culture. African-American music expresses how Black life interacts with the dominant culture. Even today's musical style of rap is built on the foundation of African music: messages about Black life, polyrhythms, and dance movements.

The musical ties in the religious aspects of Black culture by the use of an audience/ performer style that has a highly emotional interaction between Black performers and audiences uses call-and-response, similar to that of folklore and worship. In the music of African-American culture, call-and-response is most evident in the spirituals. Usually the call, sung in a particular rhythm, by the leader, is answered with a response sung by a congregation, in a matching rhythm. An example would be:

> Call: Swing low, sweet chariot
> Response: Coming for to carry me home
> Call: Swing low, sweet chariot
> Response: Coming for to carry me home
> Call: I looked over Jordan and what did I see?
> Response: Coming for to carry me home
> Call: A band of angels coming after me
> Response: Coming for to carry me home

Call-and-response also appears in the musical life of the community in jazz improvisation and rap performances by Black groups. Teachers who use African-American music connect with African-American students by using a readily identifiable part of their culture. In addition, these teachers provide contributions of African-American culture for all students. Dodds maintains, "if we believe that music is essentially concerned with living and life, music cannot be separated from education."[14] Such are the sentiments of the Tanglewood Symposium Declaration which states:

> Music of all periods, styles, forms, and cultures belongs in the curriculum. The musical repertory should be expanded to involve music of our time in its rich variety, including popular teen-age music and avant-garde music, American folk music, and music of other cultures....The music education profession must contribute its skill, proficiencies, and insights towards assisting in the solution of urgent social problems as in the inner city.[15]

Morgan challenges teachers to understand the dynamics of Black music in the lives of many of their students. "The teacher who is aware of how important music is in the lives of black people will be better able to 'connect.' "[16] Simmons reminds teachers that many Black students "are not going to respond to a Beethoven or Mozart sonata unless an effort has been made first to understand their human as well as their immediate musical needs...students are concerned about something black with which to identify."[17] Lessons that study African music, African-American composers, and African-American musical styles (spirituals, worksongs, ragtime, jazz, gospel, blues, rap, rock and roll, soul, and reggae) allow students direct beneficial experience in either singing or playing.

Weaving the Culture Together for Living and Learning

Due to the nature of the society in which Black culture was nutured, particular styles of walking, speaking, laughing, sitting, body gestures dancing, singing, and general movements were created to promote self-esteem, individuality, and a class distinction from that of white society. Within African-American culture there is a subculture as well, so that African-Americans have distinctive attributes native to individual regions. For example, a southern Black person may speak with a southern drawl (sing-song) while a Black person from

California may speak with a "valley" accent. Within other ethnic groups one may find the same regional differences, but within Black culture, the meaning of the coded language does not change. Phrases such as "that's a mean hat you've got on" or "there goes a fine sister" translate the same from coast to coast. The handshakes, the clenched fist, slapping five, and other means of body communication are universal within the Black community.

Black culture incorporates rules of addressing individuals. These rules developed during slavery because Blacks were denied titles of respect such as mister or mistress. Instead, they substituted other titles; older people were called "uncle" or "aunt" or "Brother Jones" or "Sister Jones." The Civil Rights Movement of the 1960s was instrumental in creating a new solidarity and Black men began to address each other as "brother" and Black women as "sister." This movement helped to redefine Black pride.

Prior to this time, people of African descent living in America were defined by white society as colored, negro (small "n" up to 1960, after that capital "N"), or "boy" if you were a Black man. These terms came to be accepted, at times begrudgingly, by Black society. Today, people of African descent living in America have defined themselves as Black, African-American, or Afro-American. The words colored, negro, and especially "boy" are no longer acceptable. Teachers who mistakenly refer to Black students in the terminology of the past are using derogatory language which may be viewed as racist and discriminatory.

These cultural attributes are important to know and understand, especially if one is teaching African-American students. African-American students need to feel included in the educational process. It is more complex than adding pictures of African-Americans to textbooks or celebrating Black History Month once a year. The curriculum must be strengthened to include information that relates to the ways Black students live and learn. This benefits all students because it exposes them to a variety of cultural experiences that broaden their own ethnic background.

The culture of African-American children relates more to visual, aural, and verbal senses. The creative arts in Black culture reflect a relational learning style. Relational learners achieve in an environment that is cooperative, functional, and loosely structured, where teachers and students work together to achieve a common goal. Relational learners live in a world of feelings and imagination where time consists of the moment. Relationships are very important, as are attachments to certain ideas, people, places, and things.

These students best represent themselves through sound, color, art, music, symbols, poetry, and gestures because these things represent the images of nature; they use these images to learn about themselves and the beauty around them. They use metaphoric language because thinking is done in images that do not always translate well to writing. They thrive in an environment that permits freedom of movement, expression of thought, and emotional experiences. If the learning environment does not have these things, they become anxious and frustrated.

School Environment Conflicts

A typical approach to teaching demands that students achieve in an environment that is rigid, competitive, and highly structured. This approach looks for individual, rather than group accomplishments. The teacher is the source of all information; students are usually required to sit in their seats and work independently of others leaving little room for creativity by students and little chance for interaction between teacher and student.

The conflict of the dominant culture's approach to educational systems and the relational nature of Black culture has led to the labeling of Black students as culturally deprived, culturally disadvantaged, or socially handicapped because of either a perceived correlation between socioeconomic status and intelligence or results on standardized test of achievement that may be culturally biased. This conflict appears in the classroom where teachers expect all students to fit one learning style. These teachers are not prepared to deal with children who learn differently. To improve the success of African-American children, teachers must understand how the the culture of African-American children relates to the classroom.

Many African-American children take an extraordinary amount of time in placing pencils, pens, and other articles in position before beginning to work or take an exam. They are setting the "stage" for learning by establishing a performance area.

Many African-American children tend to do better speaking than writing. The oral communication style of the culture allows for the spoken word to be more powerful and more believable. The spoken word can be dramatic, with words taking on hidden meanings known only to the participants themselves. When challenged to write, many Black students have to edit out the dramatics of the oral mode in which they speak. This means translating from very expressive body language (using hand and body gestures) to using only a pen or pencil.

African-American children can be involved in more than one thing at the same time . The nature of African-American life demands involvement in many projects to keep one from being bored. Black students tend to be multimodal and multidimensional. Their society is a combination of the visual and performing arts incorporating splashes of color from posters, paintings, and graffiti; the audio arts, such as television, stereo, radio, tape, and compact disc; and the fashion arts, such as creative hairstyles, hats, scarves, jewelry, and general adornment of the body. This is interwoven with the performance style mandated by the expressive nature of Black culture, especially in music and folklore. After-all, as Hale-Benson explains,"It is difficult to be Black and boring."[18]

Teacher as Learner

Good teachers approach learning as multifaceted. They understand the different dimensions of human perception and incorporate as many of the human senses as possible in the educational process. As Hunt says, "Good teachers have always known that students differ in how they learn. Some students learn better by listening to the teacher, some by discussion, others by working on their own."[19] The idea that the relational style of learning inherent in African-American culture is different and difference equals inferiority is wrong. The teacher who believes that African-American children lack the capacity to learn, whether such belief is based on IQ scores, socioeconomic status, race, or cultural misunderstandings of the child's behavior, ultimately undermines Black students' academic progress. Rist sees it in this manner:

> When a teacher bases her/his expectations on performance on the social status of the child and assumes that the higher the social status, the higher the potential of the child, those children of lower social status suffer stigmatization.... Yet, there is a greater tragedy than being labeled as a slow learner, and that is being treated as one.[20]

The teacher who observes and learns to accommodate African-American culture encourages a freedom within the classroom that celebrates the uniqueness of African-American children. This celebration allows African-American children to value themselves as worthy, contributing members of the society. The teacher who seeks answers about the culture from parents, leaders in the community, and African-American faculty and incorporates these into the classroom begins the process of building bridges of understanding and accommodation that all children need. Teachers and administrators who involve themselves and the Black community in programs that go beyond superficial workshops about cultural differences, racial relationship, and African-American history can develop new curriculum sources that will aid all children in becoming better citizens of the world.

What Can Be Done

Schools should "establish a functional partnership between the Black culture and school culture...teach academics and social skills and reinforce cultural heritage simultaneously."[21] This can be done through an arts based educational approach. Gilbert and Gay contend that "instructional experiences which investigate students' individual ethnic group's histories and heritage, and which help them to understand the meaning of these in shaping the present conditions and culture of their ethnic groups are most useful."[22] Elementary teachers can use stories that feature selections from different ethnic groups; multiethnic games, songs, and crafts in structured play; and music, art, and reading to increase students' awareness of ethnicity and teach intellectual skills. Through self-examination, cultural workshops, or classes, teachers can examine their attitudes about Black children (that might be based on their own biases and stereotypes) and make changes that will make them better teachers of all students. Finally, teachers can make sure that African-American culture is involved in the curriculum and their teaching style and is supported by administrators, not only on the elementary and secondary level but in colleges and universities as well.

Doing these things will ensure a culturally based educational system that prepares Black children "for entry into the mainstream culture, while it accepts, appreciates, and uses his home culture to teach him mainstream skills."[23] In addition, a culturally based educational system will help all students develop "ethnic literacy and cross cultural competency." This kind of educational environment will help students "become familiar with other races, lifestyles, and cultures and should help young people...become more sophisticated about other cultures." What is being advocated here is multiethnic education, which goes beyond the mere inclusion of Black culture in the curriculum. This includes not only studying "ethnic cultures and experiences, but also making institutional changes within the school so that students from diverse backgrounds have equal educational opportunities and the school promotes and encourages the concept of ethnic diversity."[24]

Teachers can help students master essential reading, writing, and computational skills by including examples and situations relating to the African-American world in which they live. This kind of education provides all students with skills, attitudes, and knowledge to function within their ethnic cultures, mainstream culture, and across other ethnic cultures. Multiethnic education can help reduce the pain and discrimination that African-American children experience because of attitudes of some members of mainstream society based on racism.

Multiethnic education requires teachers to give students direct experiences with cultural diversity rather than approaches that use short films or one-day celebrations. This means that teachers need to be aware of the cultural makeup of a classroom and celebrate not only differences but similarities. For the African-American child, this celebration may make the difference between success and failure.

Endnotes

1. Norman Riley, Footnotes of a culture, *The Crisis, 93*(3), (1986): p. 28.

2. Elaine Woo, "Stiffer standards for minority students," *Los Angeles Times,* 26 May 1988, p. 25.

3. Bill McAllister, U.S. reports decline in black drop-out rates: Narrowing gaps between races is "glimmer of hope," Cavazos Says, *The Washington Post ,* 15 September 1989, p. a01

4. James Banks, *Multiethnic education* (Boston: Allyn & Bacon,1988), p. 106.

5. Harry Morgan, Music—A lifeforce in the black community, *Music Educators Journal 58*(3) (1971), p. 37.

6. Jesse Goodman & Kate Melcher, Culture at a distance: Anthroliterary   approach to cross-cultural education," *Journal of Reading, 28* (1984), p. 200.

7. Janice Hale-Benson, *Black children: Their roots, culture, and learning styles* (Salt Lake City, UT: Brigham Young University Press, 1986), p. 98.

8. Lois Josephs, Electives in the English high school program: Drama and flexibility, *English Journal 60*(2) (1971), p. 246.

9. Ibid p. 249

10. Joseph White, *The psychology of blacks: An Afro-American perspective* (Englewood Cliffs, NJ: Prentice Hall.1984), p. 137.

11. Akpan Esen, The Care-Syndrome: Resource for counseling in Africa,*Journal of Negro Education* 42(2), (1973), p. 206.

12. Ruth Finnegan, *Oral literature in Africa* (Oxford: Clarendon,1975), p. 345.

13. Edward Anderson, Using folk literature in teaching composition, in *Tapping potential: English and language arts for the Black learner,* Charlotte Brooks (Ed.), (Urbana: Black Caucus of the National Council of Teachers of English)(1985), p. 219.

14. James Dodd, Music as multicultural education, *Music Educators Journal, 69* (1983), p. 33.

15. Music Educators National Conference, *Documentary report of the Tanglewood Symposium* (Washington, DC: Music Educators National Conference 1968), pp. 138-139.

16. Harry Morgan, Music—A lifeforce in the Black community, *Music Educators Journal 58*(3) (1971), p. 37.

17. Otis Simmons, Reach the bedrock of student interest, *Music Educators Journal, 58*(3) (1971), p. 39.

18: Janice Hale-Benson, *Black children: Their roots, culture, and learning styles* (Utah: Brigham Young University Press,1986), p. 35.

19. David E. Hunt, Learning styles and student needs: An introduction to conceptual level, in *Student learning styles* (Reston, VA: National Association of Secondary Principals 1979), p. 27.

20. Ray Rist, On understanding the process of schooling: The contribution of labeling theory, in *Schools and society,* John Ballantine (Ed.), (California: Mayfield 1970), p. 448

21. Shirl Gilbert II & Geneva Gay, Improving the success in school of poor Black children, *Phi Delta Kappan, 67*(1) (1985), p. 135.

22. Ibid., p. 53

23. Joan Baratz, A culturalmode for understanding Black Americans, *Black Dialects & Reading,* B.E. Cullinan (Ed.), (Illinois: Black Caucus of the National Council of Teachers of English 1974), p. 115

24. James Banks, *Multiethnic education* (Boston: Allyn & Bacon, 1988), pp. 107, 89, 38.

Marvin V. Curtis is director of choral activities and associate professor of music at Virginia Union University in Richmond, Virginia. He was previously assistant professor of music education at California State University, Stanislaus. With 25 compositions published and 16 commissions from high schools and colleges throughout the country, he is in demand as a composer, clinician, and conductor.

Early Childhood Education and the Creative Arts in New Zealand

Sue Cherrington

Ki mai koe kiau, He aha te mea nui?
Maku e ki atu, "He tangata, he tangata, he tangata."
Kotahi te kohao o te ngira
E kuhunga te miro whero, te miro ma, te miro pango.

I would like to thank the organizers of this conference for the opportunity to share with you a little of what is happening in New Zealand in the area of creative arts and cultural awareness in early childhood settings. I have brought with me some of the resources which have been developed for use in New Zealand as I think they will illustrate our approach more clearly than I can.

I have been fortunate enough to have spent the past eight weeks traveling throughout Australia and the United States on a study program observing, among other things, some of your early childhood programs. The definitions given to common terminology differ quite widely between our countries, and so it is probably time well spent to take a few moments to give some background and describe early childhood settings in New Zealand.

New Zealand has a long history of preschool education, with the first kindergartens established over a century ago. Since then it has become the norm for children to attend an early childhood program before entry to school, with over 90 percent of our four-year-olds enrolled in one of a wide variety of programs.

Traditionally our early childhood centers have offered developmentally appropriate programs—a very wide range of appropriate experiences and resources are available daily; teachers view themselves as facilitators rather than instructors; and there is an emphasis on meeting needs in all areas of a child's development rather than purely cognitive needs.

The term "early childhood education" is commonly used instead of "preschool" in New Zealand, and so we tend to focus on birth to five years when using the early childhood label. Training is specialized with a three-year teacher training course for those working with under fives, and a separate course for primary teachers who cover the 5-12 year age range.

There are four major "types" of early childhood settings in New Zealand:

Playcenters are parent cooperatives, offering several sessions per week, primarily for 2-1/2 to five year olds. Parents are expected to be highly involved in all aspects of the playcenter, and are able to work through a training process from parent helper up to a national playcenter certificate.

Kohanga Reo are Maori language nests, primarily set up to preserve the Maori language and culture by utilizing *kuia* and *kohunga* as the primary teachers of their grandchildren. *Kohanga Reo* recognize the traditional role that many grandparents play in raising their grandchildren while also acknowledging at the time of their inception that this was the last generation of fluent speakers of Maori. Many *Kohanga Reo* are located on local *marae*, alongside employment projects and other community activities, and children can attend from birth until school at five. As children have moved from *Kohanga Reo* into the primary school setting intense pressure has been placed on schools to provide bilingual teachers and classrooms.

Childcare in New Zealand encompasses a huge variety from family daycare to sessional services to fullday childcare centers. Very few childcare centers have more than 40-50 children on their total rolls - some care for infants and toddlers, some three and four-year olds only, and others a combination of both. Requirements for trained staff have not been as rigorous as for kindergartens but standards are rising rapidly, especially as government funding to early childhood education increases.

Kindergarten serves children aged three and four years, and operates with two groups of 40 children: one group attends five mornings and the other three afternoons. The remaining two afternoons are reserved for working with parents and for program planning and administration. Each kindergarten is staffed with two trained early childhood teachers, and New Zealand is currently in the process of implementing a staffing scheme to put three trained staff in each kindergarten by 1994.

Educational Administration

1989 saw a major restructuring of educational administration in New Zealand with evolution of decision-making down to individual schools and early childhood centers within national guidelines and requirements. In order to access partial government funding, early childhood centers are required to develop and negotiate a charter with the Ministry of Education. This charter covers many issues but the sections that concern us are:
1. The Curriculum, the Program, and the Learner
2. The Treaty of Waitangi, and
3. Equity.
Under the first section, the Curriculum, the Program, and the Learner, in relation to the creative arts and cultural awareness are requirements that include:
a) The curriculum will enable all children to experience an environment in which:
- They learn in appropriate ways.

- They respect the natural environment.

- Learning is not limited by race, gender, or special needs.

b) The organization of the curriculum will take into account the ethnic origins of each child, and the different characteristics and developmental needs of infants, toddlers, and preschoolers where they are present.

c) The program will include creative activities where individual expression is encouraged.

d) The program will include the use of natural materials and play in natural areas.

The Treaty of Waitangi was the founding document in New Zealand and was signed by representatives of Queen Victoria and many of the Maori chiefs 150 years ago. It established a partnership between the Maori and the Pakeha on equal terms, unlike many of the arrangements of the British Empire which sought to subjugate the indigenous peoples of the lands they colonized. The Treaty was never enshrined in New Zealand law but in recent years commitment to the principles of the Treaty has been high at a governmental level, and that commitment is filtering down through society.

So the second section, the Treaty of Waitangi, sets out the principle that: "It is the right of each and every child to be enriched in an environment which acknowledges and incorporates the dual heritage of the Treaty partners," and requires:

1) That there will be "acceptance and acknowledgement of Maori values, customs, and practices," and

2) "Management should ensure that there are opportunities available for staff, parents and *whanau* and themselves to participate in courses on cross-cultural understanding, including opportunities to extend and strengthen their knowledge and understanding of the values and language of the *Tangata Whenua*."

The third area of the charter that has a bearing on cultural awareness and the creative arts is that of equity and in this section are requirements that:

1) "Early childhood centers will reflect the values and customs of the families of children attending," and

2) "Programs and resources will be sensitive and responsive to the cultural differences among the families whose children attend the center."

There is then a strong expectation that our early childhood centers will offer programs that are culturally sensitive and that enable children and their families to develop an awareness and appreciation of both their own and others' cultures. Within these general principles and requirements both the content and the processes utilized are left unprescribed, allowing local communities and staff to determine what is appropriate for their center.

This same approach is taken with the inclusion of early childhood services into the physical education and music education syllabi, revised in 1987 and 1989 respectively. Both discuss developmental considerations for children from early childhood through to Form 7 (17 years), outline key goals and objectives, and offer a variety of ideas and resources for achieving those goals and objectives in developmentally appropriate ways. An essential component of these resources are ideas and practices for integrating *Te Reo Kori* into the music and physical education syllabi. As for the charters though, the specific content of programs is left for individual centers to determine, again based on what is appropriate for their children and community.

Celebrating Diversity

Earlier I shared two Maori proverbs—the first: "You ask me what is the most important thing, and I reply 'It is people, it is people, it is people'" and the second: "There is one eye of the needle through which pass the red thread, the white thread, the black thread."

They remind us that we have to value people above all else, and that it is important to celebrate the diversity in our society rather than to look only at what we have in common. After all, although the three threads pass through the same eye of the needle, they each remain individual. While many Maori live biculturally, generally *Pakeha* New Zealanders are taking their first tentative steps, especially in using language. Rather than attempting to develop a bicultural program on their own it is important that teachers develop relationships with the local *Tangata Whenua* so that their knowledge, skills, and values can be shared first-hand with the children in the early childhood center.

There are many ways in which children's awareness and understanding of Maori culture and values can be extended through the creative arts. The language is traditionally oral with a strong emphasis on recording events, history, and *whakapapa* through oratory, song, and storytelling. Many traditional and contemporary songs are an integral part of music sessions while the opportunity to experiment with *poi* enables young children to begin developing the motor dexterity that will allow them to use *poi* in symbolic song and dance in later childhood. Rhythm is a focal part of the music of Maori and other Pacific Island cultures, and there is evidence to show that where there is strong representation of Maori and Polynesian children in groups all children are likely to develop a strong sense of rhythm.

Poi dances and the *haka* have traditionally been performed by females and males respectively, and generally these traditions are maintained today. The extent to which children begin to learn *poi* dances and *haka* in early childhood varies considerably depending on the setting they attend.

Maori art is traditionally very symbolic and utilizes designs found in nature, for example, the fern frond. Traditional Maori art made use of naturally occurring pigments such as black, ochre, white, and red, and the designs incorporated in carvings, *kowhaiwhai* patterns, and *tukutuku* panels would trace genealogy, retell legends, and describe historical events. Because of the symbolism involved I believe it to be inappropriate for most centers to teach children specific patterns; instead many centers have consulted with their local *Tangat Whenua* who have helped them develop an appropriate *kowhaiwhai* pattern that reflects their local community. What is appropriate, however, is for center staff to ensure that they include the traditional colors as an integral part of all the art mediums they supply.

Importance of Conservation

The use of natural materials and their conservation are extremely important to the Maori, and an early childhood center that is reflecting those values will have a balance between natural and manufactured materials in all areas of the program. So, for example, the collage area might include a wide variety of leaves, flowers, shells, seed pods, pebbles, and so on, preferably arranged in natural containers such as wooden bowls or flax kits, as well as the usual collection of manufactured items such as boxes, cards, containers, bottletops, etc. Logs and tree stumps are utilized as display spaces for collections of natural objects, which are incorporated into areas such as science and nature, manipulative, math, books, and language.

New Zealand is fortunate to have substantial quantities of beautiful clay, and exploring its qualities in all states from liquid to pliable is an integral part of art programs. While most centers purchase prebagged potters clay, they can also go on clay collecting expeditions with their children, digging it out of banks ready for use. A considerable portion of the preservice teacher training art class is spent working with clay, helping teachers to feel comfortable with this natural, tactile, and oftentimes messy material.

In addition to incorporating many and varied examples of Maori art and culture into all areas of the curriculum and recognizing the value and place of natural materials in our center environment, cultural respect is also noted by not including food in art programs. It is culturally inappropriate (and I would suggest morally inappropriate) to use food for anything but its original purpose—to sustain life. There is absolutely no need to resort to using rice and pasta in collage and threading activities or to use fruit and vegetables for printmaking when so many other manufactured and natural nonfood items are available. Perhaps the worst example I have seen was the print completed by my four-year-old niece in Australia that used painted fish to make the prints with.

Using food in art programs is frowned upon in New Zealand to the extent that debate is now occurring over the use of fingerpaint made with cornflour and playdough made with flour and salt, and acceptable nonfood product alternatives to these traditional materials are being investigated. I would like to challenge those of you here today who use food in your art programs to reflect on the messages that you are sending. There may be many families attending your centers who feel uncomfortable about food being wasted in this manner.

Conservation plays a big part in any program that is being culturally sensitive. In Maori culture, land is the foundation stone and Maori people have a strong affinity with it. Land does not belong to people individually and forever, but it and its products are there to support life and must be treated carefully and with respect in order to ensure survival, both physical and spiritual. So, as well as not misusing food, when we collect natural materials for use in the program we take just what we need and return what wasn't used; we take carefully from living organisms, for example, the outer leaves of the flax bush, not any of the inner three of father, mother, and child; and we treasure and help children to appreciate the aesthetic beauty in both natural materials and objects created from natural materials.

Tikanga Maori can also be developed and extended through language and the telling of stories, myths, and legends, and through the illustrations of these tales. Maori is a traditionally oral language but many stories, both contemporary and traditional, as well as myths and legends have been reproduced in a written form in order to reach a wider audience. In keeping with the oral traditions, many are accompanied by tape recordings in both Maori and English. If you look at reproductions that illustrate some Maori legends and stories, the distinctive style and appreciation of nature and the designs found in nature are quite obvious. This style of art is quite different from traditional European art, and when incorporated into programs adds a richness to children's art and aesthetic experiences.

Tikanga Maori resources that support other areas of the curriculum do so in a manner that also supports the notion of conservation, nature, and beauty. These posters [displayed at the conference], for example, provide opportunities for children to practice counting in Maori as well as incorporating a short lyrical statement, and being, I think, absolutely stunning to look at. Other math games give children the opportunity to sort, classify, and count using pictures of *kaimoana*.

Issues Affecting Creative Arts in Early Childhood

I'd like to focus on some of the other issues that have an impact on the creative arts in New Zealand early childhood settings, namely:

1. Traditional philosophy.
2. Climate.
3. Group size and environments.
4. Entry into the primary school setting.

Traditional Philosophy

New Zealand's early childhood traditions are those of the "free-play," child-oriented approach where wide choices are given to children, and the adult's role has been to support and guide children and to facilitate discovery rather than to teach to a predetermined curriculum. The development of the whole child is a dearly held belief and if any one aspect of development has been given more weight over the years it would be that of social development. Because of this background the debate over and movement toward developmentally appropriate practices that has occurred in the United States has been much less of an issue in New Zealand. Rather than having to convince teachers that developmentally appropriate practice is the appropriate approach to take, our focus is more on fine tuning practices and helping teachers to more clearly articulate those dearly held beliefs about how children learn best to parents and the wider community.

Standardized tests are not used in preschools, and informal observations are the most widely used tools for assessing children's development and evaluating programs. Many teachers are moving toward a formalization of their procedures to ensure that they regularly monitor each child, each curriculum area, and their own performance as teachers but continue to do that monitoring using a wide range of observational techniques. Because of this developmental approach, teacher-directed activities in the art, movement, and music curriculum are kept to a minimum. Where direct instruction takes place it is usually to help children master the technique so that they can then apply their own creativity to the process, be it painting, collage, screen-printing, dance, or music making.

Climate

Before leaving New Zealand I had never seriously considered the impact that climate has on the way teachers develop and provide their programs. After all, New Zealand stretches one thousand miles from north to south, it does snow occasionally in the south, and it gets very cold when the southerly winds blow up from Antarctica. However, we do not get the several months of snow and very cold temperatures that many states face here as an annual event. I have come to the conclusion that our temperate climate is one of the reasons that we have such a strong tradition of concurrently operating indoor/outdoor preschool programs.

The overwhelming majority of our programs would be giving children the choice of working inside or outdoors for 80% plus of sessions. Outdoor play takes a wider perspective of development than just that of gross motor, and ample opportunities are provided for social interactions, cognitive and language development, and creative expression. In order to ensure that those children who prefer the outdoors do not miss out on creative experiences, materials for fingerpainting, carpentry, drawing, painting, and collage are regularly provided outdoors as well as music and movement sessions that may involve the whole group or just one or two children experimenting with sounds and songs. The involvement of the outdoor environment adds an extra dimension to all aspects of creative expression as children are encouraged to focus on the characteristics and qualities of their world through sensory experiences.

Group Size and Environments

The size of many of our preschool groups in New Zealand also has a bearing on the environment, both indoors and outside. The majority of our centers are single units with only one group of children attending at one time, and rarely exceed 40 children. As single unit centers, each has its own outdoor environment that is directly and easily accessible from the playroom, and this also promotes the integration and concurrent operation of indoor/outdoor programs. A consequence of our larger group sizes is that a far larger space is provided, and this in turn means that daily vast amounts of experiences, resources, and materials are available for children to explore and utilize. Perhaps because our early childhood staff are used to working in high adult-child ratios, they have learned to develop superb environments that encourage children to explore materials and use resources individually or with their peers. Curriculum areas are available throughout the session, not just for one hour at a time, and materials are available in larger quantities and in a larger range than I have observed in this country.

Entry into the Primary School Setting

The last major difference that I have observed between the New Zealand and the United States preschool systems is the method of entering school. In New Zealand our children enter school on their fifth birthday, regardless of when it occurs throughout the school year (although the latest legal school entry age is six years). Because of this system, there is a continuous turnover of children departing for school and new, younger children joining the group, and teachers are constantly being reminded of the range of age and developmental stages of the children in their groups. In order to meet the needs of all these children materials and resources are available for them year round, and teachers look at how they assist children to use the materials appropriately instead of becoming tied to a curriculum plan that says "we don't introduce PVA glue until January." This leads to a very rich environment that encourages the creative exploration and manipulation of materials by children, at a level appropriate to their own stage of development.

Sue Cherrington is senior teacher in the Wellington District's Kindergarten Professional Support Scheme, Tawa, Wellington, New Zealand.

Traditional Japanese Folk Songs as a Means of Children's Expression

Reiko Hata

When you hear the word "Japan," what images do you see? Some of you may well see an image of Japan as a country of so-called economic animals, or you might think of it as one of the leading countries in the world in the field of technology. Perhaps many of you still have images of a country with beautiful gardens, ladies wearing kimono, or so on. If you've been in the country, you might remember the good smell of Japanese incense. As you know, the world is becoming smaller and smaller because of rapid improvements in communication technologies. We can hear news from all over the earth almost instantaneously. The latest fashions are adopted promptly by the Japanese, and the women wear similar clothes all over Japan, no matter whether they live in a big city or in a small town. You might be surprised to know how rarely Japanese women do wear kimono. It has to be a special occasion, because kimono are usually expensive and hard to take care of. In addition, when wearing a kimono, it is hard to move and walk around freely. It doesn't suit the life we lead today.

Another important part of a culture is food. We still eat Japanese foods like sushi, tempura, and tofu and enjoy their taste very much. All the same, most Japanese families have Western-style breakfasts, with toast, eggs, coffee, and so on. Japan is filled with fast-food chains like Kentucky Fried Chicken, McDonald's, and Mr. Doughnuts. We enjoy Western foods as well as Japanese.

How about Japanese musical life? Since the Meiji Period, which was about 100 years ago, the Japanese have learned only Western music at school, with a few exceptions. This music education has been excellent, to judge from the many famous musicians who came from this background: Seiji Ozawa, Midori Goto, and Tohru Takemitsu, to name a few. Parents are very eager to provide music lessons to their children. Some 85 percent of the students at my college took some kind of music lessons when they were younger. Some attended music classes offered by Yamaha or Kawai, and some took lessons from private teachers. These lessons were all in Western music. Young people in Japan are completely absorbed by rock or folk music. Many young people seem to be listening almost 24 hours a day to their Walkman, the compact tape player with earphones.

What about the daily life of young children? The style of their life has changed greatly. When I was little, many Japanese families lived with three generations together in the same house. I sang old songs taught me by my grandmother and played traditional games with her. She also told me many folk tales. I played with my friends in the fields and yards around our houses until it got dark. I can remember that we played house, hide and seek, catch, and so on. Jumping rope was also popular. These days, families living with three generations together are rare. The number of mothers working outside of the house is increasing. Many children go to *juku,* which are private classes in school subjects that are held after school. Housing space is very limited. Children are playing with games on their personal computer these days. I am really worried about this pattern of living. I wonder whether Japanese children will be able to grow up healthy enough both mentally and physically to contribute anything to the world they have to live in.

It does seem to me that we are losing our traditional culture. However, in recent years, there is a promising trend in almost all countries in the world to reevaluate the way traditional culture is thought of. Cultures thought to be backward or otherwise undesirable are now being appreciated somewhat more fully. Things that are "ethnic" are more fashionable. In Japan, the same trend is taking place, and one aspect of it is the renewed study and analysis of Japanese traditional music. One of the findings of the study is that despite the overwhelming predominance of Western music in our lives, such as I have just described, we actually use elements of and fragments of Japanese traditional musical styles in our everyday life.

Children use certain pitch intervals for their calls or chants that are characteristic of *warabe-uta,* traditional children's folk songs (see Example 1). They use the techniques of *warabe-uta* unconsciously as a means for self-expression. This kind of musical sense probably cannot be changed easily. For example, Example 2 is a song sung when children are drawing a picture, and it is sung in every region of Japan. Analysis of the words in the song showed that the song was most likely composed within the last 30 years. Children sing this song and draw a picture not during their formal music education, but in free play as a way for self-

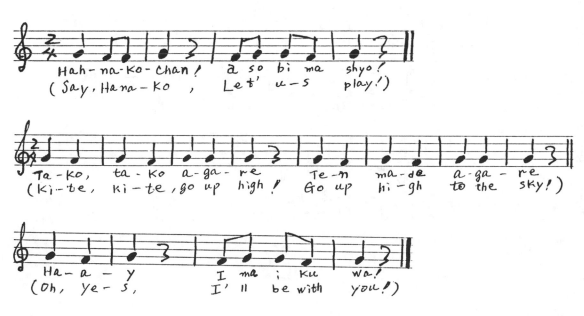

Example 1

expression. The melody and rhythm used in the song are both characteristic of those of *warabe-uta*.

Warabe-uta are very old. The term "warabe-uta" is found in old manuscripts, the oldest so far being one from 720 A.D. Even in the relatively small area of what is now called Tokyo, more than 600 songs have been collected that date from the Edo period, which lasted from 1600 to 1867. Some of the characteristics of *warabe-uta* are as follows. Like the folk songs of other nations, the composers, date of the composition, and place of origin are unknown. Most of these songs are related to children's games. The main function of the songs is to aid in the rhythmic progress of the game, so the rhymes and the meaning are frequently secondary in importance (Example 3). Many of the songs are found all over Japan, which greatly obscures the question of their place of origin. Lullabies are also placed in this category, but strictly speaking, lullabies are songs sung *to* children rather than songs sung *by* children.

Warabe-uta can generally be divided into the following categories: there are songs for use when bouncing a ball, songs for use when playing with bean-bags, songs for use in the

Example 2

game called *hanetsuki*, which is something like badminton, songs about the weather, songs about animals and plants, songs for certain special occasions, and other game songs. Some games and activities enjoyed by Japanese children include *ayatori*, *ohajiki*, *otedama*, *takeuma*, and *takoage* (see Example 4).

Example 3

お寺の和尚さん

PAN-CAKE PAN-CAKE (NABE NABE SOKO NUKE)

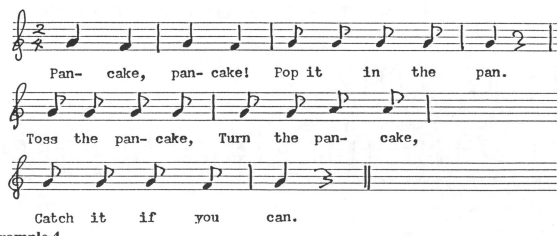

Example 4

Next, I'd like to analyze *warabe-uta* briefly in musical terms. One basic difference between these melodies and those of Western music is the tonal structure. The tonal structure of Japanese music cannot be analyzed in terms of octaves with one tonic tone. There is always one important tone in a phrase, which can be called a "nuclear tone." This tone dominates the countershapes of the phrases. All of the tones in the phrase are dominated by the nuclear tone, and they are never far from it. Thus, the nuclear tone has more of an influence on the formation of melodies than the tonic tone has on Western tonal structure. *Warabe-uta* therefore generally center on one nuclear tone and are formed of two, three, or four tones (Example 5). Relatively long *warabe-uta* have three or more phrases with one nuclear tone in each phrase.

Example 5

The rhythm of *warabe-uta* is closely connected with the rhythm of Japanese words. Changes in meter and in the division of phrases that are repeated often occur in these songs in response to the rhythm of the words being sung (Example 6). Changing meter is generally considered to be difficult, but the children do this effortlessly during play, because the change is connected with the rhythm of the words. *Warabe-uta* use the rhythm of the Japanese language in a direct, living way.

Example 6

Example 7

Children sometimes make up their own music by combining old and new musical idioms (Example7). The songs for singing during drawing seem to be fairly recent ones (Example 8).

DRAW AN OCTOPUS (MIMIZU GA SANBIKI)

First you make a line, and a line and a line.

Then you make some circ-les, round and fine

Now make some sun-beams, all in a row.

Make some lit-tle rain-drops that have no-where to go.

Now you draw a ring and there's an Oc-to-pus!

Example 8

As I mentioned earlier, musical sensibility from one's ancestors is probably not lost easily. If we want to base education of young children on what they already know, we should make more use of traditional Japanese music. By doing so, the children may be able to be creative and to express themselves in a more natural way.

Reiko Hata is professor of early childhood music education at Seiwa College in Japan. She is a member of the Early Childhood Commission of the International Society for Music Education and has had several articles on music and Japanese children published in the Society's yearbook.

Arts and Early Childhood in Finland

Riitta Heikkinen

This article consists of examples from the author's book, Nyt Mina Piirran (I Will Draw Now), published in 1985 by Weilin & Goos.

Drawing in the Air and Dark Moments

Many schools of arts, even Bauhaus, have always had exercises of expression in their program to help the students to relax before starting to draw. In teaching art to children, use of expression is natural and inspiring. Children express themselves totally by voices, motion, and expressions. For example, when young children want to tell their parents about a helicopter they have seen they go around on the floor like a helicopter.

When teaching art to children, natural sensitivity to expression is used to help the teaching. All the fancy things of a fairy tale can be drafted by drawing in the air. Children imagine to be mother birds flying around the classroom. Or with the eyes closed the shape of a circle becomes familiar by touching objects of different shapes and recognizing a ball among them.

When the motif of a picture is houses on the shore of a stormy sea, it is natural to feel the storm, be a weak plant or a strong tree, hum like the wind, or listen to the silence when the storm is over.

A child is always ready to become a Luxus Lady or a Cleaning Lady. They wash the dishes, clean. They want to fly, be a train, or a balloon. A child is always on a trip and looking for adventures.

When a group of children is concentrating on expression, a mysterious atmosphere is necessary; lights are turned off; when it is dark the imagination gets wings more easily.

See Voices, Listen to Colors

Mihail Matjusin, a Russian avant-gardist, painted pictures that were meant to be straight pictures of voices. In 1926, Matjusin wrote: "Voices vibrate in the same way as colors, the saying 'sonorous' red, for example; thin, thick, colorless, or bright voices clearly show that our eyes actually are able to hear and ears are able to see."

A child moves experiences from one area of senses to another one, uses different senses at the same time, forms conceptions through studying and experiencing. In Tsehov's novel, *At Home,* the father made surprising observations about his son's drawings and sensations. In the drawings, melodies were smoke spots, whistling was a spiral line. Sounds were closely related to form and color; when he decorated alphabets the latter L was yellow, letter M red, and letter A black.

A child senses objects alive, identifies with surroundings, and expresses himself/herself openly. When traveling by bus a five-year-old says when seeing a school building which looks deserted: "The school is sleeping now, it is tired." A child has not yet adopted the restrictions which prevent a grown up person from expressing observations openly. "These smell wonderful," say six-year-old art students and they literally stick their nose in new chairs to feel the smell of new timber.

Children are collecting things always and everywhere, whatever the object might be, a feather or a rusty can. The greatest treasure can be a small light feather wrapped in cotton in a small case. Looking for these treasures requires the senses of both vision and feeling.

In school age, the world of a child becomes estranged from sensations; reading is reading, writing is writing. We think that concepts can be formed only by words and numbers.

Still, in situations where knowledge is needed, a person acts on conditions of feelings and sense world. School teaching emphasizes learning of the language of words and numbers; learning through expression and senses is often understood as contrast to learning from books, separated from thinking. That is why the meaning of school subjects with expression is understood as relaxing moments and therapy. Only a few school lessons offer a child a possibility to make use of holistic experience.

Everybody Along

Teaching children art starts from impulse given by a teacher; the starting point can be children's play, a fairy tale, story, music, picture, motion, voice movies, model, etc. When being taught, the children sit on the floor near the teacher. First they discuss events of the week; birthdays, seeing grandmother, losing teeth. The atmosphere must be peaceful, even mysterious when necessary. Often the motif requires a short discussion. If the motif is a toy set, it is necessary to talk about the most important toys of one's own toy room.

In teaching situations ready-made pictures, such as slides, photos, and drawings, are seldom used, usually only as reference. Children should form their own opinion about contents of the motif.

When the motif is described by means of a fairy tale, the teacher tells the children a story by words. During the storytelling the characters of the story can be imitated and other things of the story can be drafted by drawing in the air. There are no pictures to look at. After this children can start working. The teacher asks the children to describe some certain events of the fairy tale, still giving children the opportunity to choose their own way to describe the event. Limiting the motif to a certain event is a way to consciously emphasize the picture's form or color, differences in sizes, darkness or lightness, etc.

If the motif is approached through motion and voice, one has to live through the situations of the motif. A child is a train, trains go through tunnels. A ball is arranged in the classroom, circus people meet each other, birds start to fly. When acting, children do not have the time to think of themselves; their energy is released to creative expression and using imagination.

In teaching art, teaching based on imagination is traditionally used to motivate the students.

A teaching guide for primary school mentions the teaching area of drama, which means putting together a picture, a word, a voice, and a motion. This area of teaching is connected to theater, mass media, and arranging school parties or performing situations. The expression exercises of this article are an essential part of the drawing event and they are not meant to be performing situations. The exercises are most suitable for teaching in childhood years and first classes of primary school.

Dialogue between a teacher and a group of children is very important. The group is a mental power. It is good if two teachers can be used in teaching situations; the first can help in care of materials and calm lively children. Then a lesson becomes an exciting play, a theater of surprises with a possibility of adventure. In teaching art, the role of a teacher must not be too dominating; two teachers reflect different views about drawing a picture through their personality and a child learns early to accept even contrary views in the area of art.

Teacher and children discuss a motif and then one child expresses it through motion. The creative expression in motion is not a performance but becomes an essential part of the drawing event.

Example: Imagination Cake

Teacher:
- Who of you have been at a birthday party?
- Was there a cake?
- What kind of cake?
- What cake do you like?

Preparing a birthday cake starts now. Children stand in a circle and draw in the air all the instruments needed for baking a cake: bowl, beater, etc. Recipe: Put some sugar and eggs in a bowl drawn in the air. Beating starts, by hands or by machine; remember the noise of beating. Add flour. Pour into the mold, and put it in the oven. Wait for the cake to become baked. Then cut it into several flat pieces.

Teacher:	• What shall we put between the pieces?
John:	• Bananas
Nicholas:	• Chocolate
Sheila:	• Cream
Walter:	• Blueberries
Ann:	• Candies
Joanne:	• Guess what my cake is made of? Chocolate, pudding, cherries, and a little imagination.

What kind of plate will the cake be put on? A decoration paper can be added; candles and a cake decoration may not be forgotten. The cakes are ready to be taken to children's own drawing desks.

Example: Up We Fly!

Children watch pictures of birds in books or film. What are a bird's head, bill, wings, tail like? There are several different birds in the pictures. Some are unfamiliar birds. The children want to know the names of all the birds in the book.

Children study flying positions of the birds. One of the birds almost hits the edge of a rock while another one flies above open sea without moving its wings.

After this the children become birds, starting from rest position. The group of birds is quiet for a moment, eyes can be closed. Then the birds start making noises, move, quack, quack . . . .
- What birds are the children?
- What do they do (look for food by pecking seed from the ground, take a resting position, scratch their feathers, quarrel)?
- Where do they live (on top of a tree, on a rock, in the grass)?

The birds fly for a moment in the classroom, then return to their nests. Now they draw bills of the birds they saw in the pictures, in the air.

Example: Children's Earthworks
(a presentation at the Holland 1990 art educator's meeting)

Having worked many years as an art teacher in children's art schools I wanted to find other methods of teaching than just sitting in the classrooms and making traditional drawings and paintings. Introducing themes into teaching art could be more than just doing the same motif with different techniques.

An an art teacher in children's summer camps I found theme teaching more and more educative. We always started the camp program by relaxing the children with exercises to activate all their senses. There is a lot of human energy beyond the conceptual thinking and language. We wanted to increase the concentration of the children by playing, making sounds, etc. If we were painting dancers, children or teachers were first dancing. Camp after camp the program grew more versatile; we not only made paintings, but painted our faces, feet, and even snow in the winter time. The working process became as important as the actual works.

Some of our themes, like "Japonism" or "The Queen of the Night," one may criticize as being superficial and cursory. I would like to call it illustrative art education; all we wanted to do was something more than just beautiful pictures—to search for holistic experiences.

The grass works was our first attempt to use new materials. Children were working in the open air at the seaside. We had an idea to make a fan using all kinds of grass and some

In summer camp programs, children can have art experiences out of doors, creating works of art by arranging natural objects in a box frame.

bast for binding. Some children had done paper fans at regular school. One girl was so good a binder, she even began to teach the technique to all of us. While looking at these fans, we can see that every little artist has his/her own personal style, every grass fan is different. Children could work with fans whenever they wanted, even in bed; that is the advantage of camp teaching.

Conclusions from Experience

While working in an experimental way you don't know what precise direction your teaching should take. It is an adventure which may succeed or may not.

Some conclusions from our experience are briefly listed here.

1. Cooperation should be developed among children as well as the ability to solve problems in concrete and active situations. Children are given the opportunity to get to feel collective experience.

2. The teacher should strive to stimulate creativity in general rather than artistic ability as such.

3. Materials can be found straight from nature and in any case they should not be too sophisticated. Children have to learn to know about the preservation of nature and ecology while walking and working in nature.

4. Working in the open air, in the middle of landscape, sensitivity to nature increases. One can feel the seasons, experience the light, etc.

5. Most of the works will be blown in the wind after the process is over, but the experience will stay in one's mind and fantasy.

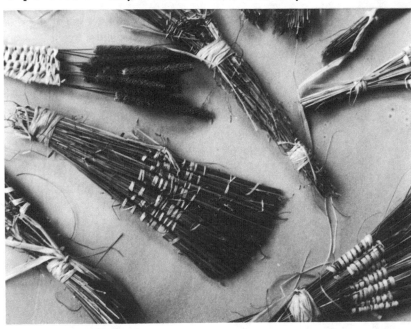

Using a material new to them, children make fans out of all kinds of grasses. Every fan is different as each young artist expresses his/her own personality.

While looking at children's works we notice that children have included symbols like a cross or a spiral in their "boxes." The same thing happened when they were making earth-paintings using mud and different kinds of sand. You could ask if we bear these symbols in our minds even in our early childhood. Do they have much the same meaning in every culture? For instance, the cross had been an important religious symbol long before the arrival of Christianity and it is believed to have an inner divine spirit. Children's works raise questions to be answered; these workshops can be as educational to teacher as to students.

Although I do not especially look for using folklore in education, I don't want to avoid it either. Everybody has played with signs made on the sand or we Finns have opportunity to draw on the snow. I can still remember the feeling of having completed a very large figure using a twig in my hand. We all have done pearls, toy pigs, and birds from yellow water lilies and straws.

Richard Long has told that he had somehow slipped into art by just doing what he liked to do without worrying how art should look. He observed how art carried the pleasures of childhood into adult life: damming streams, throwing stones by bouncing them across rivers, making sand castles. There is much of this spirit to be found in his works.

The contacts important to me are in everyday life, in nature, wild or manmade, rather than in the art world. I am interested in art and art history, but usually we don't speak so much about art—we just do what we are bound to do.

Bibliography

Fuchs, R. H. (1986). *Richard Long*. London: Thames and Hudson Ltd.

Rudofsky, B. (1964). *Architecture without architects*. New York: Doubleday Company.

Heikkinen, R. (1989). Children's TV-program, Four Steps to the Picture, Part 1: Earthworks. (Direction: I. Bergstrom-Rausku, Heikkinen, R., & Lehto, K.) Production: The Finnish Broadcasting Company.

Riitta Heikkinen is an art teacher at the Vantaa Art School for Children and Kindergarten Teachers Training School in Helsinki, Finland. She is a member of the board of the International Society for Education Through Art in Finland, author of several books on children's art, and director of children's TV programs on art.

A Creative Dance Curriculum for the Three-Year-Old

Mary-Elizabeth Manley

The creative dance curriculum for the three-year-old, like any other curriculum, must be designed to build important foundations. In order to shape such a curriculum, it is necessary to address two very important questions. First, what is the process by which the curriculum will be taught, and second, what is the nature of this process relative to the essence of the activity of the developing child?

From the early writings about art, dance, play, and the child[1] and also from Piaget's work[2] we know that for the young child the process of learning about dance should be an "ingoing" activity in which the body speaks to itself kinesthetically and experientially while it is in community with other little bodies doing the same. It is within this dance experience that those natural skills which are developing may be explored. Often these skills take on a new life and reason for being as imagination and fantasy spark less pedestrian energies in the movement.

Play is a featured characteristic of the preschool child's and more specifically the three-year-old's dance experience. The child lives within the spheres of dance and play as they interweave and provide the three-year-old with a special structure in which to experience the body dancing. As play and dance mesh with one another, the common territory seems to be a unique form of play which allows the child to enter into a journey with the dance phenomenon (see figure 1). Joseph Chilton Pearce, author of *The Magical Child,* calls it fantasy

The Intersection of Dance and Play

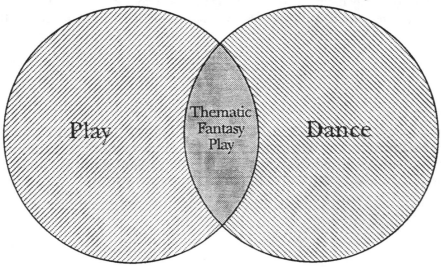

Play

Thematic
Fantasy
Play

Dance

Figure 1.

play and magical thinking,[3] while Saltz, Dixon, and Johnson define this process as thematic fantasy play. Whereas the term thematic fantasy play has been defined by these researchers as "verbal role enactment in a group,"[4] this definition seems too narrow for the creative dance setting. By changing and expanding the ideas of this definition, thematic fantasy play becomes more of an image enactment by means of the projection of natural movement.

In a creative dance class with young children in particular, the methodology employed often utilizes a theme or series of themes which can be related to natural phenomena, literature, or manmade environments. The themes, which must have significance for the group, help the teacher to guide explorations of movement concepts of body, space, time, energy, and relationships. Thus, children are able to explore and expand their movement repertoire through the ideas of a theme in a fanciful and imaginative way. Suggested and implied images shared by the teacher are absorbed and then responded to by the creative dance participants. Consequently, the resulting "natural" dance movement represents the suggested image in one way or another.

As one considers the developmental level of three year olds, it is clear that because of personal experience with their surroundings, children of this age are able to hold onto certain images. Those with particular relevance to the three-year-old will be retained long enough and with enough interest to enable the child to begin to discover dance movement possibilities with them. Much earlier than this, at two or even two and a half, a child will simply not have had enough perceptual experience to even form many images, or to recall others. With limited personal experience of the environment and the features and creatures therein, the very young child will not be enticed into the process of creative dance with the use of verbal images and fantasy. As Moira Morningstar states in her book *Growing With Dance,* "Even a two and a half year old may not remember snow, so unless it is actually snowing, there is little point in doing a snowflake dance. A six year old will not only be able to remember snow but will even be able to help in making up a story about the life of a snowflake and then translate it into an expressive dance."[5]

The shift toward retaining images for more than a fleeting moment marks the outset of centering on a dance idea, which can then be communicated through bodily speaking. This knowledge of how to share an idea as it is spoken through the dancing body accumulates very gradually. As children become more able to retrieve, recombine, and integrate images, these sources of internal knowing merged with the external stimulation of a creative dance class provide children with their first step in the process of syntax in dance. In these explorations, playful beginnings form the essence of the body words being spoken. The phrases, clauses, and sentences of a dance composition will gradually build from these tender seeds.

Beyond the fact that the three-year-old can readily engage in the process of fantasy play within the creative dance class, there are other features of this developmental stage which make it a logical age at which to introduce such activity. Children of three have a fairly well established basic movement vocabulary. Their anatomy is becoming more and more familiar to them as their kinesthetic sense gains acuity, facilitating knowledge of the neuromuscular connections needed to accomplish the basic movements. While children of three are certainly still in the process of establishing knowledge about their body image, the child's sense of the body and its parts, joints, zones, shape, and volume are generally identifiable (see figure 2). Awareness of certain joints such as the wrist, individual vertebrae of the spine, hip, ankle and toe is still gaining definition. The sides of the body are body zones which the three-year-old finds difficult to maneuver. Body shapes such as blunt (or square), twisted, or curved are yet in the fringe of the body's knowledge as are volumes such as the sense of narrowness and negative spaces in and around the body.

Remarkably, the three-year-old's range of basic movement vocabulary includes almost all of the traveling movements which form the foundation of complex dance steps used in choreography much later on. Crawling, creeping, sliding, rolling, walking, running, galloping, and jumping are very familiar. Hopping seems to appear when the ratio of strength in the legs relative to the body weight is balanced. It is then that the segments of balance, coordination, and lift of the body solidify and become identifiable as a hop. Many children of three are not "hoppers" nor are they "skippers." While the skip may appear in the child's repertoire between three and four, this is unusual. Children often continue to gallop to the rhythm of a skip until four and a half or much later, at times showing the "one legged skip" as a precursor of the normal skip pattern. In comparison, two-year-olds, still very much in the process of developing their upright balance, are struggling to develop the strength and coordination of a gallop and a jump. While a glimpse of a gallop may appear as early as eighteen months, the full form is coming into focus more often at about two and a half. The knee bounce/jiggle precedes jumping, giving the child's body a look of anticipation...somewhat like a helicopter with motor reved bouncing and vibrating furiously before takeoff. Generally then, the three-year-old must be viewed on a continuum, possessing marginally more physical finesse than the two-and-a-half-year-old. However, their slightly more advanced neuromuscular connections give their movement a more stable and refined look.

Other aspects of the creative dance curriculum which are considered under the general category of "Body Movements (see figure 2), are those movements which may be initiated as the body stays on one spot or can be layered onto a "Traveling Movement." Those actions such as shake, bend/stretch, push/pull, twist/turn, rise/sink, balance/fall, swing/sway, and bounce/ jiggle are such movements. While some of these represent opposites in the body vocabulary, others indicate a variation in the aspect of space or energy. The three-year-old has a relatively sound body knowledge of these opposites with the exception of the twist and swing as opposed to the sway. Swing requires a more controlled use of gravitational pull, giving the body or its limbs the impression of a pendulum action with equal arcing to each side of the plumb line.

While children of two certainly have absorbed much in terms of language, their understanding of what is termed "Expressive Body Actions," using words such as squirming, wiggling, freezing, exploding, stamping, tiptoeing, etc. is inadequate. There are words which will not call forth associated body movement unless imitation of the teacher is occurring (see figure 2). Conversely, the teacher of the three- and four-year-old will be able to evoke some of the associated physical subtleties of such descriptive vocabulary by asking for the child's

DANCE CURRICULUM FOR THE THREE YEAR OLD*

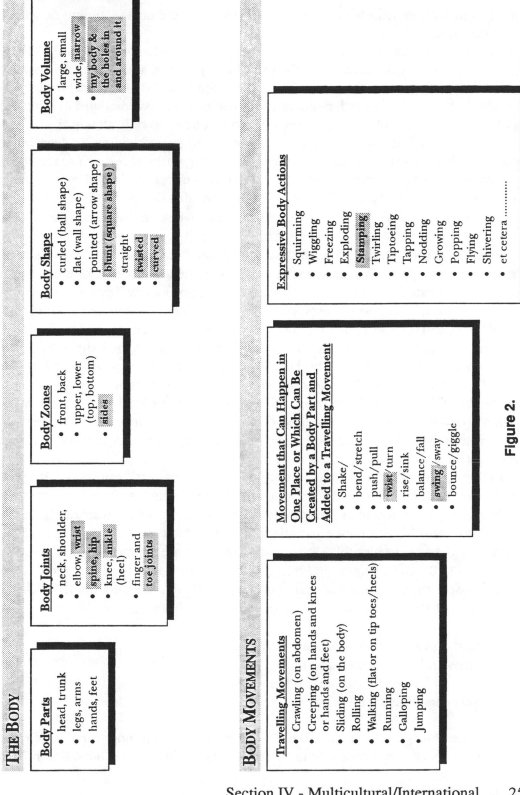

THE BODY

Body Parts
- head, trunk
- legs, arms
- hands, feet

Body Joints
- neck, shoulder, elbow, **wrist**
- **spine, hip**
- knee, **ankle** (heel)
- finger and **toe joints**

Body Zones
- front, back
- upper, lower (top, bottom)
- **sides**

Body Shape
- curled (ball shape)
- flat (wall shape)
- pointed (arrow shape)
- **blunt (square shape)**
- straight
- **twisted**
- **curved**

Body Volume
- large, small
- wide, **narrow**
- **my body & the holes in and around it**

BODY MOVEMENTS

Travelling Movements
- Crawling (on abdomen)
- Creeping (on hands and knees or hands and feet)
- Sliding (on the body)
- Rolling
- Walking (flat or on tip toes/heels)
- Running
- Galloping
- Jumping

Movement that Can Happen in One Place or Which Can Be Created by a Body Part and Added to a Travelling Movement
- Shake/
- bend/stretch
- push/pull
- **twist/** turn
- rise/sink
- balance/fall
- **swing/** sway
- bounce/giggle

Expressive Body Actions
- Squirming
- Wiggling
- Freezing
- Exploding
- **Stamping**
- Twirling
- Tiptoeing
- Tapping
- Nodding
- Growing
- Popping
- Flying
- Shivering
- et cetera ....

Figure 2.

participation without necessarily having to demonstrate the quality, timing or spatial aspect of the movement.

"Expressive Body Actions" are in fact movements of the body vocabulary which the child begins to associate with and alter by the use of energy, time, and space. These are abstract concepts of which the very young child has little comprehension. As Moira Morningstar states, "The idea that space exists independently and can be used as a medium in which to create direction, shape and pattern is a concept which can develop only slowly."[6]

Nevertheless, the creative dance experience engages children in learning how to structure each of these movement factors, often centering on the concept of space. The specific segments (see figure 3) which contribute to the overall understanding of space relationships, levels, floor patterns, body size/volume and focus, provide a rich curriculum to investigate with the three-year-old. It is from the explorations of these diverse segments that the child's mosaic of conceptual space will eventually be formed.

Comprehension of the more abstract dimensions and laws of our physical world as revealed through space, time, and weight are first experienced as felt sensations by the body, and through repeated experiences in movement. Later the brain will evaluate these sensations as an abstraction of the concept develops.[7] The sensory contrasts of weight (strong/light), flow (bound/free), and tension/relaxation show us children's use of energy and their control of that feature as they move. As indicated in figure 4, the more restrained shade of these paired sensory contrasts (strong, bound, and tension) lags behind in being perceived by the young child. The light, the free, and the relaxed movements of the body are the more habitual movement qualities of the developing child. The child of three delights in responding to the changes in quality of a simple song, tune, or series of sounds. Once again, dance exploration merges with play as the child experiments with personal body energy relative to sound and music.

In this cluster of factors, time seems to pose some enigmatic questions. It appears that one of the earliest signs of a child dancing in our Western culture is when the child instinctively responds to rhythmic sound or music with a clear, relatively fast, and steady "pulse." In fact, for the two-year-old, the dance experiences from which they seem to derive the most enjoyment are those in which this kind of instinctive response to simple rhythms is encouraged (see figure 4). Rhymes, jingles, and music with a 2/4 or a 4/4 meter are favorites. Familiar and well used rhymes or songs can be dusted off and dressed up to encourage the development of rhythm as well as body definition. Such a rhyme might be:

> Head and shoulders, knees and tums,
> Knees and tums, knees and tums,
> Head and shoulders, knees and tums,
> Eyes, ears, fingers, thumbs.[8]

Between the ages of two and three the child seems much more capable of responding within a very specific and relatively fast tempo range. Certainly this limitation relates to the

DANCE CURRICULUM FOR THE THREE YEAR OLD*

SPACE

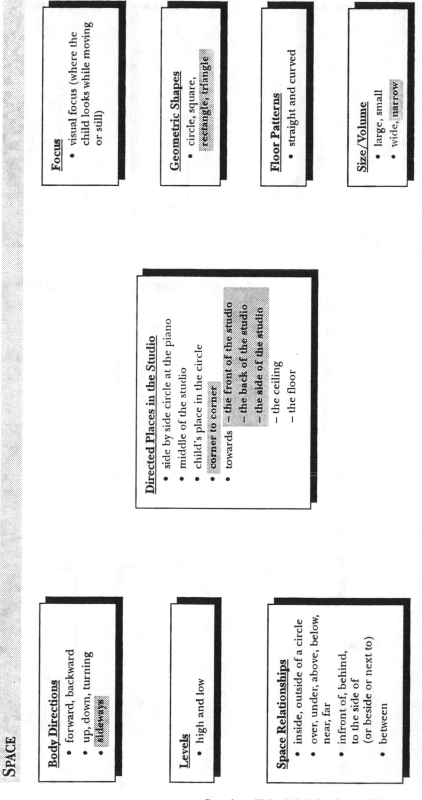

Focus
- visual focus (where the child looks while moving or still)

Geometric Shapes
- circle, square, rectangle, triangle

Floor Patterns
- straight and curved

Size/Volume
- large, small
- wide, narrow

Directed Places in the Studio
- side by side circle at the piano
- middle of the studio
- child's place in the circle
- corner to corner
- towards – the front of the studio
  – the back of the studio
  – the side of the studio
  – the ceiling
  – the floor

Body Directions
- forward, backward
- up, down, turning
- sideways

Levels
- high and low

Space Relationships
- inside, outside of a circle
- over, under, above, below, near, far
- infront of, behind, to the side of (or beside or next to)
- between

Figure 3.

DANCE CURRICULUM FOR THE THREE YEAR OLD*

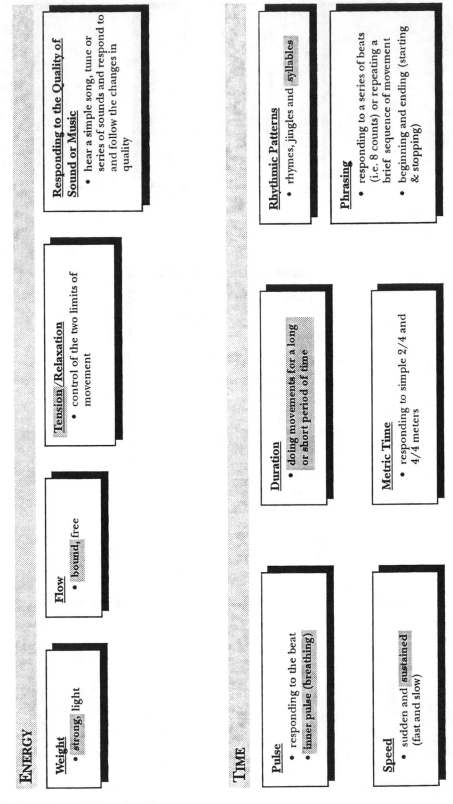

ENERGY

Weight
- **strong,** light

Flow
- **bound,** free

Tension/Relaxation
- control of the two limits of movement

Responding to the Quality of Sound or Music
- hear a simple song, tune or series of sounds and respond to and follow the changes in quality

TIME

Pulse
- responding to the beat
- **inner pulse (breathing)**

Speed
- sudden and **sustained** (fast and slow)

Duration
- **doing movements for a long or short period of time**

Metric Time
- responding to simple 2/4 and 4/4 meters

Rhythmic Patterns
- rhymes, jingles and **syllables**

Phrasing
- responding to a series of beats (i.e. 8 counts) or repeating a brief sequence of movement
- beginning and ending (starting & stopping)

Figure 4.

258   Early Childhood Creative Arts

neuromuscular control that children possess at this point in their development. Gradually the child will gain the ability to produce movements at a slower tempo, at the same time as they begin to exhibit a more distinct flow of movement.

The speed with which a movement is done and the duration of a movement being repeated seem to relate closely to the physical factors of strength and endurance. More sustained endurance of the body musculature is required to do a movement slowly. In general, it is as the child approaches four that we see this kind of sustained control begin. The duration of a movement (see figure 4), a factor considered within the whole concept of "Time" in dance movement, is quite unclear for the child of three. It is certainly not unusual to see a two- or two-and-a-half-year-old turn continuously until she/he collapses in a dizzy heap. This type of pure indulgence in the sensational quality of the movement is quite different from the aspect of controlled differentiation which a creative dance teacher will attempt to develop. Children of three have significant difficulty when they are directed to continue their movement for various gradations of time, or to identify if their movement took a long or a short time to complete. Their movement as it relates to "time passing" is not well defined.

Phrasing, an important feature of the dance phenomena, adds punctuation to the ebb and flow of a series of dance movements. In a creative dance class, phrasing (see figure 4) begins with the "freeze and dance and freeze," the start and stop in a child's body. The movement phrase then becomes identifiable as a unit or dance idea on its own. The three-year-old is actually beginning to be able to respond to the perimeters of going and stopping. At this point in their development they are able to do a simple phrase of movement from a beginning body shape through to, for example, some gallops, jumps, and a roll to a freeze. The spoken phrase might then be: gallop and gallop and gallop and gallop, jump, jump, roll, and freeze. While the three-year-old is very eager, she/he lacks the movement memory for sequencing that the four-year-old will gradually develop. Fours and fives have far greater success in being able to reflect on and remember their phrases and sequences with more facility and less prompting.

The term "relationships" is often a category within a creative dance curriculum. Typically, children gain an awareness of a diverse repertoire of relationships (see figure 5), including those physical/conceptual relationships close to their own being (body parts, different body movements and body shapes), those between the child as a dance participant and with a partner or a prop (toward and away, around and through, over and under, above and below etc.), and those social and specific dance relationships which are felt between the teacher and child and the group of dancers. All of these kinds of relationships require a certain amount of focus on others. The under-three-year-old has a difficult time responding to the requirements of group cooperation. The solution to this problem is to have the child dance with a parent or caregiver so that this natural relationship is enhanced while the focus on others is also introduced. In the "parent and tot" class, the child has the luxury of a one on one relationship as he/she experiences the framework of dance in a group setting. The parent or caregiver in this case acts as a teacher and a devoted and enthusiastic partner at one and the same time.

DANCE CURRICULUM FOR THE THREE YEAR OLD*

RELATIONSHIPS

Social Relationships

With the teacher and the members of the class:

- be a member of a group
- as a member become involved in the idea of the dance activity
- be able to co-operate and share
- take simple directions

Physical/Conceptual Relationships

With the group, a partner or a prop move:

- toward and away from
- around/through
- above & below
- between
- over and under
- before and after
- faster and slower
- alike and different

Specific Dance Class Relationships

- make a side by side circle
- move out onto the studio floor with a prop or a partner
- follow others in a line across the studio floor
- gallop, run, tiptoe etc. outside the circle
- hear a simple story or song and follow the sequence with other children
- echo the teacher's simple rhythm patterns

Shading indicates those features of the three year old's conception of dance movement which are still in the process of developing

*This curriculum guideline has been designed from personal research with preschool children in conjunction with reference to Preschool Concepts by Mary Ann Lee, Creative Dance Studio, University of Utah, Salt Lake City, Utah, 1979/80; Creative Dance in the First Three Grades by Joyce Boorman, Longman, Canada Ltd. 1969; Dance for Young Children; Finding the Magic in Movement by Sue Stinson, Reston, Virgina; American Alliance for Health, Physical Education, Recreation and Dance, 1988; and Growing with Dance; Developing Through Creative Dance from Ages Two to Six, Heriot Bay, British Columbia, Windborne Publications, 1986.

Figure 5.

A creative dance curriculum that places emphasis on the body, space, time, energy, and relationships provides a smorgasbord from which to choose in designing a year of classes for the three-year-old. There are, however, certain components within each of these areas which are better left for the child of four or five, as has been indicated with the dark shading in each of the accompanying charts. To ensure that guidelines for dance explorations are relevant for the three-year-old, the teacher must be a keen observer of physical, kinesthetic, verbal, auditory, and social development. With a curriculum guideline and a wealth of appropriate images, a teacher is then able to guide the process intelligently, giving children access to their process of creating dance as they fantasize, play, and dance.

Endnotes

1. Martin, *Introduction to the Dance*, p. 42, 133.

2. Goldstein, *Sports, Games and Play, Social and Psychological Viewpoints*, p. 3.

3. Pearce, *Magical Child*, p. xvi.

4. Goldstein, ibid.

5. Morningstar, *Growing with Dance, Developing through Creative Dance from Ages Two to Six*, p. 7.

6. Ibid., p. 6.

7. Ibid., p. 6.

8. Davenport, *Young Children's Creative Movement and Music Classes*, November 30, 1991.

References

Bettelheim, B. (1977). *The uses of enchantment: The meaning and importance of fairy tales*. New York: Vintage Books.

Cherry, C. (1971). *Creative movement for the developing child: A nursery school handbook for non-musicians*. Belmont, CA: Fearon Publishers Inc..

Dearden, R.F. (1973). *The concept of play*. In R.S. Peters (Ed.), *The concept of education* (pp. 73-71). London: Routledge and Kegan Paul.

Elkind, D. (1974). *Children and adolescents: Interpretive essays on Jean Piaget*. New York: Oxford University Press.

Fein, G. (1975). A transformational analysis of pretending. *Developmental Psychology, 11*, 291-296.

Gerhardt, L. (1973). *Moving and knowing: The young child orients himself in space*. Englewood Cliffs, N.J.: Prentice-Hall Inc.

Gould, R. (1972). *Child studies through fantasy*. New York: Quadrangle Books.

Lobel, A. (1972). *Mouse tales*. New York: Scholastic Book Services.

Lynch, Fraser, D. (1982). *Danceplay: Creative movement for very young children*. New York: Walker & Co.

Lynch, Fraser, D. (1991). *Playdancing: Discovering and developing creativity in young children*. Pennington, NJ: Princeton Book Company.

Martin, John. (1969). *Introduction to the Dance*. New York: Dance Horizons, Inc.

Morningstar, M. (1986). *Growing with dance: Developing through creative dance from ages two to six*. Heriot Bay, BC: Windborne Publications.

Pearce, J.C. (1980). *Magical child*. Toronto: Bantam Books.

Piaget, J. (1962). (trans. C. Gategno & F.M. Hodgson). New York: W.W. Norton.

Roberton, M.A. , & Halverson, L.E. (1984). *Developing children - Their changing movement: A guide for teachers*. Philadelphia: Lea and Febiger.

Ruyter, N.L.C. (1979). *Reformers and visionaries: The Americanization of the art of dance*. New York: Dance Horizons.

Sherrod, L., & Singer, J.L. (1979). The development of make-believe play. In J.H. Goldstein (Ed.), *Sports, games, and play: Social and psychological viewpoints* (pp. 1-28). Hillsdale, NJ: Lawrence Erlbaum.

Singer, J.L. (1973). *The child's world of make believe*. New York: Academic Press.

Stinson, S. (1988). *Dance for young children: Finding the magic in movement*. Reston, VA: American Alliance for Health, Physical Education, Recreation and Dance.

Sutton-Smith, B. & Shirley. *How to play with your children (and when not to)*. New York: Hawthorn Books, Inc.

Mary Elizabeth Manley is associate professor in the Dance Department at York University, North York, Ontario, Canada.

Appendix

The following articles from the Early Childhood Creative Arts Conference have been abstracted and may be available from ERIC Clearinghouse on Teacher Education, One Dupont Circle, Suite 610, Washington, DC 20036.

Achilles, Elaine and Boyer, Gretchen A., Arizona Arts and Creativity in Early Childhood

Avils, Glenna Boltuch, Multicultural Mural Projects

Barragar-Dunne, Pam, Creative Arts Activities for Ages 5 to 8, Focusing on the Self

Cambigue-Tracey, Susan, Creativity: The Antidote to Inner Poverty

Carlson, Judith B. and Robotham, Jean, Self-Directed Learning at Escuela Nueva Laboratorio

Di-Yun, Zhu, Art Eduation in the Chinese Kindergartens

Gharavi, Gloria Junkin, A Survey of the Music Abilities and Skills by Selected Preschool Teachers in Tennessee

Gilbert, Anne Green, Creative Dance Curriculum: Appropriate Activities for Ages 3-8

Heyge, Lorna Lutz, Creating a Holistic Music Experience for Young Children

Hoffman, Stevie; Kantner, Larry; Colbert, Cynthia; and Sims, Wendy, Nurturing the Expressive Arts in Chidren's Classrooms

Kalish-Weiss, Beth, Creative Arts Therapies in an Inner City School

Levinowitz, Lili M., Parent Education as a Beginning Solution to Music Childhood at Risk

Lewis, Hilda Present, The Development of Art in Early Childhood

Littleton, Danette, Cognitive, Social, and Musical Play of Young Children

McCullough-Brabson, Ellen, Celebrate Multiculturalism with Music!

Moore, Marvalene, Experiencing Music Through Movement and Instrumental Play

Ng, Margaret, Preschool Education in Malaysia with Reference to the Preschool Teacher Training

Oliver-Lewis, Irene and Ortega, Jose Francisco, The Kid Inside: Problem-Solving Together through the Arts

Pinciotti, Patricia, Creative Drama: Transforming and Mastering Reality

Reagan, Timothy, J., A Day Care Project: A Program Model Integrating the Expressive Arts into the Child Care Curriculum

Reilly, Mary Lousie, Music with Shadow Play Theatre: A Concert for the Young Listener

Reinhardt, Deborah A., The Development and Administration of a Psychomotor Measure of the Preschool Child's Music Perception

Richardson, Nancy H. and Yamagawa, Candace, Girl Scout Program: Creative Connections and Head Start

Ritchie, Lorraine, Integration--A Case Study of Early Childhood Training in New Zealand

Sayre, Nancy E., The Perfect Mix: Creative Movement and Children's Literature

Schaefer, Claire and Cole, Elizabeth, The Museum & Me: An Early Childhood Art Education Model

Spiotto, Bob, Three Rings of Learning Fun

Welsbacher, Betty, The Young Disabled Music Maker

Wright, Lin, Making and Appreciating Drama: Pretend Play Developed for the Primary Grade Child

Early Childhood Publications
From AAHPERD

Moving and Learning for the Young Child
William Stinson, Editor

Benefit from information gleaned from an important meeting of professionals in your field. This transcript of the proceedings of the Early Childhood Conference, held December 1-4, 1988, in Washington, D.C., brings you up to date on patterns of moving and learning for young children. 1990, 272 pp. Stock # 0-88314-449-2.

Dance for Young Children:
Finding the Magic in Movement
Sue Stinson

How can you develop the building blocks upon which dance activities are created? This "how to" publication helps you develop effective teaching strategies for dance education of young children. Sample ideas and lesson plans are included. An ideal resource for seasoned and beginning early childhood and elementary teachers. 1988, 161 pp. Stock # 0-88314-381-X.

The Important Early Years
Liselott Diem, Translated by Kathi Walz

Early childhood experiences are the most important ones, that is, the impressions children gain from their environment, the encouragements or restrictions they encounter, and the stimulating or limiting atmosphere within which they grow up. These early learning experiences should not be forced on a child, but should develop through self-discovery, play with others, and personal challenges. This book discusses spontaneity and sureness of movement; keen perceptual awareness; orientation in space; rational visualization and creativity in movement; comprehension of situations and independent reaction; and provides a variety of suggestions on how to promote a child's own competence, starting in the very first year of life. 1991, 88 pp. Stock # 0-88314-491-3.

Call our toll-free number for prices and ordering information: 1-800-321-0789

American Alliance for Health,
Physical Education,Recreation and Dance
1900 Association Drive
Reston, Virginia 22091